CHEAP EATS IN LONDON

SECOND EDITION
The Savvy Traveler's Guide to the Best Meals at the Best Prices.

SANDRA A. GUSTAFSON

CHRONICLE BOOKS
SAN FRANCISCO

Printed in the United States of America

SECOND EDITION
ISBN 0-8118-4283-5 (pbk.)

Cover design: Robin Weiss
Cover photograph: Mark Snyder
Book design: Words & Deeds
Original maps: Françoise St. Clair

Distributed in Canada by Raincoast Books,
112 East Third Avenue, Vancouver, B.C. V5T 1C8

10 9 8 7 6 5 4 3 2 1

Chronicle Books
275 Fifth Street
San Francisco, CA 94103

For Liz

CONTENTS

To the Reader

London—a nation, not a city . . .
    —Benjamin Disraeli

London is no longer a first-rate city with second-rate dining possibilities. The range of eating places is greater than ever. New restaurants continue to open and old favorites get better. The cooking in most has gone way beyond the staples of Yorkshire pudding, bangers and mash, and soggy puddings. There has been a growth of ethnic cuisines and the development of a new style of modern British cooking that did not exist a decade ago. Now you will find stylish Anglo-Californian cooking, new-wave Italian, French bistro, along with simply grilled meats and inventive vegetarian and fish dishes. Today, dining in London is as varied as you want to make it, and it is possible to travel gastronomically around the world without going beyond the Circle Line of the underground transport system (The Tube).

Cheap Eats in London brings you the best of London dining on a budget, with over 165 listings. I have done the advance work for you by canvassing those establishments offering the best value for your money, which is always an essential ingredient in any good meal. In *Cheap Eats in London* you will find places serving unusual Indonesian food, cheap and cheerful snack bars, historic pubs, cozy tearooms, sophisticated wine bars, and Big Splurges for special occasions. The book also answers the important questions most visitors have about the ins and outs of dining in London. You will find out where to go and what to order once you get there. What does "service charge" mean on top of the bill? Are you expected to tip, too? Because I write with first-hand knowledge of all the listings described, I have covered many miles in all types of weather and under every sort of condition. So that I will have the same service you can expect, I always dine anonymously, never asking for special treatment. Neither do I rely on advance screening teams, hearsay, or printed forms filled out by the restaurant to get my information. If I like a place, I will consider it. If I am rudely treated, the food is poorly served, the kitchen is dirty, and the restroom terrible, then the place is out, no matter how good, how cheap, or how popular it may be. A blend of good food, service, price, and ambiance inspires repeat visits. If any of these factors is missing, it is not usually a place I recommend. It is also important to judge a restaurant on its own terms. I do not expect much individual attention in a crowded, takeaway sandwich shop, nor do I look for gourmet fare in pubs. Service is another thing one must be philosophical about, especially in budget restaurants. The staff is usually young and inexperienced, and sometimes speaks limited English. England does not have the tradition, as found in France, of restaurant service as a valued profession. In England, and particularly in London, working in a restaurant is usually a means to an end, rarely a career goal.

It is important that you know *Cheap Eats in London* is *not* a book about the cheapest food in London. If you want to eat as cheaply as possible, stop reading now. On the other hand, if you are interested in top value for your dining pound, *Cheap Eats in London* is for you. If your conception of a London food bargain was formed a few years ago, or if it runs parallel with your idea of American Cheap Eats, you will find yourself very disappointed. True, London is less expensive than it was two years ago, but it is still far from *cheap* to most Americans.

In these hard times, Londoners are putting a bright face on their dim economy by making stinting stylish. Leave it to the British to maintain a stiff upper lip in every crisis! You won't find smart London diners in high-priced restaurants, unless at lunch, when they are taking advantage of the amazing set-price two-and-three-course meals offered for a fraction of the regular dinner or à la carte menus. No nonsense quality is *in*. Unending extravagance is *out.*

In selecting places to be included in the book, I limited my choices to eating establishments located within the Circle Line on the London tube system. Like many travelers, when I am in a city for a short while, I do not want to spend my time and energy traveling to a restaurant on the edge of the city, when for just about the same price, I can eat as well several bus or tube stops away.

For convenience, *Cheap Eats in London* is organized by postal codes to help you determine which restaurants are closest to your hotel or whatever tourist attraction you are visiting. You will also find restaurants listed according to the type of food they serve (American, Italian, sandwich shops, vegetarian, etc.), a list of Big Splurges for those of you with more flexible budgets, and a glossary of English food and restaurant terms. Finally, there is a page requesting your comments. I cannot overemphasize how valuable your comments are to me. They help me reconsider, investigate, question, and discover new places. Circumstances change rapidly in the food world and inevitably some of the listed restaurants will change hands, close, or hire a new chef, even in the time it takes this book to reach you. I have done my best to be accurate at press time, but I am eager to hear any news you have about changes you find or ideas you may have for future editions.

No one takes a trip to London to save money, but at the same time, you do not want to waste your money, either. Writing *Cheap Eats in*

London reinforced my view that there is plenty of good food in London—at affordable prices. But you have to know where to go, and with *Cheap Eats in London* in hand, that will be easy. I hope the book will pave your way toward wonderful dining experiences in London, will save you money, and in the bargain, inspire you to return soon. Have a marvelous time and—don't forget to write.

HOW TO USE CHEAP EATS IN LONDON

Each listing in *Cheap Eats in London* includes this information: name and address of the establishment, telephone number, postal code, tube stop, days and hours open, whether reservations are needed, which credit cards are accepted, the average price for an à la carte and a set meal, and special details about each restaurant, pub, wine bar, or tearoom.

These codes indicate which credit cards are accepted:

American Express	AE
Diners Club	DC
MasterCard or Access	MC
Visa	V

BYOB indicates that you can bring your own liquor or wine to an unlicensed restaurant.

Fourteen Tips on How to Enjoy Cheap Eats in London

1. In England, tea can be a meal in itself. If you are going to the theater or want an early evening meal, consider having afternoon tea. With a proper tea, you will enjoy dainty finger sandwiches, scones with clotted cream and jam, and rich teacakes and tarts. Afternoon tea is a lovely experience every visitor should have at least once in London.

2. Always read the menu posted outside before going into the restaurant, pub, or cafe. This prevents you from being seated before finding out you don't like anything on the menu, or worse yet, that the prices are too high. If a menu is not posted (which by law it should be), ask to see one before making the final decision whether to stay. *All* menus must clearly state the following: prices including VAT (Value-Added Tax is the British equivalent of sales tax); whether a service charge is included, and if so, how much it is; the cover charge, and the minimum if there is one.

3. Watch the fine print. A cover charge is *per person;* a minimum charge is also *per person.* A steep cover along with a hefty 12½-percent service charge on top of a three-course meal with wine, dessert, and coffee could be hard to swallow.

4. If you like fine dining without fine prices, consider going to a noted restaurant for lunch. Usually a set menu is offered, and they are outstanding values, often including dessert, coffee, service, and in some instances, wine.

5. For a cheap midday meal, try a pub. Stick with the special of the day.

6. Another cheap lunch plan is to visit a sandwich shop. If you order your food to go, you will save all service charges. If, however, you eat your food at the takeaway shop, you will pay a service charge.

7. Always order what the restaurant does best. If you are in a fish and chips takeaway, opt for the deep-fried fish and save the hamburger for another time. When you are dining a notch or

two above, always carefully consider the special of the day or the house specialty. You can bet it will be fresh and represent the best the kitchen has to offer.

8. If you are dining with children, ask if reduced prices (sometimes up to half off a regular meal) are available. Don't expect to get this for a sixteen-year-old high school halfback, but for the little ones, it can add up to a significant saving. Many restaurants will do this, but as this service is unadvertised, it pays to ask.

9. It is always better to reserve a table than to arrive and wish you had. Remember, it costs you nothing extra to reserve. If you find you will not be able to go, please call and cancel so the restaurant can rebook the table. Also remember that in busy places, tables are usually held only ten minutes, so plan to arrive on time or lose your reservation.

10. Don't be shy when it comes to asking questions. When in doubt about any aspect of a restaurant you are considering, call ahead and ask. To double-check prices, ask for the cost of a three-course meal with house wine and service. If you are a vegetarian, ask what the chef can do specifically for you. If you just walk in, your choices may be limited to steamed veggies. But, if you have called ahead, the chef may get creative. You have nothing to lose and only good value to gain.

11. If the waiter asks, "Would you like a selection of vegetables with your meal?" ask if they are included in the main course or will be extra. If they are extra, watch out—a round or two of vegetables and potatoes at £2 or £3 per person can add up in a hurry, and turn a once-reasonable meal into a budget disaster.

12. Beware of the double service-charge trick. See "Paying the Bill," page 17.

13. One of the most important tips is twofold. Tube stops can be few and far between. Consider using the bus or combining the tube and the bus. It is beyond the scope of *Cheap Eats in London* to detail all the bus routes (because their times change so frequently) in addition to the tube stops given with every restaurant listed. Here, then, are two very important pieces of advice:

   a. Buy the *Guide to London by Bus and Tube* published by Nicholson and *use it!* It will not only save you time and energy, but you will see so much more from the top deck of a London bus than you will by wearing yourself out walking miles to get to a restaurant, and then have to face the same hike back after eating.

b. Next, buy the book called *London from A to Z* (the Z is pronounced "zed"). This page-by-page street map of London tells you everything you ever wanted or needed to know about the nooks and crannies of London. If you will be in London for more than twenty-four hours and are not on a guided tour, this book is a *must*. The maps you pick up at your hotel or at a tourist office are virtually useless when it comes to finding much of anything besides Buckingham Palace and Piccadilly Circus. This street map is available at most news kiosks and at bookstores. It is a travel investment that never goes out of style or date.

14. The last two tips have nothing really to do with eating, but being aware of them will save you grief and add greatly to your trip.

a. On April 1, 1995, ALL telephone prefixes in the greater London area will change. If the number is now preceded by 071 (071-345-7875, for example) the prefix will change to 0171, followed by the current number: 0171-345-7875. If the prefix is now 081 (London outskirts), it will change to 0181.

b. A delightful way to become better acquainted with special aspects of London is to take a guided walking tour. They are all well planned and executed and led by knowledgeable guides who have trained for their positions. One of my favorites is "Legal London," where you are taken to the Inns of Court, visit the Royal Courts of Justice, and get to sit in on an actual trial at Old Bailey. There are many others, especially in the historic part of London known as The City, which introduce you to all sorts of fascinating facts and figures you would never find on your own. Check with your hotel or the London Tourist Authority for brochures. The walks last about two hours, are well worth the small fee, and go rain or shine, even if you are the only one going.

GENERAL INFORMATION ABOUT LONDON DINING

TYPES OF FOOD

The following section covers the major types of food listed in *Cheap Eats in London* restaurants.

AMERICAN

Dining American style in London may lose something in crossing the Atlantic, but for many homesick souls, a taste of home now and then feels mighty good, even if it isn't perfect in every respect. Most American restaurants in London lend themselves to party and family eating and are good places to stuff yourself without taking out a second mortgage. A typical American restaurant in London serves burgers, slabs of rib, Tex-Mex food, apple pie, chili, and cheesecake. Menus are laminated and full of jokes and puns and the decor usually includes bare wooden tables, ceiling fans, old advertisements, and other forms of nostalgia.

BRITISH

From bangers and mash to spotted dick, British food is finding new favor. When the term "British" was added to food, it used to mean mediocrity. Today, all English food is not mediocre, nor is it all meat and potatoes with gluey gravy and lumpy pudding for dessert.

For the best of Britain, start your day with a full English breakfast. At lunch, pop into a pub and try a hefty portion of steak and kidney pie or stop by a salt beef bar (corned beef) and have a freshly sliced sandwich on rye that will put to shame those made in most New York delis. If you are in a hurry, join the queue at a busy fish and chips shop and munch your fish from a paper cone just like the locals. Mid-afternoon, stop for tea. The British love their tea, usually accompanied by an assortment of finger sandwiches and delectable pastries. Then there is dinner. If you are still hungry, go to one of the big carveries and dig into a succulent roast beef served with Yorkshire pudding. Finish the feast with a warm treacle tart surrounded by soft custard. Who said British food wasn't filling *and* good?

CHINESE

Chinese restaurants in London are changing, and for the better. They are brighter, service is verging on the polite, and the quality of the cooking is improving. Many people will argue that the best ethnic food in London is found in Chinatown, a maze of streets behind Leicester Square, where local Chinese gather to eat. Their discriminating demands for authenticity keep the quality good and the prices reasonable. The advantages to eating in Chinese restaurants are many. They tend to remain open very late and all day on Sunday. Children are always welcome and a request for a knife and fork is not laughed at.

The best Chinese food is cooked quickly and simply to enhance natural flavors. Most of London's Chinese restaurants are Cantonese, offering meat and seafood specialties served with rice and the delicacy known as dim sum. Years of experience and hours of skill go into the preparation of these Cantonese snacks, yet they sell for £1.50–2.50. Most come in portions of three or four; seven sets should be large enough for two for lunch. The only drawback to dim sum is that restaurants stop serving them about 5 P.M.

FRENCH

French restaurants in London can be very expensive, with prices higher than you would pay for the same quality and service in Paris. If you do decide you want fine French food in London, and if price is any consideration, then go for lunch when the set menus are served. These will cost a fraction of the same meal served for dinner. As in Paris, nouvelle anything is *out* and hearty, homey bourgeois cooking is *in*.

INDIAN

Almost everywhere you go in London, there will be some sort of Indian restaurant. For most Americans, Indian food is exotic and different, but not for the British, who governed the subcontinent for hundreds of years. Having tandoori chicken for dinner is as normal for them as going out for a pizza is for us.

Indian restaurants have other things to offer the Cheap Eater in London. They are open late and the servings are plentiful for the money. Service is generally polite and waiters are used to explaining various dishes to novices. Indian foods blend different spices in each dish, but it is the chilies that determine how hot the food will be. With two or more in a group, it is best to order several dishes and share as you would in a Chinese restaurant. Always try the bread and ask for yogurt to help put out the fire if you get something too hot. Remember, please, that beer goes better with Indian food than wine.

ITALIAN

Italian food in London is generally reliable and predictable. The current emphasis on a high-carbohydrate diet has removed pasta from the no-no fattening category and placed it in the healthy one. In addition to pasta and pizza in every flavor and variety imaginable, you will find risotto, gnocci, thick bean soup, fish, tender veal, and often wild game in season.

JAPANESE

Bowls of Japanese noodles are the latest inexpensive food to take London by storm. These one-bowl meals are easy to make and can be topped with a variety of ingredients from a single pork slice to a jumbo prawn. At the other end of the scale are the restaurants catering to Japanese business and corporate people. These still cost a mild fortune and are best left alone, unless someone else is paying the bill.

According to an old Japanese proverb, "If you eat something you have never tasted before, your life will be lengthened by 75 days." The Japanese restaurants listed in *Cheap Eats in London* offer suggestions for good value lunches and dinners, and you are bound to find something you have never tasted.

SOUTHEAST ASIAN

Authentic Southeast Asian food need not be expensive. It is an interesting dining experience because it offers well-flavored dishes using ingredients and spices most of us don't eat on a regular basis. The dishes are not served singly in courses but all at once. It is customary to order several portions to share. If you order two or three starters and main courses with rice or noodles, you won't go away hungry. Wines don't really complement this food too well; bottled lagers are a better choice.

Malaysian, Indonesian, and Singaporean food are closely related and often appear side-by-side on the menu. Ethnic Malaysians are Muslim, so pork is not served. Bali is Hindu, so beef is out. The principal flavorings are chili, coriander, lemongrass, coconut, tamarind, and fermented, dried-shrimp paste. The simpler dishes and salads are often dressed with peanut sauce. While restaurants serving this food are not as fashionable as Thai, the cooking is as good and the prices more reasonable.

Thai cuisine is tremendously popular in London, probably because so many people spend their holidays on package trips to Bangkok and at the beaches up-country. The nice thing about a Thai meal is that it isn't always a multi-course affair. Many Thai restaurants offer single-dish meals that can be eaten there or taken out. The food has a reputation for being fiery hot, so if you cannot handle lots of heat, ask to have the chili content reduced.

Vietnamese cooking has come into its own in London. Not too long ago, there was only one small noodle shop selling *pho,* the traditional Vietnamese breakfast of noodles and beef in broth. Now there are many more offering delicate dishes that in many cases are much more sophisticated than Chinese or Thai food. If you are not used to Vietnamese cuisine, go *very* easy on the pungent fish sauce, *nuoc mam,* that is served on the side with almost everything. For most Western palates, it is an acquired taste that may take a long while to develop.

VEGETARIAN

Vegetarians continue to fare very well in London. Almost every restaurant has a vegetarian dish, including pubs, and if one is not on the menu, ask and chances are good that something can be made up for you. Also, when reserving it is smart to mention how many in your party are vegetarians, thus alerting the kitchen ahead of time. There are also ethnic cuisines that lean heavily toward vegetarian, notably Indian and Malaysian. All of the restaurants serving vegetarian food go a long way in proving that vegetarian food can be delicious *and* healthy at the same time.

HOLIDAYS

Because of the recession, more and more restaurants are staying open on holidays. However, this policy, with the exception of Christmas, Boxing Day, and Easter, varies with the wind. To avoid disappointment, be sure to call ahead to verify if a particular restaurant is open and what its holiday hours are.

Christmas Day	December 25
Boxing Day	December 26
Good Friday	Friday before Easter
Easter Sunday	Varies
Easter Monday	Monday after Easter
May Day	May 1
Bank Holidays	Legal holidays with varying dates

HOURS

Before the recession, many restaurants closed early and few took orders after 9:30 or 10 P.M. This made for slim pickings for theatergoers, who had to eat very early or not at all. Now, more restaurants are staying open all day, and most have extended their closing hours.

Mealtimes in London are similar to those in the United States: Breakfast is between 7 and 9 A.M., lunch is served between 12 noon and 2:30 P.M., and dinner anytime from 6 until 11 P.M. If the last time given for serving a meal is 11 P.M., it means you will not be able to order *after* that time, but you can be in the restaurant eating and should be allowed to enjoy and finish your meal without feeling hurried. When a restaurant closes between lunch and dinner, most want to let the help go home one hour after the last order has been taken.

Restaurants with continuous food service usually like to stop serving about one half hour *before* closing.

LICENSED AND UNLICENSED RESTAURANTS

A surprising number of restaurants in London do not have liquor licenses. In many cases you can bring your own bottle (BYOB) and will often be charged a corkage fee by the restaurant for them to pour your wine or beer. The corkage fees are usually nominal and if you buy your liquor in an off-license shop (retail liquor store) it will be much less than you would pay in a restaurant that sells wine or beer by the bottle. In a few cases all alcohol consumption is prohibited. All *Cheap Eats in London* entries clearly state if a restaurant is unlicensed and whether a corkage fee is imposed. If nothing is said about licensing, you know that the restaurant is licensed and that bringing your own liquor is not acceptable.

MIND YOUR MANNERS

1. Be patient. Relax; you are on vacation. Always remember even though you are in London where you speak the same language (more or less), you are in a foreign city with its own way of doing things. Let them do it their way—it is all part of the experience of traveling. If you insist on having things the same as they are at home, don't leave home in the first place.

2. *Please* and *thank you* still go a long way in getting good treatment and service. In London, this is especially true.

3. If reservations are recommended, take this advice seriously and make them. Many restaurants overbook, so it is imperative that you arrive *on time* or risk losing your reservation. It happens all the time. If you reserve a table and change your mind, always call and cancel.

4. If a waiter spills something on your clothing, the restaurant should offer to pay your cleaning bill.

5. Don't flash cash at the headwaiter and above all *never* tip the bar

staff in a pub. You can offer to buy them a drink, but never, never offer money.

6. Dress for success. If you are going to a nice restaurant, leave the jogging shoes and running outfits where they belong . . . in the hotel closet. Nothing brands a gauche tourist quicker and results in poor service faster than improper attire.

7. *Someone* has to sit in "Siberia" and have the new waiter trainee, but it doesn't necessarily have to be you. It seldom pays to be rude and you should always treat the restaurant staff with the same courtesy you expect to receive from them. But, whenever you dine out, always make sure you get what you are paying for. The diner who gently makes it plain when things are not right will end up having the least to complain about.

PAYING THE BILL

This can be confusing for visitors to London because there are so many things that are different from U.S. dining practices. With the following advance knowledge, you will be better armed to avoid the traps and better able to save yourself from being overcharged or confused when the bill arrives. It is very important to go over the bill carefully before paying it. Unfortunately, mistakes are rampant and do not usually favor the diner. If in doubt, always question.

PRICES

There are two prices given in the restaurant listings in *Cheap Eats in London*. If a set menu is available, the listing will state what is served for this fixed amount of money. You can expect to pay extra for the cover charge, wine, coffee, and service if they are not specifically included in the set price. The à la carte prices represent the average cost of a three-course meal that includes a starter, main course, and dessert. Drinks, the service charge, and cover charge if there is one will be extra. In determining average prices, the cheapest and the most expensive items on the menu have been avoided; therefore, you could spend more or less depending on what you order and how much you drink. All prices quoted are in British pounds and were correct at press time. You should expect a certain margin of error in the prices due to inflation, escalating food costs, and the whims of owners and chefs.

COVER CHARGE

The *cover charge* is not to be confused with the *service charge*. It is a great moneymaker to charge the customer for the bread and butter (even if you don't touch it), any flowers on the table, the tablecloth, the napkins, and who knows what else. All menus *must* state clearly the amount of the cover charge. If none is mentioned, none is imposed. The cover charge is levied per person and is listed separately on your bill, but added into the total to hike the amount of service you will pay. Thankfully, more and more restaurants are dropping this rip-off, but many Italian places are tenaciously hanging on. You can be sure that pubs, takeaway shops, and less-expensive restaurants *never* have a cover charge.

MINIMUM CHARGE

Minimum charges are given in the listings where applicable and are per person, not per couple or group. These charges may be enforced during peak periods, or in better places to discourage people from coming in only for a salad, thus occupying time and space that could be devoted to better-paying customers. If the restaurant does not state a minimum charge, you are expected to order enough to add up to at least a main course. In cafes, pubs, tearooms, wine bars, sandwich shops, fish and chip spots, and takeaway places, it doesn't matter how little you spend.

SERVICE CHARGE

The service charge *is* the tip. You are not required to leave one ha'penny more. That being said, trying to find out if the service is included on the bill is one of London's great after-dinner games. *Cheap Eats in London* clearly states in every listing what you can expect.

No service charge

This means none has been levied and you are not expected to pay any additional. You will find this in all pubs (but not necessarily in a sit-down restaurant in a pub) and in a takeaway restaurant where you do not consume your food on the premises.

_____ % service charge

This means 10 to 15 percent will be added to the total of your bill.

Service discretionary

This means the restaurant will not automatically add it, but hopes you will. The least amount you should leave in this case is 10 percent, better to leave 12½. If the evening has been extraordinary and you are feeling flush, give 15. Anything more is excessive.

If the service or food is poor, the law says you do not have to leave any service charge, even if it is included and added onto your final bill. You must, however, make your complaint to the management and explain why you are deducting the service charge.

Important! Beware of the service charge–credit card scam. This is a gouging of the customer in no uncertain terms. If the restaurant has imposed a tip and added it to your bill, but left the space on the credit card for the "tip/gratuity" blank, they are in fact charging you twice. Watch out for this because it happens with increasing regularity. If that happens to you, you should definitely deduct a portion of the original service charge to discourage such underhanded tactics. To avoid the double charge, draw a line through the space marked "tip/gratuity" and pay it in cash.

Remember, *only* if *no* service charge has been added to your final bill and if the food and service have been satisfactory are you expected to leave a tip at all.

VAT

The value-added tax is the British equivalent of a sales tax. You may think it is another extra, but it is not: it is always included in the price of any restaurant meal.

SMOKING

Nonsmokers quickly realize that there is no British surgeon general or multimillion-dollar ad campaign extolling the virtues of a smoke-free environment in eating establishments in London. During busy times, especially in pubs and smaller restaurants and cafes, the gray haze can get as thick as London fog. Where smoking is prohibited or where there is a special nonsmoking section, it has been boldly noted in the *Cheap Eats in London* listing. Otherwise—good luck!

TAKEAWAY SERVICE

Many restaurants in London prepare food to go. It is called "takeaway service." Takeaway is also a money-saver, because there is never a service charge on any food not consumed on the premises. For those of you with children or who need a fast bite on the go, this is a great convenience. If you don't want to queue for your food and are placing an order for more than a sandwich, it pays to phone ahead. This way your order will be ready at a set time and you will avoid having to waste time lining up. Takeaway service is also important to keep in mind if you are going on a train trip anywhere in Britain. The food on British Rail varies from downright terrible to simply inedible. Do yourself a favor—take your own.

TRANSPORTATION

Every listing gives the closest tube stop (London underground transport). *Close* is a relative term, because in all honesty, some of the walks are very long. Often you can do better by bus; or by combining the bus and tube you can often arrive almost at the doorstep. With a few exceptions, bus routes are not given because they change frequently and do not always run every day or at night. The best advice is to purchase two invaluable books: *The Guide to London by Bus and Tube* (Nicholson) and *London A-Z*, a book that shows every street in London in minute detail. The free maps you pick up at your hotel are useless. They don't begin to do the job when you are trying to find the street with the perfect restaurant, only to realize it is another fifteen-minute walk—in the other direction. The maps included in *Cheap Eats in London* are intended as a quick reference only. While they are useful, they are not drawn to scale, and do not indicate all of the streets.

WARNING ON PRICES

While I have made every effort to be accurate with all the prices, restaurants, managers, chefs, and especially prices, change—often overnight. It would be a safe bet to add 10 to 20 percent, particularly in 1995, to the prices quoted here. For complete certainty about a restaurant, it is always better to call ahead to check on specific details concerning hours, reservations, and prices.

WHERE TO SIT

"Do you mind sitting upstairs (or downstairs in the basement)?" invariably means being shunted to a large, more unfriendly, and often deserted room that otherwise is used for catered groups or for seating other unwary tourists. *Up-* or *downstairs* can also mean windowless rooms that get hot and unbearably smoky after one or two diners light up. If you are stuck in this Siberia, no matter how wonderful the food and service may be, something will be lost and you probably will not enjoy your meal. That is why I have mentioned the most desirable places to sit in restaurants where it makes a difference.

CHEAP EATS IN LONDON BY POSTAL CODE

Just as Paris is divided into arrondissements, London is divided into postal districts. Postal code prefixes appear on London street signs and in street addresses. The letters stand for compass directions in reference to the central district, which is divided into WC and EC for West Central and East Central. All the districts bordering the central districts are numbered 1 and continue to increase in number as they get farther from the center. If you are in London SW3, you are someplace in Chelsea, and if you are in London WC1, you are in the Bloomsbury area, probably wandering through the British Museum. If you see an address followed by W11, you will know you are *not* in the heart of Piccadilly!

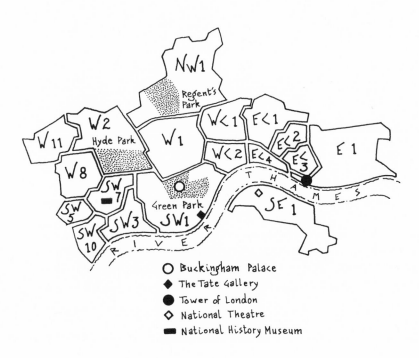

- ○ Buckingham Palace
- ◆ The Tate Gallery
- ● Tower of London
- ◇ National Theatre
- ▬ National History Museum

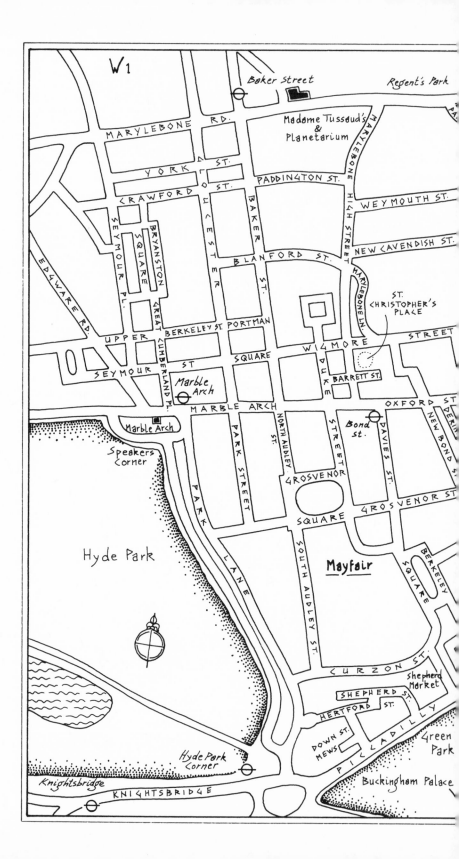

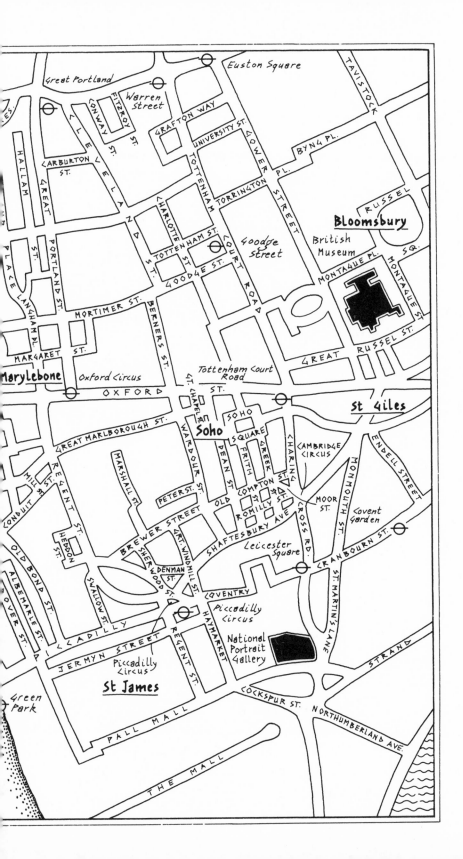

W1 ✤ MARBLE ARCH, MARYLEBONE, MAYFAIR, OXFORD STREET, PICCADILLY CIRCUS, SOHO, SPEAKER'S CORNER

Marble Arch is marooned on a traffic island, hardly noticed by frazzled car drivers and inaccessible to pedestrians. Only royalty and the King's Troop Royal Horse Artillery may pass through its central gates. It stood in front of Buckingham Palace from 1827, but was moved here in 1851.

Marylebone is located between Regent Park and Oxford Street. Britain's finest doctors have offices on Harley Street. The area's most famous resident was Sherlock Holmes who, even though fictitious, still receives letters addressed to "221b Baker Street." Also, here is Madame Tussaud's wax museum, one of the top tourist attractions in the country, and the lines that snake around the block attest to this.

Mayfair is home to elegant shops with a quiet assuredness only old money can buy. Some of the most expensive real estate in London is in Mayfair. Here you will find Grosvenor Square, the American Embassy, Bond and Regent Streets (which are synonymous with fine shopping), Buckingham Palace, and the famed Saville Row, where the man in your life can get excessively priced bespoke (custom) tailoring.

Oxford Street is lined on both sides with a variety of shops and impossible crowds. It is hardly a destination for the discriminating buyer.

All of the West End main thoroughfares go around Piccadilly Circus. It is alive night and day with crazy traffic, tourists, neon lights, and the largest Tower Records store on the planet where you can buy the Los Angeles or New York *Times*, any record made, T-shirts galore, and tickets for concerts and sporting events.

Many of London's most fashionable restaurants, clubs, and shops occupy buildings in Soho that once housed massage parlors, porn shops, and ladies of the night. Today, Soho has a cosmopolitan atmosphere with crowded streets full of bistros, cafes, avant-garde shops and galleries, and many first run theaters.

If you have an orange crate and something to say that is not obscene, or you have an urge to breach the peace, then you can do so at Speaker's Corner on Sunday. Or you can join the hecklers or just watch all the fun.

PUBS

RESTAURANTS

PUBS W1

Shepherds Tavern
50 Hertford Street, Shepherds Market, W1

TELEPHONE
071-499-3017
TUBE
Hyde Park or Green Park
OPEN
Daily
CLOSED
Christmas
HOURS
Continuous service Mon–Fri
11 A.M.–11 P.M.;
Sat 11 A.M.–3 P.M., 6–11 P.M.;
Sun noon–3 P.M., 7–10:30 P.M.
RESERVATIONS
Not accepted
CREDIT CARDS
AE, MC, V
PRICES
À la Carte: £4.50–6
VAT/SERVICE
No service charged or expected

The Shepherds Tavern once served as the wartime pub for Royal Air Force pilots. The regulars had their pewter mugs hung up behind the bar, ready for use when or if they returned. For two hundred years, the tavern has been a focal point of Shepherd Market, a bright and lively square in fashionable Mayfair, one of the most expensive residential areas in London. As is the case in most London pubs, the food is nutritious and filling rather than thrilling. When I go, I like to sit upstairs in the cozy wood-paneled room with banquette seating and a real fireplace, and order a bowl of homemade soup and a ploughman's platter, a piece of crusty bread served with one or two cheeses, an apple, and a sweet pickle. It is a light, yet satisfying meal and always sees me through until dinner.

RESTAURANTS W1

Amalfi Ristorante
29–31 Old Compton Street, W1

Amalfi has been an upscale Cheap Eat on the Soho dining scene for more than thirty years. The owner, Mr. Ramos, shows no sign of slowing down and neither do any of his Italian-speaking, somewhat brusque waiters. Clad in bright red shirts, they laugh, joke, and kibbitz with the regulars who vie for seats in the upstairs room, brightly painted with clouds on the ceiling and scenes from the Amalfi coast hand-painted on the tiled tabletops. Just off the entrance is a *pâtisserie* and a take-out counter. Downstairs are several other rooms, including one papered with Italian newspapers and photographs of Sophia Loren, and a romantic candlelit grotto hung with Chianti bottles. The best meal-deal is the £5 pasta plate. For this amazing low price you have a choice of five types of pasta topped with any of ten homemade sauces. Or, you can enjoy cannelloni, lasagna, tortellini, or risotto with mushrooms. All of these dishes come with a tossed salad and warm garlic bread. For non-pasta fanciers, Amalfi offers pizza, wonderful veal and chicken preparations, and a small selection of fresh fish. They make all of their own desserts, which are seductively displayed in the window by the takeaway counter. Try to save room. You won't be sorry when you taste your first bite of a cream-filled cake or the rich *tiramisu*.

TELEPHONE
071-437-7284

TUBE
Piccadilly Circus

OPEN
Daily

CLOSED
2 days at Christmas

HOURS
Continuous service
Mon–Sat
noon–11:15 P.M.,
Sun noon–10 P.M.

RESERVATIONS
Good idea

CREDIT CARDS
AE, DC, MC, V

PRICES
À la Carte: £6–10
Set Price: £5 for pasta,
salad, and bread

VAT/SERVICE
75p cover per person,
10% service added to bill

Bahn Thai
21a Frith Street, W1

While the fates of most Thai restaurants are variable, Bahn Thai has remained constant and is recognized as one of the best Southeast Asian restaurants in London. Little expense or effort is spared in obtaining the finest ingredients, even to the point of importing their own herbs, spices, and specialty items directly from Thailand. The food is served in the oriental manner with several dishes placed in the center of the table to be shared by everyone. Chopsticks and bowls are not used, rather forks and flat plates. Rice is piled on the plate and each dish is to be sampled by itself, never mixed with another—allowing the distinct flavors of each to stand out. Soups are eaten with the rice as a main course, and so are the spicy salads. Many Thai dishes are *very* hot, but you

TELEPHONE
071-437-8505

TUBE
Tottenham Court Road or
Leicester Square

OPEN
Daily

CLOSED
Christmas, Easter, some
holidays (call to check)

HOURS
Lunch: Mon–Sat noon–
2:45 P.M., Sun 12:30–2:30 P.M.
Dinner: Mon–Sat 6–11:15 P.M.,
Sun 6:30–10:30 P.M.

RESERVATIONS
Recommended

CREDIT CARDS
AE, DC, MC, V

PRICES
À la Carte: £18–22
Set Price: £18–25

VAT/SERVICE
£1 cover per person at night,
12½% service added to bill

MISCELLANEOUS
Takeaway

can ask to have the seasonings adjusted—either mild or turned up to "full Thai heat." The creative menu lists all the standard Thai dishes and plenty of specialties seldom seen, such as crispy frog legs and pigs trotters. The menu is marked with symbols denoting vegetarian dishes and those that are fiery hot.

Bahn Thai is one of the few restaurants I have known to provide a manual to assist and guide guests through a Thai meal. Be sure to read it. It offers sage advice on all you need to know from how to order a meal balanced in taste, texture, and flavor, to what to do if you eat too much chili.

California Pizza Company
6 Blandford Street, W1

TELEPHONE
071-486-7878

TUBE
Baker Street or Bond Street

OPEN
Mon–Sat

CLOSED
Sun, holidays

HOURS
Continuous service
noon–11:15 P.M.

RESERVATIONS
Not necessary,
unless large group

CREDIT CARDS
AE, DC, MC, V

PRICES
À la Carte: £4–9

VAT/SERVICE
10% service charge

The California Pizza Company is bright, clean, fresh, and very inexpensive if you go at the right time. It is also much more than a typical pizzeria. Their pizzas are baked on thin, crisp crusts, and topped with fresh ingredients, mostly vegetables, seafood, and chicken. All are prepared to order, baked in wood-fired ovens, giving them a mildly smoky taste. The pizzas only account for about half of the food sold here. The rest includes appetizers such as the Hollywood Bowl (clam chowder) or Surf's Up (chargrilled prawns marinated in garlic). Interesting salads, three or four imaginative pastas, mesquite-grilled catfish, baby back ribs, and a half-pound hamburger, all with clever California name tags, make up the rest of the menu. Wines from the Glen Ellen Winery in Sonoma Valley, California, and American beers are also available. Theatergoers or other early eaters can take advantage of the Happy Time between 5 and 7 P.M., when all main courses are only £4. At any time, if you are dining with children 12 or under, they get a free child-sized pizza as long as you order a main course. For desserts, try one of their "coffees with a kick," or lose yourself in one of their homemade specialties of carrot cake or the Chocolate Alcatraz, a chocolate cake which is, as the menu says, "Like the prison, you can't escape this one."

Cappuccetto Ristorante Italiano
17 Moor Street (off Cambridge Circus), W1

There is nothing prissy about the robust food you will eat at Alberto Pagano's Cappuccetto Ristorante Italiano, the oldest established restaurant in Soho with the same owner. The prices are right for Cheap Eaters, since most of the main courses include potatoes and rice and are large enough to leave you well-stuffed.

The menu reads like Italian Cuisine 101, from A—avocado *con gamberetti* (avocado with shrimp) to Z—zabaglione. In between you will find all the Italian renditions of veal, beef, and chicken. Pasta and pizza are well represented, and daily specials are written each day on the windows.

Inside there is a grotto-like room downstairs with murals on the walls of Portofino near Genoa. Upstairs, banquettes, hanging Chianti bottles, and photos crowding the walls create a warm, almost intimate feeling.

Sr. Pagano prides himself on his impressive selection of grappa. Over 187 different types are offered. If an after-dinner grappa does not suit you, by all means order one of the desserts, which are admittedly hazards to your diet willpower. All are made at his Pâtisserie Cappuccetto just across the street. To give you some idea of the volume there, eight pastry cooks begin work at 1 A.M. each morning, turning out at least 1,000 croissants a day and enough pastries to supply 140 additional restaurants. The two-room shop has a few simple wooden benches and is a good place to remember if you want a quick sandwich, a plain or filled croissant, or a dessert to die for.

TELEPHONE
071-437-2527

TUBE
Leicester Square, Tottenham Court Road, or Covent Garden

OPEN
Daily

CLOSED
Christmas, Easter Sunday

HOURS
Lunch: noon–3 P.M.
Dinner: 5:30–11:30 P.M.

RESERVATIONS
Preferred

CREDIT CARDS
AE, DC, MC, V

PRICES
À la Carte: £12–17

VAT/SERVICE
90p cover, 10% service charge

Chez Gérard
8 Charlotte Street, W1

To most people, *French* means the best, whether it is used to modify laundry, style, or cuisine. Chez Gérard, a longtime French restaurant in London, never fails to please because it always serves the *best*. Red-meat eaters adore eating here, where admittedly some of the best grilled meats and *frites* (french fries)

TELEPHONE
071-636-4975, 071-580-5495

TUBE
Goodge Street

OPEN
Daily

CLOSED
Sat, holidays
HOURS
Lunch: 12:30–2:30 P.M.
Dinner: 6:30–11 P.M.
RESERVATIONS
Better for lunch
CREDIT CARDS
AE, DC, MC, V
PRICES
À la Carte: £17–19
Set Price: £15, 3 courses;
£16, 4 courses
VAT/SERVICE
12½% service charge
added to bill

are served this side of the English Channel. The interiors of this three-restaurant Gallic chain are rustic, with paneling, quiet booths, polished wood floors, and waiters with French accents sporting wing-tipped collars, bow ties, black pants, and white aprons swooping to their toes. The set menu offers the top value, when you consider there are three appetizer and main course choices and whatever dessert you want from the pastry cart. Otherwise, you can choose from a house salad with garlic croutons and warm bacon dressing, vichyssoise, and *plats du jour* featuring French standbys of *boeuf bourguignon* and *filet de sole farci.*

Chuen Cheng Ku Restaurant
17 Wardour Street, W1

TELEPHONE
071-437-1398
TUBE
Leicester Square or
Piccadilly Circus
OPEN
Daily
CLOSED
Christmas
HOURS
Continuous service
11 A.M.–11:30 P.M.
RESERVATIONS
Suggested; no bookings taken
for Sun lunch
CREDIT CARDS
AE, DC, MC, V
PRICES
À la Carte: £9-12
Set Price: From £10 per person
VAT/SERVICE
Service discretionary

The functional Chuen Cheng Ku in London's Chinatown is *the* place to have dim sum, the Asian lunchtime treat of varieties of bite-sized appetizers. This meal provides one of the best opportunities to sample a wide range of tastes, but the experience of choosing can be frustrating. Hard-working waitresses wheel dim sum carts around the tables, chanting in Chinese the names of their offerings. Diners then take their pick of the exotic mouthfuls wrapped in leaves or delicately arranged in willow baskets. Since most of the waitresses only know the Chinese names of the food on their cart, you can study the picture menu on each table to help you decide. Actually, it is much more fun and adventurous to just point as the cart passes and enjoy the surprise.

In addition to dim sum, the long menu lists almost every Cantonese dish you have ever heard of and some you wish you hadn't (such as fried chicken blood with chili and black bean sauce). The best advice is to stick with the dim sum, served every day until 5:45 P.M. The most interesting time to go is for Sunday lunch, when you can observe extended Chinese families indulging in their favorite dim sum delicacies.

Country Life
123 Regent Street Building, entrance 1 Heddon Street, SW1

Country Life is the name to remember for very hungry Cheap Eaters who find themselves near Regent Street at lunchtime. The basement self-service cafeteria is run by Seventh Day Adventists, who also run the large health-food store upstairs. Because of their religious beliefs, you can count on a no-smoking policy and no booze being served or allowed to be brought in. The large, cavernous dining room has bistro-style tables with black chairs and dried flowers hanging from the brick pillars and arranged in pots on each table. Everything on the daily changing menu is made right here and contains no meat, fish, or dairy products. For less than £6 you can get an all-you-can-eat meal of soup, salad, homemade bread, main course, vegetables, and fruit for dessert. The ingredients for each dish are listed, so if there are some things you cannot have or do not like, you will know about it beforehand. The day I ate here I had a choice of cream of millet or chili soup, a large build-your-own salad with sprouts, seeds, and tomatoes, and for the main course, stuffed peppers, kidney bean stroganoff, or rice pilaf, all garnished with fresh vegetables and a choice of four or five homemade breads and nut butters. Believe me, it is impossible to leave hungry, or even to feel tempted by a snack for the rest of the day after doing justice to one of these square meals fit for a football halfback.

TELEPHONE
071-434-2922

TUBE
Piccadilly Circus

OPEN
Restaurant: Mon–Thurs 11:30 A.M.–2:30 P.M., Fri 11:30 A.M.–2 P.M.
Health food store: Mon–Wed 10:30 A.M.–6 P.M., 7 P.M. on Thurs, Fri 8:30 A.M.–2:30 P.M.

CLOSED
Evenings, Sat, Sun, holidays

RESERVATIONS
Not accepted

CREDIT CARDS
None

PRICES
À la Carte: £2.50–6.50
Set Price: All you can eat buffet, £5.50

VAT/SERVICE
No service charged or expected

Cranks Marshall Street
8 Marshall Street, W1

For a quick, nutritious vegetarian meal any time of day, Cranks is the name to remember. This chain of vegetarian restaurants and shops has been a front runner on the London natural food scene, introducing whole grains, raw sugar, and free-range eggs as healthy alternatives to the British staples of sausage, beans, fried eggs, and sugary snacks. The addition of organic wines, candlelit tables in the evening, and waitress service in most branches has done a good

TELEPHONE
071-437-2915

TUBE
Oxford Circus

OPEN
Mon–Sat

CLOSED
Sun, holidays

HOURS
Continuous service
Mon–Fri 8:30 A.M.–6 P.M.,
Sat 9:30 A.M.–5:30 P.M.

RESERVATIONS
Not necessary
CREDIT CARDS
AE, DC, MC, V
PRICES
À la Carte: £6.50–11
VAT/SERVICE
Service discretionary
MISCELLANEOUS
Air-conditioned; no smoking;
takeaway

deal to erase the dated feeling the chain developed in the last decade. The food is good, although some of the recipes seem a little old hat, considering the innovations in vegetarian cuisine in the past few years. Food is displayed cafeteria-style and diners can choose from a huge selection of home-baked hot and cold dishes, salads, and sweets. Particularly popular are vegetable lasagna, carrot cake, and the chestnut roast with red wine sauce.

All natural foodies will enjoy looking through Cranks' fully stocked grocery stores selling everything from vitamins and salt substitutes to the latest natural cosmetics, and cures for every condition imaginable.

Cranks St. Christopher's Place
23 Barrett Street, W1

See Cranks Marshall Street, above, for description. All other information is the same.

TELEPHONE: 071-495-1340
TUBE: Bond Street
OPEN: Mon–Sat
CLOSED: Sun, holidays
HOURS: Mon–Fri 8 A.M.–7 P.M., Sat 9 A.M.–7 P.M.

Cranks Tottenham Street
9-11 Tottenham Street, W1

See Cranks Marshall Street, above, for description. All other information is the same.

TELEPHONE: 071-631-3912
TUBE: Goodge Street
OPEN: Mon–Sat
CLOSED: Sun, holidays
HOURS: Continuous service Mon–Fri 8 A.M.–7:30 P.M., Sat 9 A.M.–7:30 P.M.

The Criterion
Piccadilly Circus, W1

TELEPHONE
071-924-0909
TUBE
Piccadilly Circus
OPEN
Daily

Just entering The Criterion will give you a high. It is, however, the *last* place you would expect to find on Piccadilly Circus amid the masses of tourists in tennis shoes and kids on their first date. Years ago it was immortalized in the first Sherlock Holmes story,

"A Study in Scarlet." At the bar, Dr. Watson met the man who would later introduce him to the great detective. Today, thanks to a brilliant renovation by Bob Payton (see Chicago Rib Shack, page 152, and Salsa!, page 104), it is one of London's most opulent and beautiful restaurants. The 120-foot-long, quasi-Byzantine marble hall, with a high, domed ceiling inlaid with gold mosaics and twinkling walls of jeweled tiles lit by a massive tulip light candelabra, is spectacular. Comfortable wicker arm chairs are placed around sixty-two tables, hand-painted by Yugoslavian muralist Filip Sotirovic. The sensational setting, along with the sophisticated Italian/American food served at reasonable prices makes this one restaurant not to be missed.

The menu changes often, but you can always expect to find caesar salad, a polenta dish, perhaps layered with wild mushrooms and dressed in an herb cream, grilled calf's liver with sage oil and onion *risotto*, homemade sausages with mash, topped with mustard and *aioli*. Showstopper desserts include the excessively rich chocolate slice and the sticky toffee pudding, a rich caramel cake surrounded by warm caramel sauce and cream, a rendition that lifts this nursery favorite to sublime heights. Service is upbeat, courteous, and prompt. All-in-all, I give The Criterion two thumbs up.

CLOSED
Christmas

HOURS
Continuous service
Mon–Sat noon–11:30 P.M.,
Sun noon–10:30 P.M.
Mon–Sat, at the bar, light
snacks from 6–10:30 P.M.

RESERVATIONS
Suggested

CREDIT CARDS
AE, DC, MC, V

PRICES
À la Carte: £15-18

VAT/SERVICE
£6 minimum charge, service discretionary

Da Corradi
20–22 Shepherd Market, W1

Da Corradi is a regular lunchtime hangout for local Mayfair office workers who enjoy the low-key atmosphere and good, affordable Italian cooking. There is often a line of people in front around noon, when the aroma of the lusty sauces flows to the sidewalk. The freshly prepared food is worth the wait, especially the daily specials of lasagna, tortellini, or *risotto alla paesana*, which disappear as quickly as they are brought out steaming from the kitchen. All the pastas and sauces are made here by Giuseppe Corradi and his family. They even go so far as to pick their own mushrooms for the wild mushroom pasta sauce.

TELEPHONE
071-499-1742

TUBE
Green Park

OPEN
Mon–Sat

CLOSED
Sat afternoon, Sun, holidays

HOURS
Breakfast: 7–11:30 A.M.
Lunch & Dinner:
noon–10:30 P.M.

RESERVATIONS
For lunch if arriving at peak time

CREDIT CARDS
AE, MC, V
PRICES
À la Carte: £5.50–8
VAT/SERVICE
10% service charge added
to bill
MISCELLANEOUS
Takeaway

When I asked him where he picked the mushrooms, he told me it was a secret location even the Pope couldn't get out of him.

Flowers on small, close-together tables add a splash of color to the rustic coziness of the two-floor Shepherd Market favorite. In the early morning, stop by for a cappuccino, a bowl of real porridge, the kind that is slow-cooked with milk, not zapped in the microwave, or a typical English breakfast. It is a good spot for dinner if you have an early theater ticket or don't want to be fashionably correct and eat after 8 P.M.

Dell'Ugo
56 Frith Street, W1

TELEPHONE
071-734-8784
TUBE
Leicester Square
OPEN
Mon–Sat
CLOSED
Sun, holidays, Sat lunch for the
2 top-floor restaurants
HOURS
Cafe/Bar: 11 A.M.–11 P.M.
Bistro: 11:30 A.M.–3:30 P.M.,
7 P.M.–12:15 A.M.,
closed Sat lunch
Restaurant: 11:30 A.M.–
3:30 P.M., 5:30–11 P.M.,
closed Sat lunch
RESERVATIONS
Essential
CREDIT CARDS
AE, DC, MC, V
PRICES
À la Carte: Cafe/Bar, £4-7;
bistro and restaurant, £9–15
VAT/SERVICE
Service discretionary

It has been said that Chef Antony Worrall-Thompson starts up new restaurants as often as some men buy a new tie. One of his latest ventures—Dell'Ugo, named after one of his favorite olive oils—is not an Italian restaurant as the name suggests, but a trendy Soho address with an eclectic menu and clientele. It is located in a three-story building with each level devoted to a separate restaurant. The ground-floor bar and cafe serves snacks like *crostini, bruschetta,* and salads to a fashion-conscious audience of the under-thirty set. As the evening wears on, the crescendo rises and by 10 P.M., the place is packed to the walls and in full, very loud, form. The next floor up is slightly more serene, at least from a noise level, but it has one wall of wildly abstract-painted naked ladies cavorting about. On the top floor, Renaissance murals, heavy linens, and dark, polished-oak set a formal, more quiet tone. These two floors share one good menu and the food *is* good. No, make that terrific. Start by ordering a basket of country breads with *tapenade, anchoiade,* and olives, or the Mediterranean: hand-rolled mozzarella, chargrilled vegetables, and basil *panino*. Most appetizers, soups, and salads can be ordered in large or small portions. If it is on, try the plum tomato and basil tart with rocket (arugula) and Parmesan slivers tossed over the top. Or skip the appetizers altogether and choose one of the remarkably inexpensive meals called One Pot

Dining. I like the crispy duck confit on a stew of white beans or the braised oxtail with new potatoes and savoy cabbage. Chargrilled meats, pastas, steaks, and the Cafe dell'Ugo Burger on tapenade toast with fries fill out the imaginative menu. Certainly not to be overlooked are the desserts, especially the tangy lemon tarte with *crème fraîche* or the banana cream pie with passion fruit sauce.

Ed's Easy Diner
12 Moor Street, W1

"We are only as good as the last meal we served," states the sign on the wall at Ed's, one of the best diners in London. The eating is as good as the people-watching, which provides an intense look at the latest fashion fads for trendy groupies. Seating is around a circular bar where you will be served mainstream American fast food that will take you back to the days when expanding waistlines and elevated cholesterol and fat levels were not on our lists of things to worry about. All the favorites are here: burgers with cheese, grilled onions, chili, or bacon served with a side of fries and a bottle of catsup and washed down with a thick malt or a pint of Beck's beer. On Saturday and Sunday morning, stop by for brunch. Order the Hash Deluxe, hash browns topped with two fried eggs, bacon rashers, and a grilled tomato. It comes with toast, juice, and as much coffee as you can drink. The gum-chewing staff is friendly, the jukebox blares all the fifties and sixties popular tunes and it all adds up to a nostalgic experience for everyone.

TELEPHONE
071-439-1955

TUBE
Leicester Square or Tottenham Court Road

OPEN
Daily

CLOSED
Christmas

HOURS
Continuous service Mon–Thurs 11:30 A.M.–midnight, Fri 11:30 A.M.–1 A.M., Sat 9 A.M.–1 A.M., Sun 9 A.M.–11 P.M.

RESERVATIONS
Not accepted

CREDIT CARDS
None

PRICES
À la Carte: £5.50-8

VAT/SERVICE
No service charge, but "the staff accepts bribes."

MISCELLANEOUS
Takeaway

Europa Restaurant
37 Albermarle Street, W1

A smartly dressed lunch crowd fills this homey Italian restaurant skillfully run by Carlo and Tony. The interior is not particularly inspiring: a takeaway counter graces the front entrance and in back, hard-back chairs are arranged around pink linen-draped tables, and calendar art lines the walls. On the plus side, the location is strategic for fine shopping and the tabs are very reasonable for this posh area. On top

TELEPHONE
071-409-1580

TUBE
Green Park

OPEN
Mon–Sat

CLOSED
Sun, Christmas

HOURS
Continuous service
Mon–Fri 7 A.M.–11 P.M.,
Sat 8 A.M.–8 P.M.
RESERVATIONS
Not necessary if you avoid
peak lunch hour
CREDIT CARDS
MC, V
PRICES
À la Carte: £8–11
VAT/SERVICE
70p cover per person, service
discretionary
MISCELLANEOUS
No-smoking section; takeaway

of that, the robust Italian fare is generously served and very, very good. The restaurant has long hours with continuous service, making it one to remember for an early mid-week breakfast, a quick takeaway, or a full meal at an odd hour. The special menu changes daily and offers several main courses liberally garnished, enabling diners to enjoy a full meal and not spend more than £10 or £11. In the evening, the rush is over and tranquility sets in. Simple starters of iced melon or minestrone make the perfect prelude to a zesty pizza or the sophisticated *petto di pollo polifemo*—breast of chicken stuffed with Parma ham in a sage, mushroom, and tomato sherry sauce. If you don't see the dish you want on the menu, ask and the chef will try and prepare it. Desserts are basic, but if you insist, order ice cream or the fresh fruit cocktail.

The Fountain Restaurant at Fortnum & Mason
181 Piccadilly (entrance within the store or via Duke Street at the corner of Jermyn Street in the back), W1

TELEPHONE
071-734-8040, ext. 492
TUBE
Green Park
OPEN
Mon–Sat
CLOSED
Sun, holidays
HOURS
Breakfast: 7:30 A.M.–11 A.M.
Lunch: 11:45 A.M.–3 P.M.
(minimum charge £5)
Afternoon tea: 3 P.M.–6 P.M.
Dinner: 6 P.M.–11 P.M.
RESERVATIONS
Accepted after 6 P.M. for
dinner only
CREDIT CARDS
AE, DC, MC, V
PRICES
À la Carte: £5–12
VAT/SERVICE
Service discretionary

There are two other restaurants in Fortnum & Mason, but my favorite, and the best for Cheap Eaters, is the ground-floor Fountain Restaurant. This is the type of place that brings back memories of special lunches after a morning of shopping with your grandmother or maiden auntie—gloves and good manners are definitely in vogue here. The large dining room is cool, light, and airy with pretty murals depicting the travels of Mr. Fortnum and Mr. Mason on their worldwide quests for the finest coffees and teas to sell in their Piccadilly store. The long menu details all sorts of wonderful choices for breakfast, lunch, afternoon tea, and dinner with something for everyone. There is a glittering array of ice cream delights starting with at least a dozen sundaes, followed by milk shakes, ice cream sodas, frappes, and floats. The restaurant also has the advantage of being open through the dinner hour in a location that is convenient for light pretheater dining. Before you leave the store, you must explore the famous food hall, renowned for its clerks wearing formal morning coats and its fantasy picnic hampers that are still considered the only way to dine at proper British sporting events.

MISCELLANEOUS
No-smoking section; air-conditioned

Hungry's
37a Crawford Street, W1

Two Little Indians, Love Me or Liver Me, Cheese Just My Type, Tongue Fu, and Steak a Claim are just five of the one hundred sandwiches with silly names that are made daily at Hungry's, a neat, little, blue and white restaurant with only eleven small tables. The names may provoke a few laughs, but the generously filled sandwiches are serious business here and are some of the best in the area. All the meat is cooked in-house, the bread is fresh, only real mayonnaise is used, and every sandwich is made to order. There are no cellophane-wrapped ham and cheese numbers lurking in tired masses here! If you are not in the mood for a sandwich, try the soup of the day, a salad, the hot special, or a huge jacket potato (baked potato) smothered in cheese, chili, and onions. Desserts are not made here, so they can be safely skipped.

Great breakfasts are served from "Dawn to Distraction" which actually means 11:30 A.M. They range in size from the Full House, fried eggs, bacon, sausage, tomato, and toast, to the Je T'Aime, a warm croissant served with butter and jam.

If your eyes were bigger than your stomach, doggie bags are available. Everything can also be packed to go and will be delivered free if the order exceeds £10.

TELEPHONE
071-258-0376, 071-723-4010
TUBE
Baker Street
OPEN
Mon–Sat
CLOSED
Sun, holidays
HOURS
Mon–Fri 7 A.M.–4 P.M., Sat 8:30 A.M.–2:30 P.M. serving breakfast only
RESERVATIONS
Not accepted
CREDIT CARDS
MC, V
PRICES
À la Carte: £1.75–5
VAT/SERVICE
Service discretionary
MISCELLANEOUS
Takeaway; unlicensed; no public toilets or place to wash your hands

Ikkyu
67a Tottenham Court Road, W1

Ikkyu is in an unpretentious, rather shabby basement location on Tottenham Court Road. The cooking can be overseen from the low wooden bar and is a good initiation to those unfamiliar with Japanese food. The grilled fish set-lunch comes with rice pickles and miso soup and features your choice of sardines, mackerel, pike, herring, or salmon. It is a buy for less than £7. Other set-lunch meals feature sushi,

TELEPHONE
071-636-9280
TUBE
Goodge Street
OPEN
Mon–Fri, Sun
CLOSED
Sat, holidays
HOURS
Lunch: Mon–Fri 12:30–2:30 P.M.
Dinner: Sun–Fri 6–10:30 P.M.
RESERVATIONS
Not necessary
CREDIT CARDS
AE, DC, MC, V

PRICES
À la Carte: £5–10
Set Price: £5–7
VAT/SERVICE
Service charge at lunch, discretionary; 10% service for dinner
MISCELLANEOUS
Takeaway

sashimi, deep fried chicken, and grilled pork in a ginger-soy sauce. All include rice and miso soup and seconds on these are free. The atmosphere is hectic and hurried, but it is friendly, and for Japanese food, as cheap as it gets.

Indian YMCA Cafeteria
41 Fitzroy Square, W1

TELEPHONE
071-387-0411
TUBE
Warren Street
OPEN
Daily
CLOSED
Holidays
HOURS
Breakfast: Mon–Sat 7:45–8:45 A.M., Sun 8:30–9:30 A.M.
Lunch: Daily 12:30–1:45 P.M.
Dinner: Daily 7–8 P.M.
RESERVATIONS
Not accepted
CREDIT CARDS
None
PRICES
À la Carte: £3.80–5
VAT/SERVICE
No service charged
MISCELLANEOUS
Unlicensed; no smoking

For the nearest thing to Indian home cooking, eat at the Indian YMCA Cafeteria, where you will rub elbows with students at breakfast and dinner, and budget-conscious office workers and neighborhood Indians at lunch. While certainly not the place to entertain your boss, it is one place to keep in mind if you like simple Indian food.

The philanthropically priced meals are geared to the two hundred Indian students who stay at this YMCA while studying in London. Naturally, any attempt at decor is out, and the choices for each meal are very limited. The breakfasts are usually English style, but once a week an Indian dish is added. One of the popular Indian breakfast dishes is *upma*, a southern Indian dish made from cereal and vegetables. It is interesting, but not something I am anxious to have too often. Things pick up at lunch. Two meals are offered: a vegetarian and a meat dish, each served with rice or *chappathi*. Dal and condiments are on the shared tables. The dinner dishes vary among tandoori chicken, mutton stew, and spicy prawns as well as a vegetarian selection. Desserts are absolutely forgettable, mostly canned fruit or sticky Indian sweets.

The Lindsay House
21 Romilly Street, W1

See The English Garden, The English House, and The Lindsay House (SW3), page 134, for description. All other information is the same.
TELEPHONE: 071-439-0450
TUBE: Leicester Square
OPEN: Daily
CLOSED: Sun lunch, Christmas and some holidays (call to check)

HOURS: Lunch: Mon–Sat 12–2:30 P.M.; Dinner: Mon–Sat 6 P.M.–midnight, Sun 7–10 P.M.

RESERVATIONS: Necessary

CREDIT CARDS: AE, DC, MC, V

PRICES: À la Carte: 3 courses & coffee, £32. Set Price: Mon–Sat 2 courses & coffee, £11; 3 courses & coffee, £15.75; Sun dinner, 3 courses & coffee, £17.75

VAT/SERVICE: Service discretionary

The Lucky Spot
14 North Audley Street, W1

Whenever I see a line of people waiting to get in to eat somewhere, I know they are on to something Cheap Eaters should know about. Such is the case at the tiny hole-in-the-wall eatery called The Lucky Spot. Seating is at small booths by the sandwich counter and in the back. When the weather is right, there are a few tables on the sidewalk in this quiet corner of London near the American Embassy. Pinstriped suits dominate the lunch scene, when most diners are refugees from nearby offices. They arrive in droves for one of the forty-two varieties of freshly made sandwiches or the hearty Italian hot dishes that pay no mind to waistline considerations. If you want peace with your meal, avoid the madhouse between noon and one. Be aware, however, that if you go later, demand may have exceeded supply and they may be out of some things. In the morning they offer breakfast, and in the afternoon, tea and pastries.

Even though they are open until 6:30 P.M., economy would have to be a top priority to make this a dinner selection.

TELEPHONE
071-493-0277

TUBE
Marble Arch or Bond Street

OPEN
Mon–Sat

CLOSED
Sun, holidays

HOURS
Breakfast: 7 A.M.–noon
Lunch: noon–3 P.M.
Tea: 3–6 P.M.
Dinner: 5–6:30 P.M.

RESERVATIONS
Not accepted

CREDIT CARDS
None

PRICES
À la Carte: £2.50–5

VAT/SERVICE
No service charged or expected

MISCELLANEOUS
Takeaway; unlicensed, BYOB, no corkage

Malaysian Dining Hall
44 Bryanston Square (in the basement), W1

When was the last time you had rice slowly simmered in coconut milk and topped with anchovies and chili peppers for breakfast? Or how about *roti-chanai,* a flattened green pancake served with curry or dal (lentils)? All this and more are yours for the asking at the Malaysian Dining Hall, a little-known student

TELEPHONE
071-723-9484

TUBE
Marble Arch

OPEN
Daily

CLOSED
Christmas

HOURS
Breakfast: 8:30–10:30 A.M.
Lunch: noon–3 P.M.
Dinner: 5–9 P.M.

RESERVATIONS
Not accepted

CREDIT CARDS
None

PRICES
À la Carte: £1.80–3.50

VAT/SERVICE
No service charged

MISCELLANEOUS
Unlicensed

canteen subsidized by the Malaysian government. Open for breakfast, lunch, and dinner every day except Christmas, this haven for Malaysians far from home serves some of the best Malay and Indonesian food in London. If you ordered everything in sight, you would have trouble spending more than £4. The menu changes daily, the standards are high, the food is fresh, and the cafeteria, filled with students, elegant diplomats, extended families, and tourists in the know, has a friendly atmosphere. For an unusual and mighty inexpensive dining experience, this one is hard to top.

Mayfair Greek Taverna
5–6 Down Street, W1

TELEPHONE
071-491-3810, 071-409-1315,
071-499-1383

TUBE
Green Park or
Hyde Park Corner

OPEN
Daily

CLOSED
Christmas, Easter

HOURS
Continuous service
noon–midnight

RESERVATIONS
Preferred for dinner

CREDIT CARDS
AE, DC, MC, V

PRICES
À la Carte: £15
Set Price: *mezes*, £10–16;
Greek feast, £15 per person,
minimum 2 people

VAT/SERVICE
Service discretionary

A big thank you goes out to those *Cheap Eats* readers who wrote to me about this exceptional Greek restaurant in Mayfair. The Mayfair area of London is not known for its low-cost, budget-conscious restaurants. It is nice, therefore, to know about this worthy exception. Despite its smart address, it is basically a neighborhood restaurant with a loyal local following. The neat, clean, and spacious interior has low lighting, dark wood, well-spaced tables with fresh flowers, and candles glowing in the evening. Black-and-white photographs and drawings of Greece adorn the walls, and green plants hang down from the ceiling. The wide-ranging, well-annotated menu offers à la carte dishes, vegetarian specialties, a Greek and a fish *meze*, and if you want to go full tilt, a mammoth Greek feast with fifteen different dishes.

Greek cooking is an often-forgotten food culture, dwarfed between Italy and the Middle East. While it has never been grand in the manner of France, it offers a rustic, rural style of cooking that many enjoy. When dining here, look for *tzatziki* (yogurt with cucumber, garlic, and olive oil); *tabouleh* (crushed wheat with parsley, tomatoes, onions, and fresh mint); vine leaves stuffed with meat, rice, and herbs; grilled lamb kebabs; *moussaka; kleftiko* (lamb seasoned with oregano); and *halva* or *baklava* for dessert. Who knows, you may be like one reader who ate here four nights out of his five-day stay in London.

Melati
31 Peter Street, W1

"We wish you selamat datang," says the waiter and the message at the top of your menu at this special restaurant in Soho. This ritual toast is said at the beginning of a meal in Indonesia and Malaysia, where the highly spiced food has been influenced by the Chinese, Indians, and Dutch who settled there through the centuries. The deliciously exotic food served at Melati will provide fascinating eating for those willing to experiment with the unusual, bearing in mind that most dishes can have the level of the hot spices tailored to individual tastes. The menu is long and the choices will undoubtedly bewilder the novice. When in doubt, ask your waiter to help you put together a typical meal. Whatever you do, do not overlook the famous bean curd omelette, the *gado-gado*—an Indonesian salad topped with peanut sauce, or the deep-fried garlic chicken with chili, an absolute must-have for any garlic lover. Beef eaters will want to sample the *rendang*—beef cooked in a hot, spicy coconut gravy. For a lighter meal, try *sayur campur ayam*—mixed vegetables cooked with chicken slices. Having lived in the Far East, I have sampled many a Malaysian and Indonesian meal, and I can honestly say that the food at Melati is as good as anything I had in Kuala Lumpur or Jakarta.

TELEPHONE
071-437-2011
TUBE
Piccadilly Circus
OPEN
Mon–Sat
CLOSED
Sun, holidays
HOURS
Lunch: noon–2:45 P.M.
Dinner: 6–11:30 P.M.
RESERVATIONS
Advised
CREDIT CARDS
MC, V
PRICES
À la Carte: £12–15, minimum charge £5 in evening
Set Price: £30 for 2 includes starters, main course, dessert, coffee
VAT/SERVICE
10% service charge added to bill
MISCELLANEOUS
Takeaway

Mildreds
58 Greek Street, W1

Jane Muir and Diane Thomas became friends while working together in various restaurants in London. During that time they decided: "We could run a better restaurant." The result is Mildreds, their joint effort and one of the most popular vegetarian restaurants in London. Their original and nourishing menu offers daily specials and boasts seasonal organic produce, free-range eggs, and organic wines cleverly combined and attractively presented in enormous servings.

The menu always lists soups, salads, several hot dishes, and divine desserts. On Tuesday, look for the

TELEPHONE
071-494-1634
TUBE
Tottenham Court Road
OPEN
Mon–Sat
CLOSED
Sun, holidays
HOURS
Continuous service noon–10 P.M.
RESERVATIONS
Not accepted
CREDIT CARDS
None

Mexican bean burritos with guacamole, sour cream, and a side salad. On Thursday, it is the Vegetarian Wellington with spinach, cream cheese, and mushrooms. The homemade ice cream is wonderful, but for true decadence, hope that the banana, chocolate, and sherry trifle is on the menu. Whenever you eat at Mildreds and whatever you order, you will realize quickly that natural foods can be a dining experience to savor.

PRICES
À la Carte: £5–8.50, minimum charge £3 at peak hours

VAT/SERVICE
10% service added for 6 or more; otherwise, discretionary

MISCELLANEOUS
Takeaway, 40p less per entrée

New Piccadilly Cafe Restaurant
8 Denman Street, W1

TELEPHONE
071-437-8530

TUBE
Piccadilly Circus

OPEN
Daily

CLOSED
2 days at Christmas, Easter Sunday

HOURS
Continuous service noon–9:30 P.M.

RESERVATIONS
Not accepted

CREDIT CARDS
None

PRICES
À la Carte: £5–7

VAT/SERVICE
Service discretionary

MISCELLANEOUS
Unlicensed; BYOB, no corkage; takeaway

As you walk down the short street only a block from Piccadilly Circus, you can't possibly miss this budget diner's dream: it is the one with the big, red neon sign flashing the word "EATS" in the front window. There is nothing even remotely interesting about the restaurant decor. In places, the floors are worn through to the bare boards, and the yellow formica tables set in aging booths have obviously held many a hungry soul. There is a wall lined with post-cards sent by long-time customers to owner Lorenzo Marioni and his sister, Rosita, who has held court at the cash register since they opened in 1951. Service by waiters wearing starched white jackets can be good, or downright rude. If you get one with a flip-pant attitude, complain to Lorenzo because he needs to know from all sources that a few of his waiters need a crash course at Dale Carnegie. Despite this draw-back, do not pass up this oasis of economy, which is filled throughout the day with locals, show people, and thrift-minded tourists who stoke up on the heaping portions of chicken, steak, veal, pork, pasta, pizza, omelettes, salads, and desserts. From beginning to end, you can be well fed and out the door for around £5–7.

Ninjin
244 Great Portland Street, W1

If you did not know about it, the Ninjin would be an easy address to miss. Located just around the corner from the Great Portland Hospital, where the

Duchess of York gave birth to Princess Bea and Princess Eugenie, this former mah-jongg club has been turned into a smart basement restaurant that is a good place for those new to Japanese food to begin exploring. Some Japanese restaurants make the mistake of tailoring their food to Western tastes, thus changing the authenticity of their cooking. The approach at the Ninjin is not to compromise, but to offer simple Japanese cooking in great abundance. For the most authentic experience, go for dinner when Japanese businessmen are here in full force. If you are dining alone, sit at the wrap-around counter facing the open kitchen and watch the fast-moving chefs perform their kitchen magic. The most economical plan is to order one of the many set meals, which come with appetizer, miso soup, rice, pickles, and fresh fruit. All you have to do is select your main dish from a long menu featuring sashimi, vegetarian tempura, salmon grilled with teriyaki sauce, deep-fried oysters, *shabu shabu*—beef and vegetables cooked at your table, fifteen different noodle and rice dishes, and ten or more vegetables. The wine and spirits have high price tags. Order instead a bottle of sake or a round of Kirin beer to complement your feast.

TELEPHONE
071-388-4657

TUBE
Great Portland Street

OPEN
Mon–Sat

CLOSED
Sun, holidays

HOURS
Lunch: noon–2:30 P.M.
Dinner: 6–10:30 P.M.

RESERVATIONS
Only for large parties

CREDIT CARDS
AE, DC, MC, V

PRICES
À la Carte: £15–18
Set Price: £10–30

VAT/SERVICE
Service discretionary

MISCELLANEOUS
No children under 10 allowed at dinner

O'Keefe's
19 Dering Street, W1

O'Keefe's is the type of restaurant you always hope to discover, and when you do, jealously guard as your own secret place for fear popularity will go to its head. Until now, O'Keefe's has been frequented by savvy London insiders who know a good meal when they find it. If you are going, better book a table way ahead. When I finally got in, I understood why; food this good usually brings a tidal wave of instant regulars who eat here every day.

The open kitchen along one wall serves as a backdrop for the minimalist white interior of this corner location that operates as a restaurant, deli, and takeaway counter for imaginative food, beautifully prepared and nicely presented. The menu changes daily

TELEPHONE
071-495-0878

TUBE
Bond Street, Oxford Circus

OPEN
Mon–Sat for breakfast, lunch, and tea; Thurs for dinner

CLOSED
Sun, holidays

HOURS
Mon–Fri 8 A.M.–5 P.M., Thurs until 10:30 P.M., Sat 10 A.M.–5 P.M. in winter, 6 P.M. in summer
Breakfast: 8 A.M.–noon
Lunch: noon–3 P.M.
Dinner: Thurs *only* 7:30–10:30 P.M.

RESERVATIONS
Recommended
CREDIT CARDS
None
PRICES
À la Carte: £12–17
Set Price: Thurs dinner
only, £16
VAT/SERVICE
Minimum charge £6 per person
from noon–3 P.M.;
service discretionary
MISCELLANEOUS
Takeaway

and only the freshest ingredients are used, such as Devon chocolate, pork from the Heal Farm, and the best seasonal produce. The flavors of each dish are clearly defined. Everything comes through from the courgette (zucchini) and Parmesan soup or the *bruschetta* with black olive and tomato salsa to the sage *focaccia* with roast pork, grilled red onions, arugula, and Cumberland sauce.

If you go for an early morning bite, the homemade muffins and Chelsea buns go fast, so don't be late. For lunch, you have a choice of ordering something to go from the deli/takeaway counter, or sitting down to an à la carte meal. For dinner there is a three-course, set-price menu available *only* on Thursday night.

The Original Carvery at the Cumberland Hotel
Marble Arch, W1

TELEPHONE
071-262-1001
TUBE
Marble Arch
OPEN
Daily
CLOSED
Never
HOURS
Lunch: Mon–Sat noon–
2:30 P.M., Sun noon–3 P.M.
Dinner: Mon–Thurs 5:30–
10 P.M., Fri & Sat 5:30–
10:30 P.M., Sun 6–10 P.M.
RESERVATIONS
Suggested for Sunday lunch
CREDIT CARDS
AE, DC, MC, V
PRICES
Set Price: £16 for lunch, £17
for dinner
VAT/SERVICE
Service discretionary
MISCELLANEOUS
Children under 5 free,
age 5–16 half price

"Help yourself" is the motto at these Forte Carvery Restaurants, where traditional English food is served for a modest financial investment. This is genuine value for the money, especially when you consider that you may eat as much as you like—or can—with second and third helpings encouraged. Children under five are free and those between five and sixteen are half price. Plan to arrive with a giant-sized appetite to properly tackle the dazzling buffet tables laden with hors d'oeuvres, salads, and succulent roasts of beef, lamb, pork, turkey, and ham with all the trimmings, along with a wide selection of vegetables and potatoes. Vegetarians are not ignored; there are always two or three hot non-meat dishes available. To round it all off, the dessert trolley has fruit, pastries, cakes, trifle, hot puddings, ice cream and sorbets, and a selection of English cheeses. If you just cannot make up your mind, ask for the "taster plate," which has a little of everything. Carvery Restaurants are big and bright in the best hotel-style with large, well-spaced tables properly set with linens and heavy cutlery. Sunday lunch seems to be the busiest time, so book ahead on that day.

The Original Carvery
at The Regent Palace Hotel
12 Sherwood Street (off Piccadilly Circus), W1

See The Original Carvery at the Cumberland Hotel for description. All other information is the same.

TELEPHONE: 071-937-4751
TUBE: Piccadilly Circus
OPEN: Daily
CLOSED: Never

Pappagalli's Pizza
7–9 Swallow Street, W1

Wholemeal pizza cooked to order, freshly sauced pastas, pizza pies filled with mozzarella, tomato, sausage, pepperoni, mushrooms, peppers and onions, stuffed garlic bread, plus a large help-yourself salad bar have made Pappagalli's a family favorite for years. The brick-walled interior has been created from old church fittings, with New England church pews making up the booths, a baptismal font used for the salad bar, and an ornate pulpit housing the cashier. Chicago-style pizzas are large enough for two and they will give you a doggie bag if you cannot finish all of yours. Pasta-lovers can order either wheat or spinach fettuccini, linguini, or fusilli covered with any of nine homemade sauces. If you are not in the mood for something Italian, order from the Potato Parlor and have a large baked potato slathered with ham, cheese, chili, or cottage cheese and chives. There is also a very reasonable two-course set menu that includes pasta, pizza, or a meat course and a glass of wine. After all of this, if you can even contemplate dessert, there are monster sundaes, fudge brownies, and Mississippi mud pie.

TELEPHONE
071-734-5182

TUBE
Piccadilly Circus

OPEN
Mon–Sat

CLOSED
Sun, holidays

HOURS
Continuous service
noon–11 P.M.

RESERVATIONS
Not necessary

CREDIT CARDS
AE, MC, V

PRICES
À la Carte: £8–12
Set Price: £8.95, 2 courses and
glass of wine

VAT/SERVICE
10% service added to bill

MISCELLANEOUS
No-smoking section; takeaway;
Happy Hour 5:15–7:15 P.M.

Pasta Fino
27 Frith Street, W1

One of the best seats in the house is on a stool at the tiny bar in the storefront exhibition kitchen where you can watch chefs turning out the homemade pastas. The spry can climb down the steep

TELEPHONE
071-439-8900

TUBE
Piccadilly Circus or
Leicester Square

OPEN
Mon–Sat

CLOSED
Sun, holidays

HOURS
Lunch: noon–3:30 P.M.
Dinner: 5:30–11 P.M.

RESERVATIONS
Suggested on weekends

CREDIT CARDS
AE, MC, V

PRICES
À la Carte: £9–12

VAT/SERVICE
10% service added to bill for
parties of 5 or more, otherwise
discretionary; minimum charge
£3 during peak hours

MISCELLANEOUS
Takeaway; children's portions;
dry pasta and fresh sauces
available to go

spiral staircase and sit in the bright red, white, and green *cave* below. At night, candles soften the room somewhat. Wherever you sit in this pasta paradise you will have a wonderful meal without putting a major strain on your wallet.

Begin with *Agliata,* an antipasto of crisp raw vegetables served with their own creamy garlic dip. Or try the homemade soup of the day or the *Misto all'Italiana,* a selection of Italian salami and ham with mozzarella. The most popular pasta orders are the Fettuccine Carbonara, pasta ribbons tossed in eggs and cream with chunks of smoky bacon, or the *Conchiglie Pollo,* diced chicken with peppers in a white wine sauce served on pasta shells. They also serve melt-in-your-mouth gnocci, a rich lasagna, superb ravioli, and six types of pizza. There are the usual Italian desserts: gelati, whipped cream cake, and *tiramisu,* but the most unusual is the *pasta finale.* This is fresh chocolate pasta with vanilla ice cream, covered in hot chocolate sauce and whipped cream. After this you will need to walk for a week, but it will have been worth it.

Paul Rothe & Son
35 Marylebone Lane, W1

Paul Rothe & Son specializes in sandwiches, and oh, what sandwiches they are!

TELEPHONE
071-935-6783

TUBE
Bond Street

OPEN
Mon–Fri

CLOSED
Sat, Sun, holidays

HOURS
Continuous service
8 A.M.–6 P.M.

RESERVATIONS
Not accepted

CREDIT CARDS
None

PRICES
À la Carte: £1.50–4

VAT/SERVICE
No service charged

MISCELLANEOUS
Unlicensed; takeaway: orders
called in by 11 A.M. are ready
for pickup at noon

For over ninety-three years, nothing much has changed in this grocery-lined deli within a short walk of the Wallace Collection and shopping on New Bond Street. The Rothe family is on hand every day, making all of the cheese spreads, chopping the chicken livers, roasting the beef and turkey, and then using the bones for some of the best soup you will ever drink from a styrofoam cup. As you can tell, formality is out, but good lunchtime food is in at this citadel of Cheap Eating, where the queue begins around noon. The homemade potato salad or a side of cole slaw goes well with any sandwich order. Pass on the desserts, unless you like homemade fruit cake.

Pizzeria Condotti
4 Mill Street (off Conduit Street), W1

Delicious pizza served in upscale surroundings is exactly what you can expect at the classy Pizzeria Condotti, just off Regent Street. It looks expensive: well-spaced tables with starched linens and fresh flowers, walls hung with a superb collection of signed contemporary art, polite service—and all they serve is pizza? That's right. And they are *not* expensive. The pizzas are crisp, the toppings imaginative, the salads big and beautiful, and the desserts worth jogging an extra fifteen minutes for. All the pizzas come with a mozzarella and tomato base; extra toppings are available, and only free-range eggs are used. Favorites include The Veneziana with onions, capers, olives, pine nuts, and sultanas. The Venice in Peril fund gets 15p for every one sold. I like the simple Pizza Condotti topped with ricotta and Gorgonzola cheese and the La Reine with ham, olives, and mushrooms. Dessert decisions are never easy, but I am finally down to the dense chocolate fudge cake or a scoop of creamy *tartufo* ice cream made with chocolate liqueur. A light Italian wine or a bottle of Peroni beer makes a perfect accompaniment to the meal, and a bracing espresso the best ending.

TELEPHONE
071-499-1308

TUBE
Oxford Circus

OPEN
Mon–Sat

CLOSED
Sun, holidays

HOURS
Continuous service
11:30 A.M.–midnight

RESERVATIONS
Not accepted

CREDIT CARDS
AE, DC, MC, V

PRICES
À la Carte: £9–12

VAT/SERVICE
Service discretionary for parties of 1 to 5, then 12½% added

MISCELLANEOUS
Takeaway

Plexi's
1b St. Christopher's Place, W1

Plexi's is located on St. Christopher's Place, just a minute or two away from one of the major hubs of London shopping along Oxford Street and New Bond Street. This picturesque pedestrian walkway is lined with smart boutiques and snappy restaurants that seem to come and go as fast as they open. Plexi's is different. You won't see it advertised anywhere and very few visitors know about it. However, it has a twenty-five-year history of outlasting the neighborhood competition. It is nothing fancy, mind you. Just two or three tables outside, a small room on the street level, and a romantic brick-walled cellar downstairs laid out with pretty tablecloths, candles, and fresh flowers on every table. Its popularity is based on

TELEPHONE
071-935-1047

TUBE
Bond Street

OPEN
Mon–Sat for lunch and dinner

CLOSED
Sun, holidays

HOURS
Lunch: noon–3 P.M.
Dinner: 6–11 P.M.

RESERVATIONS
Not necessary

CREDIT CARDS
AE, DC, MC, V

PRICES
À la Carte: £11–15
Set Price: Lunch, 2 courses, £5;
dinner, 2 courses & coffee, £8

VAT/SERVICE
10% service added to bill

its congenial atmosphere and consistently good food, which is reasonably priced. The menu offers tried-and-true staples of British cuisine plus daily specials. I like to start with a crock of the homemade pâté spread on slices of fresh bread. For the main course, Plexi's veal escalope cooked in egg and breadcrumbs with a paprika and Parmesan cheese sauce always pleases. So does the beef casserole in red wine sauce and the fresh Scotch salmon poached in lobster cream sauce and served on a bed of spinach. The best dessert is one of the calorie-charged pancakes filled with fresh fruit, laced with liqueur and covered with whipped cream or ice cream. Worthy alternatives are the homemade cheesecake or the Lovable Lush Lemon Pie.

Rabin's Nosh Bar
39 Great Windmill Street, W1

TELEPHONE
071-434-9913
TUBE
Piccadilly Circus
OPEN
Mon–Sat
CLOSED
Sun, Jewish and all other holidays
HOURS
Continuous service
11 A.M.–10 P.M.
RESERVATIONS
Not accepted
CREDIT CARDS
None
PRICES
A la carte: £4–9
VAT/SERVICE
Service discretionary
MISCELLANEOUS
Unlicensed; takeaway

If you did not know about Rabin's, believe me you would never give it a second glance. Located in the heart of the West End's theater district and frequented by actors and critics, it was started by Phil Rabin in 1948. At eighty-two, he still drops in to check on things, which are expertly run and owned by Mark Weiner and his father-in-law, Simon Weston. It looks like dozens of other sandwich shops in London, with only a few tiny tables and hard chairs, a crowded deli case, and long lines at lunch. But—corned beef lovers take note. The best hot or cold corned beef in London is served right here. Yes, of course they also have chopped liver, fried gefilte fish, and chicken soup, but the one and only dish to remember here is the corned beef, which is brought up from the kitchen every twenty minutes during rush hour, carved right in front of you, and served on fresh rye bread with a crunchy pickle, or piled high on a plate with a helping of fries or *latkes,* potato pancakes made with egg and onion. Rabin's is open from eleven in the morning until ten at night, so there is plenty of time to indulge.

Note: Don't expect to see the term *corned beef* in England. Here it is called *salt beef.*

Raw Deal
65 York Street, W1

Cozy, clean, cheap, and above all, good for you! This is the unbeatable combination awaiting you at Raw Deal, a super vegetarian restaurant that has come into its own now that watching what you eat is the popular thing to do.

Every day, Julia Dabrowski and Sophi Tetmajer, who have been serving health-conscious regulars for more than a quarter century, dish up bountiful salads, unusual soups, as well as hot, savory main dishes. Desserts to tempt even the most rigorous dieter might include apple charlotte, pear or banana flan, apricot crumble, or papaya gateau, an unusual cake made with sponge and filled with papayas, homemade raspberry jam, and cream, then dusted with nuts. I like to eat here because no white sugar is used, the orange juice is freshly squeezed, and half portions are offered so that I can sample more dishes in one meal. The seasonal menu changes daily, so you never have a chance to tire of having the same old thing.

The light-green interior walls combine with lush hanging plants and big picture windows to create an open and welcoming atmosphere. In the evening, candles add a nice touch, and on sunny days, two tables on the sidewalk offer ringside seats for the passing parade.

TELEPHONE
071-262-4841

TUBE
Baker Street

OPEN
Mon–Sat

CLOSED
Sun, holidays

HOURS
Continuous service
10 A.M.–10 P.M.

RESERVATIONS
Accepted for dinner only

CREDIT CARDS
None

PRICES
À la Carte: £5–8; minimum charge £2 at peak times; 10p cover per person at dinner

VAT/SERVICE
Service discretionary

MISCELLANEOUS
No-smoking section; unlicensed, BYOB, no corkage; takeaway

Richoux—Mayfair
41a South Audley Street, W1

The detailed menu has something for every taste, time of day, and budget. Breakfast, morning coffee, lunch, afternoon tea, dinner, or a late supper—if you are hungry, Richoux will serve you, and in style. The key locations across from Harrods, on Piccadilly, and in Mayfair make these restaurants even more attractive for shoppers, cinemagoers, and sightseers who want a dignified place to relax over a full meal or just a simple cup of herbal tea. The restaurants began in 1909 as *pâtisseries* and candy shops. To this day they still serve some of the best pastries and most irresistible chocolates you will taste.

TELEPHONE
071-629-5228

TUBE
Bond Street or Green Park

OPEN
Daily

CLOSED
Christmas

HOURS
Continuous service
Mon–Fri 8:30 A.M.–11 P.M.,
Sat 8:30 A.M.–11:30 P.M.,
Sun 10 A.M.–7 P.M.

RESERVATIONS
Not necessary

CREDIT CARDS
AE, MC, V
PRICES
À la Carte: £4–12.50,
minimum service charge £5 per
person noon–3 P.M.—at
discretion of management
VAT/SERVICE
Included
MISCELLANEOUS
Takeaway for all foods
including pastries, candies,
and preserves

The settings are all rather old-world, with sweet waitresses serving everyone with a smile. This is the place where you will see older women with gloves who remember how tea should be served, young mothers sharing an hour of animated conversation while their babies doze in nearby strollers, and office workers catching up on the morning newspapers while enjoying a full English breakfast. They all know it is difficult to go too far wrong here.

Richoux—Piccadilly
172 Piccadilly, W1

See Richoux—Mayfair for description. All other information is the same.

TELEPHONE: 071-493-2204
TUBE: Piccadilly Circus
OPEN: Daily

Rock Island Diner
2nd floor, London Pavillion, Piccadilly, W1

TELEPHONE
071-287-5500
TUBE
Piccadilly Circus
OPEN
Daily
CLOSED
Christmas
HOURS
Continuous service
noon–11:30 P.M.
RESERVATIONS
Not accepted
CREDIT CARDS
AE, DC, MC, V
PRICES
À la Carte: £6–9
VAT/SERVICE
Service discretionary

Fasten your seat belts for a trip to the Rock Island Diner, a jumping joint right on Piccadilly Circus. Bobby-soxed waitresses, a '54 Chevy suspended over the bar, and a rollerskating staff set the tone for this 100% American diner. Music, dancing, games, competitions, raffles, badges, balloons . . . you name it and it all adds up to fun for all the family. The music is ear shattering, especially from 6 P.M. to midnight when the live DJ turns up the volume on the fifties and sixties sounds. However, if you are a teenager, or with one, and prepared to stand in line to get in, especially on Friday and Saturday nights, this is one stop you won't want to miss. The food is basic and comes in daunting portions. Look for chili, barbecued meats, burgers, hot dogs, fries, and corn on the cob, all served in paper-lined plastic baskets. There are also malts, milk shakes, and a fully stocked bar, which some of you may need to get through this one. Every Saturday and Sunday until 5 P.M., one child eats free from the "Dinner Mites" menu for each adult buying a main course.

Smollensky's Balloon
1 Dover Street, W1

If you are looking for a great place to take your family for a treat, the American-owned and -inspired Smollensky's Balloon is the ticket. Providing a taste of home for faraway wanderers of all ages, the two locations offer something for every member of your party. During the day, music from the thirties and forties plays in the background. At the Dover Street site, a pianist sings and plays low-key jazz favorites in the evening. There is a children's menu, highlighted by "Kids' Kocktails" and "Kids' Dessert Konkoktions." On weekends, a strolling magician keeps the children busy, and at 2:30 in the afternoon, all the little ones are invited upstairs for a Punch and Judy show. There is a clown who will paint willing faces, free helium balloons, and a variety of T-shirts. If you go to the Smollensky's Balloon on The Strand, you will find the same good food and service, plus dancing from 9:30 P.M. on Friday and Saturday nights and live jazz on Sunday at 8 P.M. Here there is a play area for tots under seven and Nintendo games for the older ones.

Mom and Dad can relax through it all at a comfortable banquette, sipping a classic cocktail and enjoying the main draw on the menu: perfectly grilled steak served with one of seven sauces and golden fried potatoes. Dieters must beware of the dazzling dessert lineup. Grandma Smollensky's Peanut Butter Cheesecake comes with this warning: "Even if you hate peanut butter, believe me, if you love cheesecake, this one is really special." So is Erna's Chocolate Mousse, which comes in a large bowl. If you finish your first helping, there is no charge for the second.

TELEPHONE
071-491-1199

TUBE
Green Park

OPEN
Daily

CLOSED
Christmas

HOURS
Continuous service
Mon–Sat noon–midnight,
Sun noon–10:30 P.M.

RESERVATIONS
Suggested

CREDIT CARDS
AE, DC, MC, V

PRICES
À la Carte: £15–20

VAT/SERVICE
8% service added to bill; for parties over 10, 5% surcharge (13%)

The Star Café
22 Great Chapel Street, W1

The food served at The Star Café is designed to inspire confidence in these hard-edged economic times. The concise, no-nonsense menu is a varied catalog of pasta, meat and fish dishes, omelettes, sandwiches, and breakfast items. The café has been on this

TELEPHONE
071-437-8778

TUBE
Tottenham Court Road or Oxford Circus

OPEN
Mon–Fri

CLOSED
Sat, Sun, holidays
HOURS
Breakfast: 7–11:30 A.M.
Lunch: noon–4 P.M.
Afternoon snacks, late lunch
specials, cold beer, tea
until 6 P.M.
RESERVATIONS
If 4 or more
CREDIT CARDS
None
PRICES
À la Carte: £4–6.60
VAT/SERVICE
Service discretionary
MISCELLANEOUS
Takeaway for sandwiches and
hot meals

site for more than sixty years, and under the same family ownership from the beginning. The area is made up of film and photo labs and the employees from these offices make up the backbone of the clientele. According to management, British film stars also stop in whenever they are in the neighborhood. Best seating is in action central on the main floor, where tables are covered with oilcloth and a vase of fresh flowers fills the esthetic void. Here you can also enjoy the impressive collection of pre–World War II enamel advertising signs that cover the walls. Service is swift, the food reliable, and the prices well within budget . . . and isn't that what *Cheap Eats in London* is all about?

Stockpot—Soho
18 Old Compton Street, W1

TELEPHONE
071-287-1066
TUBE
Piccadilly Circus
OPEN
Daily
CLOSED
Christmas
HOURS
Continuous service
Mon–Sat 11:30 A.M.–
11:30 P.M.,
Sun noon–11 P.M.
RESERVATIONS
Not accepted
CREDIT CARDS
None
PRICES
À la Carte: £6–7, minimum
charge £2.20 during peak hours

Each Stockpot is individually managed, but all the locations operate on the same theory—volume. Here you can fill up on lumberjack portions of international standards in areas of the West End and Chelsea where getting even a snack for under £15 can be a gastronomic challenge. The Basil Street location around the corner from Harrods is a welcome relief for shoppers who have spent their bundle at the famed department store. The Panton Street restaurant is a dining oasis near the theater district, while the King's Road site offers respite from the many fast food bars and cafes that infest the Chelsea area.

The interiors of all the Stockpots are bare and a little harsh, with only green plants accenting the pine tables and chairs. The youthful staffs seem jolly and efficient, even when put to the test with a full house and a queue waiting to be seated. Daily mimeographed handwritten menus offer something for everyone from your fussy five year old who won't consider anything but spaghetti, to Aunt Alice who is clinging to her Weight Watchers regime. The best advice is to stick with the daily specials, an omelette, or anything that must be cooked and served immediately. Stay away from anything that sounds complicated. Please note that *every* Cheap Eater in London knows about the Stockpot's great food bargains, so expect a wait, especially at lunchtime.

Topo Gigio Restaurant
46 Brewer Street, W1

So many tourists told me about Topo Gigio, that I could not believe I would like it. Finally, on my last night in London I had dinner here before going to the theater and was happily surprised.

The Italian waiters in red sweater vests and black pants are attentive without being condescending and service is brisk without being rushed. The tables, covered in bright red cloths, are turned several times an evening. The busiest times are before the theater and just after the last curtain call. You will find a good mixture of visitors and regulars, most of whom are served their favorite Italian dishes without ever consulting the menu. Portions are modest, so you can safely order several courses plus dessert and not feel too full. When ordering, consult the daily specials and for dessert, have the *tartufo,* a scoop of creamy ice cream bathed in a dark chocolate coating.

TELEPHONE
071-734-5931

TUBE
Piccadilly Circus

OPEN
Mon–Sat

CLOSED
Sun, holidays

HOURS
Continuous service
noon–10 P.M.

RESERVATIONS
Suggested

CREDIT CARDS
MC, V

PRICES
À la Carte: £15–22

VAT/SERVICE
10% service charge added
to bill

Wong Kei
41–43 Wardour Street, W1

Wong Kei boasts three floors of the rudest waiters in London, serving some of the best-value Chinese food in Soho. Customers enter through an open kitchen displaying ducks and chickens in the windows, to be herded indiscriminately to tables by waiters shouting "Sit here, not there!" Singles and couples are seated on the ground floor, while larger parties are ushered to one of the barn-like rooms upstairs that tend to be a bit quieter. When it is time to go, you are told, "You pay now and get out." Long a student and bargain-eater's paradise, some feel the institutional interior and outrageous behavior of the waiters is simply too much. Others think it is part of the so-called charm, and put up with it as a price to pay for the cheap and consistently good food. The set meal at

TELEPHONE
071-437-8408

TUBE
Leicester Square

OPEN
Daily

CLOSED
Christmas

HOURS
Continuous service
noon–11:30 P.M.

RESERVATIONS
Large groups only

CREDIT CARDS
None

PRICES
À la Carte: £5–7.50
Set Price: £6, 3 dishes,
rice, and tea

£6 per person is a buy with four to six dishes, depending on the number at the table who order it. Wong Kei is famous for its noodle soups—everything from fish ball to roasted duck and barbecued pork, which for speed, taste, and interest beat a trip to McDonald's any day.

The Wren at St. James's
197 Piccadilly or 37 Jermyn Street, W1

TELEPHONE
071-437-9419
TUBE
Piccadilly Circus
OPEN
Daily
CLOSED
Christmas
HOURS
Continuous service
Mon–Sat 8 A.M.–7 P.M.,
until 8:30 if there is
an evening concert;
Sun 10 A.M.–5 P.M.
RESERVATIONS
Not accepted
CREDIT CARDS
None
PRICES
À la Carte: £2–6
VAT/SERVICE
Service discretionary
MISCELLANEOUS
No smoking inside; takeaway

If you are looking for an economical meal near Piccadilly Circus, consider The Wren at St. James's Church. This whitewashed cafeteria is an unassuming adjunct to Sir Christopher Wren's seventeenth-century church. Everyday, backpacking tourists and budget-conscious office workers line up for the simple, vegetarian food. The choices seldom change, except for the daily hot specials. Hearty soups served with wholemeal rolls, casseroles, potato pancakes, lasagna, quiches, salads, and baked potatoes with a variety of toppings fill you nicely. Teatime offers scones, cold flapjacks, heavy-duty cakes, and cookies. For breakfast, you have a choice of tea and cold toast, a Danish, a bowl of muesli, or a croissant with jam and butter. The atmosphere is unhurried and pleasant, especially on a warm day if you sit at an outside table under one of the massive shade trees. Lingering is never discouraged, making it an ideal place to regroup after a hard morning of sightseeing. Because the cafe is owned and operated by the church, all the profits go directly to the church.

Food is not the only reason to visit the most fashionable church in London, which Wren called his ideal parish church. The inside is magnificent, especially the decorated plasterwork and the wooden altar intricately carved by Grinling Gibbons. Every Wednesday at lunchtime there are free concerts and usually one or two nights each week, as well. Shophounds should know that the paintings hung in the cafeteria are for sale, and a fleamarket and crafts sale is set up on the Piccadilly Street forecourt on Friday and Saturday from 9–6.

Young Cheng
76 Shaftesbury Avenue, W1

For many people, the best ethnic food to be found in London is Chinese. For all of us, it is also some of the cheapest. At Young Cheng on Shaftesbury Avenue, smart Chinese diners crowd in from noon until almost midnight at this storefront restaurant in the theater district. The chef stands in a tiny corner kitchen in the front window, chopping, boiling, and stir-frying just as fast as he can. If he runs out of any ingredients, he runs two doors down to the Chinese greengrocer and grabs what he needs and hurries back. Not every dish works, but if you stick to their specialties of baked spareribs, barbecued meats, and tofu dishes, you will have a pleasant, satisfying, and cheap meal. Bear in mind that all lunches come with rice or noodles, thus keeping your Cheap Eats tab even lower.

The second location on Lisle Street (page 105) is larger and a little tonier, but definitely not as *real* or full of interesting regulars as the Shaftesbury site. However, the special three-course set menus for about £10 per person offer good value and, of course, the food is just as good.

TELEPHONE
071-437-0237

TUBE
Leicester Square

OPEN
Daily

CLOSED
Christmas

HOURS
Continuous service
noon–11:45 P.M.

RESERVATIONS
Not necessary

CREDIT CARDS
AE, V

PRICES
À la Carte: £6–9
Set Price: £20 for two persons

VAT/SERVICE
Service discretionary

TEAROOMS W1

Maison Sagne
105 Marylebone High Street, W1

Stanley Comras and Ray Hall have been the proud owners of this elegantly old-fashioned *pâtisserie* on the Marylebone High Street for more than thirty-five years. Guests are warmly greeted by "Mr. Stanley," while Ray works behind the scenes creating fantastic marzipan works of art and wonderful chocolates and pastries that must be seen and tasted to be believed. Little has changed in the decor or on the menu since the tearoom first opened its doors in the early twenties and that is just the way the loyal customers like it. Whenever something is worn out, modern replacements are never installed; exact replicas are made

TELEPHONE
071-935-6240

TUBE
Baker Street or Bond Street

OPEN
Mon–Sat

CLOSED
Sat afternoon, Sun, holidays

HOURS
Breakfast: 9 A.M.–noon
Lunch: noon–2:30 P.M.
Afternoon tea: 3–5 P.M.

RESERVATIONS
Not accepted

CREDIT CARDS
None
PRICES
À la Carte: £3.50–7.50
VAT/SERVICE
Service discretionary
MISCELLANEOUS
Unlicensed; no smoking;
takeaway

instead. As a result, the atmosphere is more like an old club than a fussy tearoom.

If you arrive early in the morning, you will join local office workers sipping cups of filtered coffee and trying to resist the warm Danish pastries and famous buttery croissants. During the noon rush, doctors, dentists, and shoppers are served creamy omelettes, chicken and mushroom *vol au vent,* or frankfurters and potato salad by old-staff waiters in crisp white coats. Everyone knows they must save room for the best part: a sampling of the desserts. The strawberry tarts and heavenly macaroons are my favorites, but others wouldn't miss the cream éclairs and buttery cakes. Whatever you order will be delicious and I guarantee you will come back for more during your stay in London.

Pâtisserie Cappuccetto
8–9 Moor Street (off Cambridge Circus), W1

See Cappuccetto Ristorante Italiano, page 29, for description.

TELEPHONE: 071-437-9472
TUBE: Leicester Square, Tottenham Court Road, or Covent Garden
OPEN: Daily
CLOSED: Christmas, Easter
HOURS: Continuous service, 7:30 A.M.–8 P.M.
RESERVATIONS: Not accepted
CREDIT CARDS: None
PRICES: À la Carte: £1.50–3.50
VAT/SERVICE: 10% service charge
MISCELLANEOUS: Takeaway

Pâtisserie Valerie
44 Old Compton Street, W1

TELEPHONE
071-437-3466
TUBE
Piccadilly Circus or Tottenham
Court Road
OPEN
Daily
CLOSED
Holidays

Pâtisserie Valerie has been voted the best tearoom in London, and after one visit to either location it is easy to see why. The Soho location first opened its doors in 1926, when Belgian-born Madame Valerie decided to introduce continental pâtisserie to the English. It was an instant success, and remains so to this day. The impossibly crowded room, with

Toulouse-Lautrec cartoons painted on the walls, has shared tables, people standing in the aisles, and rushed waitresses reaching over diners' heads and under their noses. The newer location in Knightsbridge, just down Brompton road from Harrods is more relaxed and spacious, and has the added advantage of being licensed for beer and wine. It also has a changing display of national and international art, which is all for sale. Of course, the main attraction is the pastry, but not to be overlooked are the creamy omelettes, the perfectly toasted sandwiches, and a variety of individual quiches and well-dressed salads. If you are not in the mood to brave the throngs in the middle of the day, go at an off time, perhaps first thing Sunday morning for homemade cinnamon toast and a pot of tea, or during the week around 6 P.M. for a light supper and a slice of the unforgettable chocolate truffle cake with chocolate mousse filling.

Richoux—Mayfair and Piccadilly

See pages 49–50.

HOURS
Continuous service
Mon–Fri 8 A.M.–8 P.M.
Saturday 8 A.M.–7 P.M.
Sunday 10 A.M.–5:30 P.M.

RESERVATIONS
Not necessary

CREDIT CARDS
AE, DC, MC, V only for orders of £10 or more

PRICES
À la carte: £2.50–3.50 for tea and pastry, £5.50–8 for light meal with pastry and beverage

VAT/SERVICE
12½% suggested

MISCELLANEOUS
Not licensed

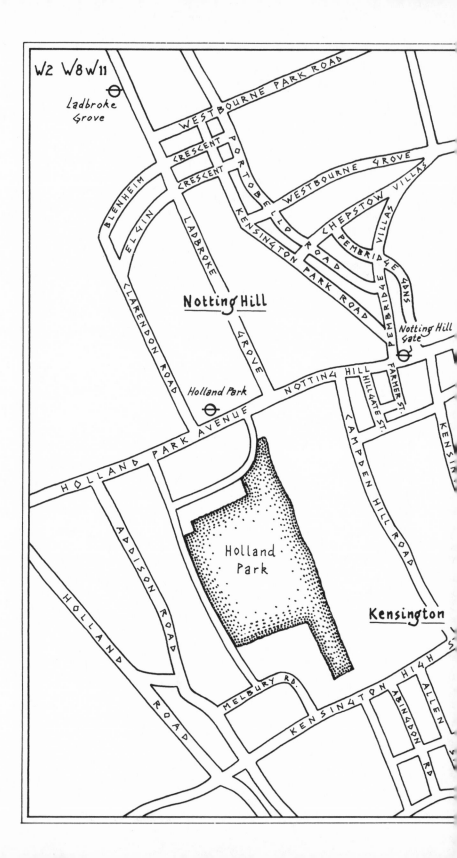

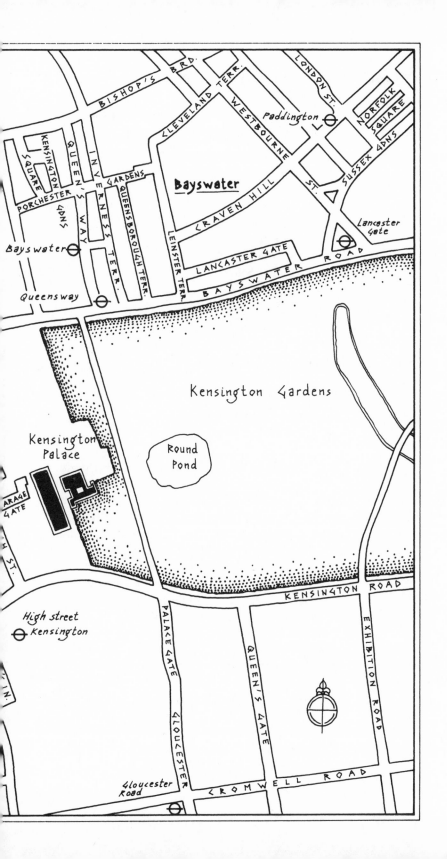

W2 ✤ BAYSWATER AND PADDINGTON

Bayswater runs along the northern end of Hyde Park and includes Paddington Station, a major train terminal with connections to the North. The area is full of Indian and Pakistani restaurants.

RESTAURANTS

TEAROOMS

RESTAURANTS W2

Halepi
18 Leinster Terrace, W2

TELEPHONE
071-262-1070, 071-723-4097

TUBE
Queensway

OPEN
Daily

CLOSED
Christmas

HOURS
Continuous service
noon–12:30 A.M.

RESERVATIONS
Essential for dinner

CREDIT CARDS
AE, DC, MC, V

PRICES
À la Carte: £13–18

VAT/SERVICE
12% service charge
added to bill

You won't find Halepi mentioned in many guide books or listed in London dining directories, and that is the way its loyalists want to keep it. Owned and run by the Kazolides family since 1966, Halepi offers typical Greek-Cypriot food in a rustic setting with long rows of closely placed tables covered with bright cloths, Greek bouzouki music in the background, and a native crowd both for business lunches or in for a long party evening. The main difference between Greek mainland cooking and Greek-Cypriot food is that Cyprus pulls in a Middle Eastern flavor to its food due to its historic links with Turkey and its proximity to Lebanon, Syria, and Israel. The emphasis is always on meats and grills.

If you are starved, or with a group prepared to share several dishes, order an appetizer. Otherwise, concentrate on the grilled kebabs of chicken, lamb, or beef, or perhaps one of their specialties. If you like lamb, you are in heaven. Try *klefticon*, oven-cooked baby lamb seasoned with aromatic spices; *moussaka*, minced lamb and eggplant layered with béchamel sauce; or *dolmades,* vine leaves stuffed with lamb and rice. Another top choice is *afelia,* pork filet cooked with wine and spices and served with both potato and rice. For dessert? Naturally you will have their home-made *baklava,* those melt-in-your-mouth layers of flaky pastry filled with honey and ground nuts.

Khan's
13–15 Westbourne Grove, W2

Mention good, cheap Indian food in London and the place that is always suggested first is Khan's on Westbourne Grove. Despite the service, which has been called "diabolically rude," the uncomfortable, jammed-together seating, and the long weekend queues, everyone has a good time in this big, bustling and noisy restaurant that seats three hundred and fifty diners at one time under a magic cloud-like ceiling mural. A great deal of food is prepared ahead, which enables lightning service and encourages speed eating. Don't worry, the turnover is so fast that you will not run the risk of getting something that has languished past its prime in a lukewarm pot on the back burner. The astonishingly cheap tandoori chicken is wonderful; so is the house specialty, Butter Chicken, prepared in a butter, cream, nut, and masala sauce. Hardy taste buds will want to consider chicken *jalfrezi,* a hot curry that requires an extra beer to put out the fire. Vegetarians love the *chana masaladar,* chick peas spiced with garlic, ginger, lime juice, and onions. For dessert, order the refreshing orange or lemon sorbet.

TELEPHONE
071-727-5420

TUBE
Bayswater

OPEN
Daily for lunch and dinner

CLOSED
Christmas, holidays

HOURS
Lunch: noon–3 P.M.
Dinner: 6 P.M.–midnight

RESERVATIONS
Advised for large parties

CREDIT CARDS
AE, DC, MC, V

PRICES
À la Carte: £6.50-11;
minimum charge £4

VAT/SERVICE
10% service charge added
to bill

MISCELLANEOUS
Takeaway

Nahar Cafeteria—Mara House
190 Sussex Gardens, W2

Open for lunch and dinner daily and for breakfast on the weekends, the Nahar Cafeteria is always filled with local Malays who have adopted it as their home-away-from-home in London. Given the astounding low prices and quality food, every Cheap Eater in London will soon be beating a path to the door . . . provided they can find it. Don't be put off by the gloomy basement location and hard-to-find entrance

TELEPHONE
071-402-8129

TUBE
Paddington

OPEN
Daily

CLOSED
Christmas, Malaysian
holidays (call to check)

HOURS
Breakfast: Sat & Sun 8–10 A.M.
Lunch: Daily noon–3 P.M.
Dinner: Daily 6–10 P.M.

RESERVATIONS
Not accepted

CREDIT CARDS
AE, DC, MC, V

PRICES
À la Carte: £2.50–6
Set Price: £3–4

VAT/SERVICE
No service charged or expected

MISCELLANEOUS
Unlicensed

next to a steep staircase. Once inside this cheap eatery, you are in for some delicious food. Every day there are five or six special dishes offered, all neatly written on a wipe-clean formica board. For less than £5 you could have a bowl of noodles covered with chunks of seafood or fried rice, the vegetable of the day, and a main course of fish curry, garlic chicken, prawn in sambal sauce, a hot sauce of chili, onion, garlic, and ginger, or mutton rib soup. Vegetarians need not worry, especially with the fresh bean tofu served with a chili or peanut sauce. Desserts are not to be overlooked, as is the case in most Malay restaurants. Try the *tepeng bungkus,* a coconut custard with a fried coconut filling, all steamed in a banana leaf, or the pièce de résistance, fried banana with ice cream. If you are here for breakfast on Saturday or Sunday, you can look forward to coconut rice and a sort of filo pastry filled with chicken or beef curry, all washed down by Malaysian tea, a frothy mix of tea, cinnamon, and condensed milk. Glasses of rosewater, a sweet, lightly spiced water, are on the house whenever you dine here.

Norman's Restaurant
7 Porchester Gardens (off Queensway, opposite Whiteleys Shopping Center), W2

TELEPHONE
071-727-0278

TUBE
Bayswater or Queensway

OPEN
Daily

CLOSED
Christmas

HOURS
Continuous service
8:30 A.M.–11:30 P.M.

RESERVATIONS
Not accepted

CREDIT CARDS
None

PRICES
À la Carte: £2.50–6
Set Price: £5

VAT/SERVICE
Service discretionary

Set in a fifties' time warp that includes decor, food, and prices, Norman's is about as *real* a cafe experience as you will have in this part of London, just off the busy Queensway shopping street. Look for the placard standing outside listing daily specials, go down three steps, and you will be in a knotty-pine room with fourteen formica-topped tables surrounded by velvet-covered, black metal chairs. Bridie, who has been at the helm for thirty-plus years, greets the old-timers who arrive for early morning coffee, the daily special, a teatime treat, or breakfast any time of day. Don't look for upscale dishes such as prosciutto with melon or sophisticated veal preparations. The food leans toward battered and fried, with heavy emphasis on fried liver with bacon, onions or sausage, fried fish, spaghetti, pork chops, and hamburger steak with onions and fried eggs. All dishes include potatoes and one vegetable and are served in growing-boy portions.

Poons
205 Whiteleys Shopping Center, Queensway, W2

For the best Chinese food in London, go to Chinatown. No fewer than thirty restaurants lie huddled around this maze of streets just behind Leicester Square. Some of the best barbecued and wind-dried meats you will have are found at the Poons restaurants. The location on Lisle Street was their first. It is still an unpretentious hole-in-the-wall that is a favorite with the local Chinese community. With only four round oilcloth-covered tables upstairs, sharing is expected, and you will get to know the other diners quickly, which could be a help when trying to decide between the salted wind-dried duck with rice or the roasted crisp pork belly. The Leicester Street branch was the first expansion from the original location. The menu is basically the same with a few specialty dishes added. There is more space, but the prices are slightly higher, the decor Chinese-functional, and the crowds legion.

For special occasions, try one of the other Poon branches, especially the newest, just-opened in The City. This restaurant represents state-of-the-art Chinese cooking and serving. Many of the dishes have never been prepared in this country. In addition to a serene dining room, there is an eighty-seat, fast food section dedicated to nearby office workers who haven't time for a more leisurely lunch. No matter which Poons branch you choose, the comprehensive menus featuring fine Cantonese cuisine will make the meal one you will remember and want to have again.

TELEPHONE
071-792-2884

TUBE
Bayswater or Queensway

OPEN
Daily

CLOSED
Christmas

HOURS
Continuous service,
noon–11 P.M.

RESERVATIONS
Not necessary

CREDIT CARDS
AE, DC, MC, V

PRICES
À la Carte: £12–18;
Set Price: £12–16 per person

VAT/SERVICE
Service discretionary

MISCELLANEOUS
MSG omitted on request

Texas Lone Star Saloon
117a Queensway, W2

For a taste of home, Texas-style, grab your boots and Stetson and head for the Texas Lone Star Saloon. While hardly the spot for the first date of a possible new romance, it is a great place to go with your pals

TELEPHONE
071-727-2980

TUBE
Queensway

OPEN
Daily
CLOSED
Christmas
HOURS
Continuous service
Mon–Wed noon–11:30 P.M.,
Thurs–Sat noon–12:15 A.M.,
Sundays and holidays noon–
11:15 P.M.
RESERVATIONS
Essential after 7 P.M. but not
accepted Fri or Sat night
CREDIT CARDS
None
PRICES
À la carte: £4–11
VAT/SERVICE
10% service charge; minimum
charge after 7 P.M. £4
MISCELLANEOUS
Takeaway; live music Mon–Sat
nights; sweatshirts and T-shirts
for sale

any day of the year except Christmas. Close your eyes and imagine a Texas honkytonk with wagon-wheel lights and pine booths where you are served by waitresses named Sally Sue, wearing tight jeans and even tighter T-shirts and you will have this one down pat. During the day, country music straight from KJ 97 FM in San Antonio, Texas, keeps everyone happy and humming along with Loretta Lynn, Conway Twitty, and Dolly Parton. From Monday–Saturday night, live bands and bluegrass singers have them lined up to get in.

The food is as real as the atmosphere and naturally comes in Texas-sized portions. Slabs of barbecued ribs with cole slaw, three-alarm chili, 1¼-pound T-bone steaks with mounds of fries, burritos, tacos, burgers, and desserts like Mississippi mud pie keep everyone off a diet. There are between twelve and fourteen lunch specials, ranging in price from £2.85 for Coyote Pete's onion rings with a salad, to a 5-oz. grilled prime steak and fries going for £4.95. In between there is a toasted turkey sandwich, potato skins filled with cheese and bacon, and half a Cajun-spiced chicken with fries or a salad. Libations include Michelob and Dos Equis beers, zombies, Singapore slings, and a deadly brew called the One-Pot-Screamer, a mix of white tequila, vodka, orange juice, and grenadine.

TEAROOMS W2

Pâtisserie Française
127 Queensway, W2

TELEPHONE
071-229-0746
TUBE
Bayswater or Queensway
OPEN
Daily
CLOSED
2 days each at New Year's,
Easter, Christmas

I found the Pâtisserie Française early one Sunday morning as I was on my way to the Whiteleys Shopping Center not far away. I was first drawn to the tempting window display of all my favorite French goodies: big, buttery croissants, *pain au raisin, pain au chocolat,* brioche, glistening fruit tarts, and creamy mousse-filled cakes. Once inside, there is more: everything from apple strudel to scones and a variety of fabulous wholemeal breads. In back is a dining area where you can sit and enjoy one of the bakery treats, or order breakfast from 8 A.M.–3 P.M. They also serve quiche lorraine, hot soup, salads, a plat du jour, three-decker sandwiches on their great bread, and savory and sweet crepes. Given the high quality of the food, which is all made right here and is head and shoulders above anything else on this street, it is no wonder it is usually SRO every day from morning to night.

HOURS
Continuous service
Counter for takeaway: 7 A.M.–8 P.M. Dining Room: 8 A.M.–8 P.M.

RESERVATIONS
Not accepted

CREDIT CARDS
None

PRICES
À la Carte: £1.50–6

VAT/SERVICE
Service discretionary

MISCELLANEOUS
Takeaway for all pastries

W8 ✤ KENSINGTON

This is a gracious and sheltered residential area where Princess Diana lives in the lovely Kensington Palace. Kensington High Street is regarded as one of the major shopping areas and a magnet for the new, the weird, and the far-out. Kensington Church Street is lined with pricey antiques shops.

PUBS W8

The Britannia
1 Allen Street, W8

TELEPHONE
071-937-1864

TUBE
High Street Kensington

OPEN
Mon–Sat

CLOSED
Sun, holidays (call to check, they may decide to stay open)

HOURS
11 A.M.–11 P.M.; noon–2:30 P.M. for hot food; dinner, cold food only

If you have time for only one typical neighborhood pub, the Britannia would be a good choice. No loud music, banging slot machines, or boisterous behavior from the patrons will mar your stay in this old-fashioned, friendly spot a block from Kensington High Street. Managers John and June Eaglestone have been at the Britannia for over a decade, and in pub management, that is a record. They have that special talent for making people feel welcome, whether on their first or fiftieth visit.

The large bar is accented by an impressive collection of Toby mugs and vintage English china plates. In the back is a glassed-in summer garden conservatory with hanging plants and picnic benches. The pub food includes casseroles, lasagna, fish and chips on Friday, and if you are lucky, June's own steak and kidney pie made with Guinness stout. No hot meals are served in the evenings, but you can always get a salad, toasted sandwiches, or a ploughman's lunch plate. For dessert, the only thing to consider is June's homemade apple pie.

RESERVATIONS
Not accepted

CREDIT CARDS
None

PRICES
À la Carte: £4.50–6.60

VAT/SERVICE
No service charged or expected

MISCELLANEOUS
Children allowed only in garden area

RESTAURANTS W8

The Ark
122 Palace Gardens Terrace, W8

What has kept the faithful returning to this bastion of good cooking for so long? Not fussy haute cuisine, but ample portions of the type of cooking that has always been standard fare in France. It would be hard not to enjoy The Ark's onion soup, marinated mushrooms, or the spinach salad with bacon and avocado as starters. The favorite main course is the rack of lamb with herb gravy. A close second is bouillabaisse. The fresh fish of the day is always reliable and so are any of the plats du jour. Vegetables and potatoes are extra, but not very much. The servings are so large that one dish of carrots or spinach is enough for two to share. The wine list is simple and concise, with the house white or red the best buys. Everyone orders a *pot au chocolat* or the hot butterscotch sundae for dessert. By 9 P.M. every night it is SRO, so plan ahead for this reliable Cheap Eat.

Please note: Well worth the additional outlay is their second location off Kensington High Street. Here the two-floor restaurant is more formal and expensive by about £3–5 per person for the more subtle French cooking.

TELEPHONE
071-229-4024

TUBE
Notting Hill Gate

OPEN
Daily for lunch and dinner

CLOSED
Sun lunch, Christmas

HOURS
Lunch: Mon–Sat noon–3 P.M.
Dinner: Sun 6–11 P.M.

RESERVATIONS
Essential at dinner, advised at lunch

CREDIT CARDS
AE, DC, MC, V

PRICES
À la Carte: £13–15

VAT/SERVICE
Service discretionary

The Ark

35 Kensington High Street (enter off the footpath leading from Kensington High Street to Kensington Court), W8

See The Ark, Palace Gardens Terrace, previous page, for description.

TELEPHONE: 071-937-4294
TUBE: High Street Kensington
OPEN: Daily
CLOSED: Sun lunch from Oct–Easter, Christmas
HOURS: Lunch noon–3 P.M. Dinner: 7–11:15 P.M.
RESERVATIONS: Advised
CREDIT CARDS: AE, DC, MC, V
PRICES: À la Carte: £16–25; Set Price: Lunch, £11 for 2 courses, £14 for 3
VAT/SERVICE: £1 cover per person; service included for parties of 6 or more, otherwise discretionary

Café Flo

127–129 Kensington Church Street, W8

TELEPHONE
071-727-8142
TUBE
Notting Hill Gate
OPEN
Daily
CLOSED
Christmas
HOURS
Breakfast: 9–11:30 A.M.
Lunch: noon–3 P.M.
Snacks: 3–5 P.M.
Dinner: 5–11:30 P.M.
RESERVATIONS
Preferred
CREDIT CARDS
MC, V
PRICES
À la Carte: £5–12
Set Price: Sunday lunch, 3 courses and coffee, £13; 2 courses and coffee, £7.95; Mon–Fri, 2-course lunch, £6
VAT/SERVICE
Service discretionary

If the traffic was not rushing by on the wrong side of the street, you might think you were sitting in a café in the heart of the Left Bank in Paris. Café Flo reminds me of dozens you see in Paris, right down to the approved bistro-style tables and chairs and proper French toilet. I like the Kensington Church Street location best because it is larger and more relaxing. That is not to say the one on St. Martin's Lane in the theater district isn't good; it is just very small and you are forced to sit elbow-to-elbow with your neighbor. At both locations, the menu changes seasonally and always offers all the recognizable French dishes: salad *frisée aux lardons-oeuf mollet* (curly endive with bacon pieces topped with a poached egg), steak and *frites* (french fries), creamy omelettes, and *croque monsieur.* For dessert, indulge in an airy *oeufs à la neige,* floating island, *crème brulée,* or the tarte du jour. Both sites are good to keep in mind for a nice breakfast. Besides the usual full English breakfast, you can have scrambled eggs with smoked salmon, fresh fruit and yogurt, pancakes with maple syrup, along with croissants, orange juice, and good coffee.

Costas Grill
14 Hillgate Street, W8

Budget-conscious Londoners have been noshing on fish and chips for decades. The fish is usually cod, haddock, plaice, or any other white fish, deep fried in batter until golden. It comes to you crunchy on the outside and moist inside. Accompanied by an order of chips (french fries) it makes a satisfying meal.

Costas Grill is a Greek-owned spot near Notting Hill Gate, best known for its fish and chips, and that is what you should stick to when dining here. If you don't fancy fish, their homemade sausages with onion or garlic flavoring are worthy alternatives. For variety's sake, try a Greek starter, say octopus in oil and vinegar or the *taramosalata*. If you are still hungry after all of this, the hot apple or banana fritters complete the cholesterol festival very nicely.

TELEPHONE
071-229-3794
TUBE
Notting Hill Gate
OPEN
Tues–Sat
CLOSED
Sun, Mon, holidays
HOURS
Lunch: noon–2:30 P.M.
Dinner: 5:30–10:30 P.M.
RESERVATIONS
Essential
CREDIT CARDS
None
PRICES
À la Carte: £7–10
VAT/SERVICE
Service discretionary
MISCELLANEOUS
Reduced prices for children on request; takeaway for fish and chips only

Geales Fish Restaurant
2 Farmer Street, W8

For more than half a century, the Geales family has been serving fresh fish in their two-room country-style dining room near Kensington Palace (home of Princess Diana). Their fish and chips are not only relatively inexpensive, but touted by many as the best in London. The fish is sold according to size and weight and the selection is basic: cod, haddock, plaice, and salmon being the best sellers. The batter used is made with beef drippings, which gives it a distinct texture, yet doesn't overpower the fish. Everything you will eat is à la carte, from appetizers and main courses, to chips, salad, tartar sauce, pickles, and dessert. You are asked to pay when the food is delivered. That may be strange to some of us, but it has been working here for years.

TELEPHONE
071-727-7969
TUBE
Notting Hill Gate
OPEN
Tues–Sat
CLOSED
Sun, Mon, holidays, last 2 weeks in August
HOURS
noon–3 P.M., 6–11 P.M.
RESERVATIONS
Not accepted
CREDIT CARDS
MC, V
PRICES
À la Carte: £7–10
VAT/SERVICE
15p cover per person, service discretionary

The Original Carvery at the Kensington Close Hotel
Wright's Lane, W8

See The Original Carvery at the Cumberland Hotel, page 44, for description. All other information is the same.

TELEPHONE: 071-937-4751
TUBE: High Street Kensington
OPEN: Daily for lunch and dinner
CLOSED: Never
HOURS: Lunch: Mon–Sat noon–3 P.M., Sun noon–3:30 P.M. Dinner: Daily 5:30–10:30 P.M.

Palms
3–5 Campden Hill Road (off Kensington High Street), W8

See Palms, page 100, for description. All other information is the same.

TELEPHONE: 071-938-1830
TUBE: High Street Kensington
OPEN: Daily
CLOSED: Christmas
HOURS: Continuous service, 9:45 A.M.–11:30 P.M. Breakfast: 9:45 A.M.–noon, 1 P.M. on Sun
RESERVATIONS: For more than 8
CREDIT CARDS: MC, V
PRICES: À la Carte: £7–12
VAT/SERVICE: 12½% service added to bill

TELEPHONE
071-937-0120
TUBE
High Street Kensington
OPEN
Daily
CLOSED
Christmas
HOURS
Continuous service noon–midnight. Buffet served Mon–Sat *only* from 12:15–2:30 P.M.
RESERVATIONS
Suggested
CREDIT CARDS
AE, DC, MC, V
PRICES
À la Carte: £18-30; lunch buffet, £11. Set Price: From £15.50–28 per person
VAT/SERVICE
No cover charge or service for buffet lunch; £1.60 cover per person on à la carte and set meals; 15% service for all à la carte and set meals
MISCELLANEOUS
Takeaway

Phoenicia
11–13 Abingdon Road (off Kensington High Street), W8

Middle Eastern meals do not follow the Western pattern of three courses plus coffee or tea. They start and end with *meze:* a variety of small dishes of vegetables, salads, meats, and pastries, accompanied with olives and unleavened pita bread to scoop up the food. Lebanese food, in particular, is a delightful collection of flavors from all over the Middle East.

The outstanding Cheap Eats attraction at Phoenicia, a Lebanese restaurant, is the all-you-can-eat *meze* buffet lunch served every day but Sunday. Huge tables are laden with salads, tabouleh, hommus, pita bread, lamb, chicken fixed numerous ways, vegetables, and cheeses. If you have never tried Lebanese food, this is the perfect beginning.

Budgeteers should beware of the à la carte menu, which if you are not careful, can get way out of hand.

Stick & Bowl
31 Kensington High Street, W8

If you linger too long, the waiter at Stick & Bowl may ask you to leave to make room for the next person. With only four tables downstairs and four upstairs, you can see this is not the place for a leisurely meal. It is, however, absolutely unbeatable for fast Chinese Cheap Eats while shopping along Kensington High Street. The most expensive meal (#10) comes in under £5. For that you will get one spring roll, one prawn, two spare ribs or sweet and sour pork, fried rice, and a vegetable. There are fifty-five other possibilities ranging from soup (sweet corn, won ton, chicken noodle, or sweet and sour) to nuts (lichees served either in a bowl or made into a drink).

TELEPHONE
071-937-2778

TUBE
High Street Kensington

OPEN
Daily

CLOSED
Christmas

HOURS
Continuous service
11 A.M.–11:30 P.M.

RESERVATIONS
Not accepted

CREDIT CARDS
None

PRICES
À la Carte: £4–6
Set Price: £4.50

VAT/SERVICE
No service charged or expected

MISCELLANEOUS
Takeaway

TEAROOMS W8

The Muffin Man
12 Wright's Lane, W8

Soups, salads, and sandwiches, a variety of addicting cakes, tea breads, and scones, plus continuous service from breakfast through teatime keep The Muffin Man humming from Monday to Saturday. I like to sit in the upstairs loft, which holds four tables. Although it can get a bit stuffy, it is an intimate and cozy choice for a lovers' chat or an hour of good gossip.

In the morning, order the scrambled eggs with smoked salmon and two toasted buttered crumpets with orange marmalade. For lunch, the Original Muffin Man sandwich is always a good choice: toasted wholemeal bread loaded with roasted chicken, crisp bacon, lettuce, tomato, and cucumbers. For a lighter meal, try a cup of their homemade soup or the Muffin Man Rarebit. If I am there for tea, I order a pot of their specially blended tea and either a slice of passion cake, a dense carrot cake loaded with walnuts and raisins, or the Queen Mother's Cake, fruit cake with dates and brown sugar.

TELEPHONE
071-937-6652

TUBE
High Street Kensington

OPEN
Mon–Sat

CLOSED
Sun, holidays

HOURS
Continuous service
8:15 A.M.–6 P.M.
Lunch: 11:30 A.M.–6 P.M.

RESERVATIONS
Not necessary

CREDIT CARDS
None

PRICES
À la Carte: £2–6; minimum charge £1.50 from 12:30–2:30 P.M.

VAT/SERVICE
Service discretionary

MISCELLANEOUS
No-smoking section; low-fat and vegetarian butter available; unlicensed; takeaway; half portions for children

Everything is almost perfect at The Muffin Man until it is time for the loo. This requires a trip down steep, poorly lighted stairs to what must once have been a mop closet. Improvements are always intended, but are yet to be executed.

WINE BARS W8

Benedicts Restaurant Wine Bar
106 Kensington High Street, W8

TELEPHONE
071-937-7580
TUBE
High Street Kensington
OPEN
Daily
CLOSED
Christmas
HOURS
Continuous service
Mon–Sat noon–10:30 P.M.,
Sun noon–2:30 P.M., 5–10 P.M.
RESERVATIONS
Not necessary
CREDIT CARDS
AE, DC, MC, V
PRICES
À la Carte: £5–12
VAT/SERVICE
Service discretionary

Directly opposite the Kensington High Street tube station is Benedicts. The second-floor wine bar and restaurant delivers much more than first appearances on the street would suggest. After entering a small open doorway, you climb two sets of stairs and find yourself in a darkly paneled, rather dimly lit room. The theme is Irish, thus the pictures of well-fed monks and priests adorning the walls. It is a popular lunchtime spot, especially with local office workers and shoppers along Kensington High Street (see "Cheap Chic" in *Cheap Sleeps in London*).

The best thing about eating here is that you can order an appetizer or a salad with a glass of wine for either lunch or dinner and be treated as well as if you ordered the most expensive three-course meal. The seasonal menu offers few exciting surprises, but the food is well prepared and nicely presented. The best appetizer is always the golden fried mushrooms stuffed with cream cheese, herbs, and garlic. Main-course choices range from a short list of daily and weekly specials to the usual grilled steaks, fish, meat pies, omelettes, and lasagna. All dishes are garnished with vegetables and potatoes. Desserts are made elsewhere, with the exception of the cheesecake and crêpes. A better choice is the excellent Irish coffee.

W11 ✤ NOTTING HILL GATE

Notting Hill Gate is a beautiful residential area with grand villas lining the streets. On Saturday morning, shoppers should not miss the famous Portobello Road street market. It dates back to the nineteenth century when gypsies traded horses here. Today, the street is lined with stalls selling everything from good quality jewelry, bric-a-brac, second-hand linens, and antiques to cheap imports and questionable silver.

RESTAURANTS

RESTAURANTS W11

Books for Cooks & Ristorante
4 Blenheim Crescent, W11

When I found Books for Cooks & Ristorante, I knew I had hit the jackpot in more ways than one. The restaurant, flat, and shop are under the ownership and skillful management of Clarissa Dickson-Wright, who ran the place for years for Heidi Lascelles. Ms. Wright really knows her cookbooks. She stocks London's largest inventory of cookbooks— old, new, obscure, well-known, ethnic, gourmet, or cookbooks written in Yiddish, French, German, or in countless other languages—if it has to do with cooking, she has it, or knows about it and will order it for you and ship it to your home address.

Those who appreciate good food should never consider leaving London without sampling a meal served in the tiny four-table Ristorante in the back of the shop. The menu changes daily according to the whims and fancies of the rotating chefs. All use only the best seasonal ingredients to create their deliciously inventive dishes. Just thinking of the warm fusilli with sundried tomatoes, grilled peppers, and ricotta cheese, the cream of quail soup, the pizza with baby artichokes and fresh tomatoes, or the cod seasoned with coriander and served with an array of fresh vegetables makes me phone for lunch reservations the minute I arrive in London.

TELEPHONE
071-221-1992

TUBE
Notting Hill Gate or Ladbroke Grove

OPEN
Mon–Sat

CLOSED
Sun, holidays

HOURS
Shop: 9:30 A.M.–6 P.M.
Ristorante:10:30 A.M–5 P.M.
Lunch: 1–3:30 P.M., pastries all day long

RESERVATIONS
Advised, and essential on Saturday

CREDIT CARDS
AE, DC, MC, V

PRICES
À la Carte: £10 for 3 courses

VAT/SERVICE
Service discretionary

MISCELLANEOUS
Cooking demonstrations usually held between 11 A.M. and 1:30 P.M., call ahead to verify; Unlicensed, no corkage

If you have time, be sure to call ahead to find out when a famous chef will be demonstrating in the upstairs test kitchen. Here you will have a ringside seat to the performance and be invited to taste the results.

Special: If you are a true cook, or even if you only microwave, consider staying in the two-bedroom flat located above the shop. It is attractively decorated with English country furniture and fabrics and is the sort of place you can move right into and call home for a long or short stay. (See *Cheap Sleeps in London* for details.)

Mr. Christian's
11 Elgin Crescent, W11

TELEPHONE
071-229-0501
TUBE
Ladbroke Grove or Notting Hill Gate (for Portobello Market)
OPEN
Daily
CLOSED
Christmas, holidays
HOURS
Continuous service Mon–Fri 7 A.M.–7 P.M., Sat 6 A.M.–6 P.M., Sun 9:30 A.M.–2 P.M.
RESERVATIONS
Not accepted
CREDIT CARDS
None
PRICES
À la Carte: £1.75–4
VAT/SERVICE
No service charged or expected
MISCELLANEOUS
Takeaway

After a Saturday morning spent braving the crowds at Portobello Market, join the queue at Mr. Christian's and sample one of the best sandwiches in London.

During the week this is a delicatessen serving morning croissants and muffins and mid-day sandwiches, salads, and hot specials alongside a stunning assortment of salamis, cheeses, pâtés, and vintage olive oils. On Saturday, when the market is in full swing, it hits its stride as the food spills onto the sidewalk with a dazzling display of a rotating selection of international breads that are sold whole or sliced into sandwiches wolfed down by hungry shoppers. If it is available, be sure to sample their English sourdough bread—a specialty that takes five days to make and lasts up to eight days.

Note: Portobello Market operates as an antiques market on Friday and Saturday, but it is best on Saturday morning from 8 A.M.–1 P.M. when the street stalls are open.

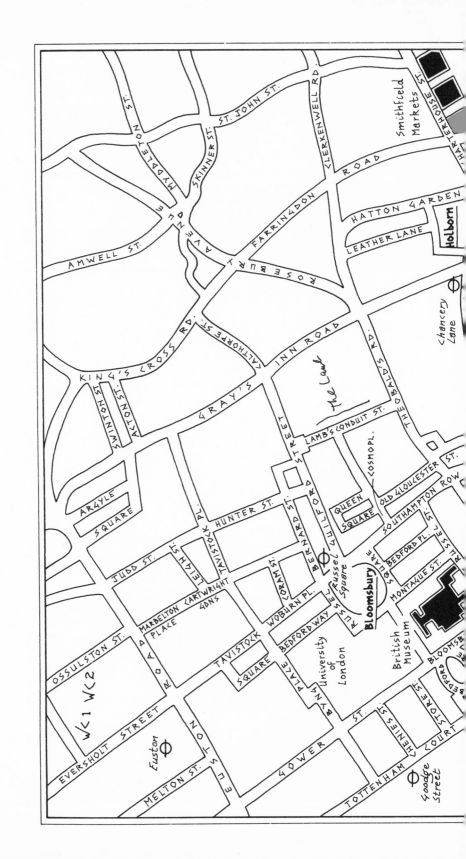

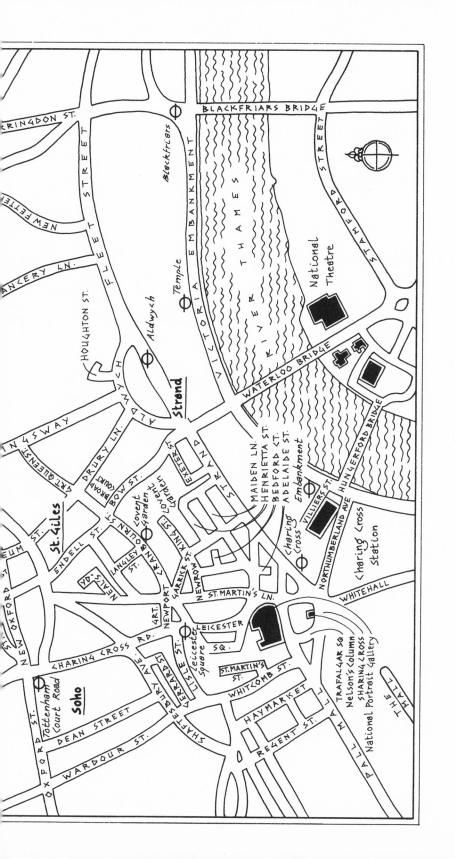

WC1 ✤ BLOOMSBURY, RUSSELL SQUARE

Known as intellectual London, this is a good location with a quiet atmosphere for being so central. It is the former home of the famed Bloomsbury Group, which included biographer Lytton Strachey, novelist Virginia Woolf, economist John Maynard Keynes, and poet T.S. Eliot. The cornerstones of the area are the British Museum and Russell Square, which is London's second largest after Lincoln's Inn Fields. University of London buildings are scattered throughout the area.

PUBS WC1

Lamb
94 Lamb's Conduit Street, WC1

TELEPHONE
071-405-0713

TUBE
Russell Square

OPEN
Daily

CLOSED
Holidays

The Lamb is a magnificent pub in the heart of Bloomsbury, the part of London made famous in the twenties and thirties by the Bloomsbury Group of writers that included Leonard and Virginia Woolf, Lytton Strachey, and John Maynard Keynes. Aside from the beautiful green-tiled exterior, the most striking feature of the pub is the horseshoe bar with its original etched-glass "snob screens" still in place. These rotating screens were used in Victorian days to shield the pillars of society when they were drinking with women of dubious distinction. In the rest of the pub the wood-paneled walls are decorated with a fascinating display of Hogarth prints and sepia photographs of half-forgotten stars of the Victorian music halls and theaters. On a more current note, there is a large photo of the Queen Mum with a glass of beer in her hand. The seating throughout is comfortable and you can always hear what is being said. The Lamb is one of the rare pubs that does not have piped-in music, a blaring jukebox, or banging slot machines drowning out the gentle hum of conversation. In addition to the great atmosphere, the Young's beer is good, the lunchtime food is above average, there is a no-smoking section, and the generally upscale crowd is very friendly.

Note: When you leave the pub, head up Lamb's Conduit Street and you will come to Coram's Field, a lovely park dedicated to children. The sign at the entrance tells all: "Adults may only enter with a child. If you see an adult who happens to be on their own, please contact a member of the Coram's staff."

HOURS
Mon–Sat 11 A.M.–10 P.M.;
Sun noon–3 P.M.,
7–10:30 P.M. Food service:
noon–2:30 P.M. (hot food).
Sunday lunch (roast beef, pork, or lamb) noon–2:30 P.M.

RESERVATIONS
Not accepted

CREDIT CARDS
MC, V

PRICES
À la Carte: £4–5

VAT/SERVICE
No service charge

Museum Tavern
49 Great Russell Street, WC1

The Museum Tavern is a splendid pub with oak paneling, velvet benches, etched glass, and wooden tables on the sidewalk in the summer. It is one of the oldest pubs in Bloomsbury, first opening for business in the early eighteenth century. For over two hundred and sixty years, it has continued to offer ales, wines, spirits, food, and hospitality to visitors and locals alike. Located opposite the British Museum, it was Karl Marx's watering hole during his London days, and is also rumored to have been one of the gathering places for Virginia Woolf and her Bloomsbury Group, and for Oscar Wilde and his friends. It is a free house, which means it can serve any brewery's beer, thus you will find a wide choice of real ales. Because it is such a convenient place for resting tired

TELEPHONE
071-242-8987

TUBE
Holborn or Tottenham Court Road

OPEN
Daily

CLOSED
Christmas

HOURS
Mon–Sat 11 A.M.–11 P.M., Sun noon–10:30 P.M. Food service: lunch 11:30 A.M.–2 P.M.

RESERVATIONS
Not accepted

CREDIT CARDS
AE, DC, MC, V

PRICES
À la Carte: £5.50–8

feet after tramping the corridors of the British Museum, it is wall-to-wall crowded at lunchtime. So, for the best food selection and a seat, arrive early.

Queen Charlotte's Restaurant & Pub
1 Queen's Square, WC1

TELEPHONE
071-837-5627
TUBE
Russell Square
OPEN
Daily
CLOSED
Christmas and some holidays
HOURS
Mon–Sat 11 A.M.–11 P.M.
Sun noon–3 P.M., 7–10:30 P.M.
Food service: Lunch noon–
2:30 P.M. (restaurant and pub),
dinner 5:30–9:30 P.M.
(restaurant only)
RESERVATIONS
Not necessary
CREDIT CARDS
MC, V
PRICES
À la Carte: Pub, £5–7;
restaurant, £11
Set Price: £7–11
VAT/SERVICE
Service discretionary in
restaurant, not charged or
expected in pub

The history of Queen Charlotte's Restaurant & Pub goes back to 1710, when the first tavern was licensed to operate on the site. When the mentally ill George III was confined to a hospital on Queen's Square across the street, his consort, Queen Charlotte, used the underground cellars at the pub to store delicacies for her sick husband. The cellars are still used to store beer kegs and are said to be haunted by ghosts of the past. History and ghosts aside, the best part about this pub today is that it serves hot lunches *and* dinners. In addition to the familiar pub food downstairs, the upstairs dining room has both à la carte and set menus highlighting the house specialty, homemade pot pies. These meals-in-themselves are filled with fish, vegetables, beef, lamb, or chicken and come garnished with potatoes and two seasonal vegetables or a salad. The best Cheap Eat is the Queen's Choice, a set three-course meal with choices of three appetizers, three pot pies, dessert, and coffee, all for less than £12.

RESTAURANTS WC1

Cosmoba
9 Cosmo Place (off Southampton Row), WC1

TELEPHONE
071-837-0904
TUBE
Russell Square
OPEN
Mon–Sat
CLOSED
Sun, holidays
HOURS
Lunch: 11:30 A.M.–3 P.M.
Dinner: 5:30–11 P.M.

It is always nice to go back to a good Cheap Eat and find it better than ever. That is how I found Cosmoba, situated on the same side of a pedestrian lane that sports a trendy wine bar and a haunted pub. Cosmoba is the one the locals will tell you about as having good value for money. It is a plain, family-run restaurant serving homey Italian food that is definitely worth a second trip. Fortunately, the old, uninteresting, and dusty decor has been brightened by a coat of white paint, pictures of Italy on the wall, and

Italian music playing in the background. The strings of wine bottles are mercifully gone, replaced by brighter lighting and one or two green plants. It is all a definite improvement.

The menu is still comfort reading for all Italian food fans. There is a long list of antipasti with everything from stuffed zucchini and homemade pâté to a mixed salami plate or melon with Parma ham. Follow that with veal, chicken, steak, or one of the weekly specials such as grilled calf's liver or lamb steak in a tomato, garlic, and olive sauce. Pasta is well represented, with lasagna and ravioli, or spaghetti, tagliatelle, and penne served with a variety of sauces. Desserts tend to be mundane and can be skipped without any pangs. As you can see, nothing is very sophisticated, but it all tastes good, is generously served, and will not end up ruining the day by shattering your budget.

RESERVATIONS
Not necessary
CREDIT CARDS
None
PRICES
À la Carte: £9–14
VAT/SERVICE
Service discretionary

The Fryer's Delight
19 Theobalds Road, WC1

You will know you are close when you pass people in the street munching their cod wrapped in unlined newsprint. You will also recognize it by the line of people on the sidewalk waiting to get to the counter, and by the cars double-parked in front with drivers dashing in to pick up an order. Fast food British style began with fish and chips (french fries). Today you can find fish and chips shops all over London that vary little in price, but are oceans apart in quality. One of the best is The Fryer's Delight. The cooking is done right in front of you in a tiny room with zero decor. What counts is their specialty: deep-fried chicken or fish and chips served in heaping portions you will have a hard time finishing. If you order takeaway, it will be wrapped in plain white paper and handed to you. If you are eating your food here, place your order at the counter, find a seat at one of the five plastic covered booths with bright orange table tops and your heaping plate will be brought to you by the motherly waitress. A order of rock cod and chips with a huge slab of buttered bread will set you back less

TELEPHONE
071-405-4114
TUBE
Holborn
OPEN
Mon–Sat
CLOSED
Sun, holidays
HOURS
Continuous service noon–10 P.M.; takeaway, noon–11 P.M.
RESERVATIONS
Not accepted
CREDIT CARDS
None
PRICES
À la Carte: £3.50–4.50
VAT/SERVICE
No service charged or expected
MISCELLANEOUS
Takeaway

than £4 and will be one of the best Cheap Eats you will enjoy in London.

The Greenhouse
Basement of 16 Chenies Street, Drill Arts Center, WC1

TELEPHONE
071-637-8038
TUBE
Goodge Street
OPEN
Mon–Sat
CLOSED
Sun, holidays
HOURS
Continuous service
Mon–Fri 10 A.M.–10 P.M.,
Sat 10 A.M.–9 P.M.
Women only, Mon 6–10 P.M.
RESERVATIONS
Not accepted
CREDIT CARDS
None
PRICES
À la Carte: £2–7
VAT/SERVICE
No service charged or expected
MISCELLANEOUS
No smoking; unlicensed,
BYOB, no corkage

For the last ten years, interest in vegetarian food has increased considerably in London and there are now a number of specialty restaurants that offer excellent vegetarian cuisine at prices most Cheap Eaters can afford. The Greenhouse in the basement of the Drill Arts Center is one of the most popular, despite its laid-back, almost hippy air. Seating is on plain wooden chairs around wooden tables in a white-washed room filled with ads and posters for fringe plays, off-beat art exhibitions, new age classes, and yoga lessons. There is no written menu, but the dishes, which change daily, are listed on a blackboard behind the counter. In addition to the special of the day, there is usually quiche, soup, a selection of salads, and one vegan dish. The desserts are special, especially the fruit crumble or the trifle. For an informal, low-budget yet imaginative meal, it will be hard to do better.

Konaki
5 Coptic Street, WC1

TELEPHONE
071-580-9730, 071-580-3712
TUBE
Tottenham Court Road
OPEN
Mon–Fri lunch and dinner,
Sat dinner
CLOSED
Sat lunch, Sun, Christmas
HOURS
Lunch: Mon–Fri noon–3 P.M.
Dinner: Mon–Thurs 6–
11:30 P.M., Fri–Sat 6–midnight
RESERVATIONS
Recommended on weekends
CREDIT CARDS
AE, DC
PRICES
À la Carte: £16–22
Set Price: £26, *meze* for two

Some of the best Cheap Eats restaurant tips come from readers who write to me about their discoveries. That is how I found out about Konaki, located about ten minutes from the British Museum. The interior is serene, compared to most Greek restaurants, with lots of flowers, beamed ceilings, comfortable seating, and lights on each table in the evening. On Friday and Saturday nights there is live piano music from 8 P.M. on. The food is Greek, and while not brilliantly gourmet, it is good and filling, especially the *meze* for two at £26. This gargantuan feast is composed of three courses with a choice of ten to fifteen starters, lamb cutlets, chicken, or pork *souvlaki* (pork kebabs) for the main course, all the fresh pita bread you can eat, and dessert. If you order à la carte, the moussaka is one of their specialties and one of the best I've ever had. You need to be a meat eater to dine here successfully because there isn't much on the menu for a dedicated vegetarian.

VAT/SERVICE
50p cover per person, 12% service added to bill

The Museum Street Cafe
47 Museum Street, WC1

The Museum Street Cafe draws enlightened diners to its minimally decorated space. The small dining room has maybe ten bare wood tables and hard-seated bistro chairs. Coat hooks, an umbrella stand, and a large vase of fresh flowers complete the spartan scene. The food, however, is anything but spartan. The simple cooking, with top quality ingredients and bold flavors, is expertly prepared and will soon convince you that English food can be very good. A limited three-course menu is posted on a blackboard and changes daily so the regulars never get bored. Homemade wholemeal bread served with a tub of butter keeps you going until the starters arrive. They might be a roasted red pepper tart with olive and anchovy butter, or an asparagus salad, topped with shrimp in a light vinaigrette dressing. Fresh pork sausage with mustard grain sauce or a simple grilled monk fish with a sundried tomato mayonnaise serve as main courses. Round off your repast with the warm apple brown betty or the pressed chocolate cake and I am sure you will agree with all the devotées of this restaurant: this is *wonderful* food. Lunchtime is a packed-out, frantic time. Better to go in the evening when the service by the attractive staff is less hurried and the clientele more eclectic.

TELEPHONE
071-405-3211

TUBE
Tottenham Court Road or Holborn

OPEN
Mon–Fri for lunch and dinner

CLOSED
Sat, Sun, holidays

HOURS
Lunch: 12:30–2:15 P.M.
Dinner: 7:15–11 P.M., last order 9:15 P.M.

RESERVATIONS
Absolutely essential

CREDIT CARDS
None

PRICES
À la Carte: None
Set Price: Lunch, 2 courses £12, 3 courses £15; dinner, 3 courses £21

VAT/SERVICE
Service discretionary

MISCELLANEOUS
Unlicensed, BYOB, no corkage. Note: You can buy liquor around the corner at Victoria Wine.

My Old Dutch Pancake House
131 High Holborn Street, WC1

One hundred and five varieties of the 1½-foot-wide Dutch pancakes, stuffed with everything under the sun, are served daily on genuine Delft blue pancake plates to hungry people who love a hearty bargain. In these *pannekoeken,* ingredients are cooked into the batter rather than being rolled inside or spooned over the top. The many fillings are based

TELEPHONE
071-242-5200

TUBE
Holborn

OPEN
Daily

CLOSED
Christmas

HOURS
Continuous service
noon–11:15 P.M.

RESERVATIONS
For 6 or more

CREDIT CARDS
AE, DC, MC

PRICES
À la Carte: £6–10

VAT/SERVICE
10% service added for parties
of 6 or more, otherwise
discretionary; minimum charge
£3.50 during busy times

around cheese, ham, bacon, vegetables, fish, herbs, ice cream, and fresh fruit. It is true: some people actually have room for dessert, selecting from thirty sweet pancakes and seven waffle creations, including a summertime treat with fresh strawberries and whipped cream piled on top.

The restaurant's interior is high-degree Dutch kitsch, with masses of hanging plants, scrubbed pine tables, blue-and-white-tiled fireplaces, and antiques displayed on shelves around the ceiling. Sometimes, there are used (that means chipped or cracked) *pannekoeken* plates for sale.

Neals Yard Dining Room
14 Neals Yard, WC1

TELEPHONE
071-379-0298

TUBE
Covent Garden

OPEN
Mon–Sat

CLOSED
Sun, holidays

HOURS
Continuous service
Mon–Fri noon–8 P.M.,
Sat noon–6 P.M.

RESERVATIONS
Not accepted

CREDIT CARDS
None

PRICES
À la Carte: £5–7

VAT/SERVICE
Service discretionary

MISCELLANEOUS
No smoking; unlicensed,
BYOB, no corkage

Neals Yard Dining Room is a haven for Cheap Eaters searching for good healthy dishes at prices that won't take big bites out of their budget. The dining room is a cooperative that serves international vegetarian dishes. It is located above the Neals Yard Remedies shop and overlooks the busy courtyard ringed with juice bars, sandwich places, an excellent health food store, and the Neals Yard Bakery, which features their own stone-ground wholemeal flour in all their products.

To eat here you must be an adventurous diner willing to try new food combinations and able to tackle oversized portions. The menu features dishes from Mexico, Turkey, India, Sri Lanka, West Africa, and the Middle East with the occasional British pudding thrown in for good measure. If you opt for the West African meal, you will have a stew made from sweet potatoes and vegetables cooked in a creamy peanut sauce and served over steamed rice. Accompanying this will be beet salad and a fresh banana on the side. Lighter appetites can be satisfied by filled tortillas, several salad choices, or a bowl of rich soup. The Polish lemon and raisin cheesecake is tempting, but the fresh chocolate cake with orange slices is the finale to remember.

October Gallery Cafe
24 Old Gloucester Street, WC1

The October Gallery Cafe is run by two hard-working, creative women who alternate days with shopping and cooking. Polished wooden tables are set in the art gallery that displays changing avant-garde art "from around the planet." In warm weather, you can sit outside in the plant-filled patio of this former Victorian school building. While the art will appeal to a distinct few, let me assure you that the vibrant food will appeal to everyone. The changing menu allows the cooks to take advantage of the freshest seasonal products, which they use with verve and style in everything they prepare. I started with a cream of leek and potato soup and for the main course had a broccoli and cheese roulade, followed by the best rhubarb crumble you can imagine. Other choices that day included Moroccan lamb and couscous, free-range chicken tarragon, orange and almond cake, and plum tart. Everything is made daily and in small quantities, so there are never any leftovers. For best selection, arrive when they open because the locals are on to this one.

TELEPHONE
071-831-1618

TUBE
Holborn

OPEN
Tues–Sat for lunch only

CLOSED
Sun, Mon, holidays

HOURS
Lunch: 12:30–2:30 P.M.

RESERVATIONS
Not accepted

CREDIT CARDS
None

PRICES
À la Carte: £4–8

VAT/SERVICE
No service charged or expected

MISCELLANEOUS
Unlicensed, BYOB, no corkage

The Original Carvery at the Forte Crest Bloomsbury
Coram Street, WC1

See The Original Carvery at the Cumberland Hotel, page 44, for description. All other information is the same.

TELEPHONE: 071-837-1200
TUBE: Russell Square
OPEN: Daily
CLOSED: Never

Poons
50 Woburn Place, WC1

See Poons Restaurants, page 63, for description.
TELEPHONE: 071-580-1188
TUBE: Russell Square
OPEN: Daily

CLOSED: Holidays
HOURS: Lunch: noon–3 P.M. Dinner: 6–11:30 P.M.
RESERVATIONS: Advised in the evening
CREDIT CARDS: AE, DC, MC, V
PRICES: À la Carte: £15–20
VAT/SERVICE: No service added, discretionary
MISCELLANEOUS: Will omit MSG if requested

Wagamama
4 Streatham Street (off Coptic Street), WC1

TELEPHONE
071-323-9223
TUBE
Tottenham Court Road
OPEN
Mon–Sat
CLOSED
Sun, holidays
HOURS
Lunch: Mon–Fri noon–
2:30 P.M., Sat 1–3:30 P.M.
Dinner: 6–11 P.M.
RESERVATIONS
Not accepted
CREDIT CARDS
None
PRICES
À la Carte: £4–8
VAT/SERVICE
Service discretionary
MISCELLANEOUS
No smoking

Wagamama has taken London by storm.

Welcome to Wagamama where the philosophy is "positive eating, positive living." What is Wagamama? A fast food Japanese noodle bar with a few rice dishes for diners not into noodles. Reservations are not taken and dining is communal on long tables set in a basement dining room with all the charm of a high school gym. The atmosphere is always lively, especially at night when vast hordes queue for up to an hour to get in. A friendly staff wearing black baseball caps and grey Wagamama T-shirts take orders on infrared electronic pads. The order is then immediately transmitted to the kitchen where all dishes are individually prepared. There are no starters or desserts. For most, one bowl of noodles is enough with a side order of *gyoza*, the typical accompaniment to ramen, consisting of a mix of cabbage, carrots, water chestnuts, and garlic-grilled dumplings. With prices around £6–7 a head for a dish of ramen noodles topped with vegetables, meat, or fish, you probably won't object to the wait for a seat or to sharing a table.

Woolley Brothers Food Hall
33 Theobalds Road, WC1

TELEPHONE
071-405-3028
TUBE
Holborn
OPEN
Mon–Fri
CLOSED
Sat, Sun, holidays

Sandwich shops are a sixpence a dozen in central London. These popular food outlets appeal to office workers on tight time schedules, cabbies on the run, and offer a chance for visitors to rub elbows with the locals, or at least to exchange smiles.

On Theobalds Road there are several sandwich shops, but the one to remember is the Woolley Brothers Food Hall. Everything served in this spic-and-span spot is made according to their own recipes in the huge kitchen below. The ingredients are the best, the food creative, and the results worth many repeat visits. Because there is only one small table in the back courtyard, you should plan on taking your food with you.

Every day there are sixteen sandwich choices, plus two specials; ten or more salads that come in small, medium, and huge and range from "Hazeldorf—like his brother Wal, but with hazelnuts, celery, and raisins," to "Lively Rice—organic and wild rice with peanuts, parsley, and raisins in a sweet pickle dressing." Pies, pastries, baked potatoes with two dozen toppings, and wonderful daily soups complete the food picture at this top-drawer Cheap Eat in London.

HOURS
Continuous service
7 A.M.–3:30 P.M.

RESERVATIONS
Not accepted

CREDIT CARDS
None

PRICES
À la Carte: £1.50–4

VAT/SERVICE
No service charged or expected

MISCELLANEOUS
All takeaway

WC2 ♣ CHARING CROSS, CHINATOWN, COVENT GARDEN, HOLBORN, LEICESTER SQUARE, STRAND, TRAFALGAR SQUARE

All distances in London are measured from Charing Cross, the official center of London on the south side of Trafalgar Square. Book lovers won't want to miss a stroll down Charing Cross Road, which is loaded with fascinating second-hand booksellers.

Gerrard Street is the main street of Chinatown. It is a pedestrian walkway framed by massive, scrolled dragon gates. The area is loaded with restaurants, shops, and oriental markets selling everything imaginable.

Covent Garden is where the slick and chic meet to eat and drink in the enticing variety of restaurants that are close to most major West End theaters. By 1974, the Eliza Doolittle flowergirls and the famous fruit and vegetable markets had moved to a new location at Nine Elms. The market reopened as a collection of trendy shops filled with foreigners in a carnival atmosphere. It is one of the liveliest parts of London, especially on Sunday, when most shops are open here.

Holborn was the thirteenth century route for the transport of goods to the City. Here you will find Leather Lane, a busy market selling everything from fresh fruit and vegetables to sweaters and Levis; Hatton Garden, the center of London's diamond trade; the London Silver Vaults; several ancient pubs; and the oldest Catholic church in London—St. Etheldreda's.

Great people watching is yours for the looking anywhere around Leicester Square. It is an area perpetually jammed with tourists flocking to one of the many cinemas that ring the square, or just standing around watching street performers. Here you will also be able to stand in a long line for half-price tickets at a kiosk in the center. Don't think you will get tickets for any of the top shows for half-price because they are never sold here. You can get a ticket for a lesser-known show or something on the fringe.

The Strand is a commercial area with incessant traffic and not much to hold a visitor's interest.

Trafalgar Square is framed by the National Gallery, National Portrait Gallery, and St. Martin in the Fields Church. The Nelson Monument stands in the center of the square.

PUBS

RESTAURANTS

PUBS WC2

The Chandos

29 St. Martin's Lane, WC2

I like The Chandos pub because it is a good place to get a meal anytime of day or a nice place to relax after a tour of the National Portrait Gallery. You can stop by for a full English breakfast, a bowl of chili for lunch, hot apple pie in the afternoon, a grilled steak

TELEPHONE
071-836-1404
TUBE
Charing Cross
OPEN
Daily
CLOSED
Christmas
HOURS
Breakfast: 9–10:30 A.M.
Lunch: 11 A.M.–2:30 P.M.

Tea 2:30–5:30 P.M. Dinner: 5:30–9:30 P.M. Drinking Hours: Mon–Sat 11 A.M.–11 P.M., Sun noon–3 P.M., 7–10:30 P.M.
RESERVATIONS
Not accepted
CREDIT CARDS
AE, DC, MC, V
PRICES
À la Carte: £3–9
VAT/SERVICE
No service charged or expected

in the evening, or a pint or two of beer anytime. The dark interior, alcove booths, and soft-leather chesterfield couches lend themselves to restful moments and quiet conversations.

The pub was named after Lord Chandos, who once owned all of Trafalgar Square. It is now the flagship pub for Smith's Brewery, the oldest independent brewery in Yorkshire.

The Globe
37 Bow Street, WC2

TELEPHONE
071-836-0219
TUBE
Covent Garden
OPEN
Mon–Sat
CLOSED
Christmas
HOURS
Continuous service
Mon–Sat 11 A.M.–11 P.M., Sun noon–3 P.M., 7–10 P.M. Lunch: noon–3 P.M., hot food, cold snacks otherwise Dinner: Not served
RESERVATIONS
Not accepted
CREDIT CARDS
None
PRICES
À la Carte: £4–7
VAT/SERVICE
No service charged or expected

The history of The Globe goes back to the seventeen hundreds when the Bow Street Runners (London's first police) ran through the cellar taking captured fugitives back to Westminster where they were dealt with accordingly. This is now a subdued pub where no loud music or pinball mania will jar your sensibilities or shatter your ears. I like to sit upstairs, which is like a library with a fireplace, comfortable chairs, and a small bar. The food is above the average pub standard, thanks to the culinary talents of Tom Adams and his son and wife, who now manage The Globe. Tom is a real history buff who loves old pub lore, so if you can get him to tell you some stories, you will be in for a treat.

The Sherlock Holmes
10 Northumberland Street, WC2

TELEPHONE
071-930-2644
TUBE
Charing Cross
OPEN
Daily
CLOSED
Christmas
HOURS
Continuous service
Mon–Sat 11 A.M.–11 P.M.; Sun noon–3 P.M., 7–10:30 P.M. Downstairs pub: Lunch noon–3 P.M.; snacks, sandwiches, and burgers 3–10:30 P.M.

No self-respecting Sherlock Holmes devotée will be able to resist this pub, a shrine to the great detective and his creator, Sir Arthur Conan Doyle. Inside are countless mementoes that will thrill any fan, including photos of famous actors who have played the role of the sleuth on stage and screen. The first-floor restaurant has a perfect replica of Holmes's cluttered 221b Baker Street study with its book-lined walls, his deerstalker cloak and hat hanging on a hook, a sofa covered with papers, and a model of the man himself. Why is a pub so totally devoted to Sherlock Holmes so far from Baker Street? As all real Holmes buffs will tell you, it was across the street in the Northumberland Hotel (now the War Office) where Holmes met Sir Henry Baskerville.

One must be reminded that this *is* a pub and food *is* served. Downstairs is primarily for basic pub food, sandwiches, and serious drinking. The upstairs serves proper meals, including Sunday lunch in the summer. The mainly English-based dishes served here are named after characters in the stories and reflect better cooking than you will find in most pub restaurants. In the summer, tables and umbrellas are set up outside.

Restaurant: Mon–Sat noon–3 P.M.; Sun noon–3 P.M., 7–10:30 P.M.

RESERVATIONS
For upstairs restaurant

CREDIT CARDS
AE, DC, MC, V

PRICES
À la Carte: pub £2.50–5; restaurant £9–15

VAT/SERVICE
No service charged or expected in pub; discretionary in restaurant

MISCELLANEOUS
T-shirts available £7.95–14.95

RESTAURANTS WC2

Café Flo
51 St. Martin's Lane, WC2

See Café Flo, page 68, for description.

TELEPHONE: 071-836-8289
TUBE: Leicester Square
OPEN: Daily
CLOSED: Christmas
HOURS: Breakfast: 9–11:30 A.M. Lunch: noon–3 P.M. Snacks: 3–5 P.M. Dinner: 5–11:30 P.M.
RESERVATIONS: Preferred
CREDIT CARDS: MC, V
PRICES: À la Carte: £5–12; Set Price: Sun lunch, 3 courses and coffee £13, 2 courses and coffee £7.95; Mon-Fri 2-course lunch £6
VAT/SERVICE: Service discretionary

Cafe in the Crypt at St. Martin in the Fields
St. Martin in the Fields Church on Trafalgar Square, WC2

St. Martin in the Fields is the parish church for Buckingham Palace. You probably won't run into the Queen taking tea at the Cafe in the Crypt, but you will meet countless others who have come to appreciate the relaxed atmosphere and the good food value offered. This underground restaurant is a roomy

TELEPHONE
071-839-4343
TUBE
Charing Cross
OPEN
Daily

CLOSED
Maundy Thurs, Good Fri,
2 days at Christmas, New
Year's Day

HOURS
Mon–Sat 10 A.M.–8 P.M.,
Sun noon–6 P.M.
Coffee: 10 A.M.–noon
Lunch: noon–3:15 P.M. daily
Tea: 2:30–5:30 P.M. daily
Dinner: Mon–Sat 5–7:30 P.M.,
no dinner Sun. Bookstore:
Mon–Sat 11:30 A.M.–7:30 P.M.,
Sun noon–6 P.M.
Courtyard market:
9 A.M.–6 P.M. daily

RESERVATIONS
Not accepted

CREDIT CARDS
MC, V

PRICES
À la Carte: £4–9, includes
service charge

VAT/SERVICE
Service charge included

MISCELLANEOUS
No-smoking section

place, with vaulted ceilings, plain wooden slat furniture and a no-smoking section. The location on Trafalgar Square puts you across from the National Gallery and the National Portrait Gallery and in close walking distance to Piccadilly, Covent Garden, and many West End theaters. The straightforward home-style cooking is varied and ample. The choices change for every meal, so you will never be faced with a dinner dish that was better at lunch. In addition to the thick soups and hot main dishes, there is also a cold buffet counter with beautiful salads and tasty desserts that make nice alternatives to a heavier meal.

All the profits from the restaurant are used to support the church's charities, especially those that take care of the poor and the homeless. Shoppers will want to devote a few minutes to the well-stocked bookstore and art gallery and take a quick stroll through the Courtyard Craft Market directly behind the church. The merchandise is largely T-shirts and cheap Indian clothing, but now and then there is a stall with something more interesting.

Cafe Pacifico
5 Langly Street, WC2

Let's face it—if you love Mexican food, going without it can cause deep longing. For years, the Mexican food scene in London ranged from grim to nonexistent. Not any longer. With Cafe Pacifico firmly entrenched on the scene, favorites such as margaritas, quesadillas, chiles rellenos, chimichangas, tacos, enchiladas, and fajitas are all within easy reach in Covent Garden. To really appreciate the place, give it a chance to build some momentum and arrive after 8 P.M. The loud and active crowd will not appeal to the Sun City set, but for people mixing and matching, it's a knockout. *Warning:* Keep an eye on the tab; it can mount up in a hurry if you order several drinks.

TELEPHONE
071-379-7728

TUBE
Covent Garden

OPEN
Daily

CLOSED
Holidays

HOURS
Continuous service
Mon–Sat noon–11:45 P.M.,
Sun noon–10:45 P.M.

RESERVATIONS
Not accepted *after* 6 P.M.

CREDIT CARDS
MC, V

PRICES
À la Carte: £13–16

VAT/SERVICE
12½% service charge added to
bill

Cafe Pasta
184 Shaftesbury Avenue, WC2

Cafe Pasta serves pleasant Italian food that is perfect for a quick meal. While the dishes can hardly be labeled original, they are filling and inexpensive. The pastas are made from fresh ingredients and are prepared to order, although almost all are cream based and mildly seasoned. Best choices include fusilli with gorgonzola sauce, *penne al cavolfiore* (penne with cauliflower in a chili, cream, and tomato sauce), or the baked lasagna. The best starter is smoked mozzarella cheese on garlic bread. The frozen chocolate cake studded with cognac-soaked raisins and chocolate chips surrounded by fresh cream is a dessert for which you will happily extend your caloric boundaries. If you go during an off-meal time, say in the morning or late afternoon, there is a small menu for these times featuring plain or filled croissants, French bread sandwiches, and pâtisseries. The ambiance in the two locations is relaxed and low key. There is an exhibition kitchen in one and sidewalk dining when the weather permits in the other.

TELEPHONE
071-379-0198

TUBE
Tottenham Court Road

OPEN
Daily

CLOSED
Christmas

HOURS
Continuous service
Mon–Sat 9:30 A.M.–11:30 P.M.,
Sun 9:30 A.M.–11 P.M.

RESERVATIONS
Not accepted

CREDIT CARDS
None

PRICES
À la Carte: Snacks £2–5,
meals £7–12

VAT/SERVICE
Service discretionary; for six or
more 10% service added to bill

Cafe Pasta
2–4 Garrick Street, WC2

See Cafe Pasta, above, for description. All other information is the same.

TELEPHONE: 071-497-2779

TUBE: Leicester Square

Chez Gérard
119 Chancery Lane, WC2

See Chez Gérard, page 29, for description. All other information is the same.

TELEPHONE: 071-405-0290

TUBE: Chancery Lane

OPEN: Mon–Fri

CLOSED: Sat, Sun, holidays

HOURS: Breakfast: 8–11:30 A.M. Lunch: noon–2:45 P.M. Tea: 2:45–5:30 P.M. Wine bar: 5:30–10 P.M. Dinner: 6-10 P.M.

RESERVATIONS: Better for lunch

Cranks Charing Cross
8 Adelaide Street, WC2

See Cranks, page 31, for description. All other information is the same.

TELEPHONE: 071-836-0660
TUBE: Charing Cross
OPEN: Mon–Sat
CLOSED: Sun, holidays
HOURS: Mon–Fri 8 A.M.–7:30 P.M., Sat 9 A.M.–6 P.M.

Cranks Covent Garden
11 The Market, Covent Garden, WC2

See Cranks, page 31, for description. All other information is the same.

TELEPHONE: 071-379-6508
TUBE: Covent Garden
OPEN: Daily
CLOSED: Holidays
HOURS: Continuous service, Mon–Sat 9:30 A.M.–8 P.M., Sun 11 A.M.–7 P.M.

Cranks Leicester Square
17–19 Great Newport Street, WC2

See Cranks, page 31, for description. All other information is the same.

TELEPHONE: 071-836-5226
TUBE: Leicester Square
OPEN: Daily
CLOSED: Holidays
HOURS: Continuous service, Mon–Wed 8 A.M.–8:30 P.M., Thurs–Fri 8 A.M.–10 P.M., Sat 10 A.M.–10 P.M., Sun noon–7 P.M.

Diana's Diner
39 Endell Street, WC2

TELEPHONE
071-240-0272
TUBE
Covent Garden
OPEN
Daily
CLOSED
Christmas
HOURS
Continuous service
Mon–Sat 7 A.M.–8 P.M.,
Sun 8 A.M.–6 P.M.

You will need a stein of beer and a double chin to do justice to the overflowing plates of food served at this meat-and-potatoes cafe on the edge of Covent Garden. When you arrive, don't be put off by Diana's Diner's plainness, with narrow wooden tables, fake flowers, and a deli case positioned by the front entrance. Cafes like this one have been around since time began and are havens for Londoners in search of plenty to eat without plenty to pay. Entrées are a familiar lot: roast beef, chicken, or turkey with two vegetables; spaghetti with meat sauce; omelettes and chips (french fries); liver and bacon; homemade steak and kidney pie; sandwiches; baked potatoes with ten or more fillings; salads and fruit crumbles slathered in cream. These are the English staples the neighborhood locals have been thriving on at Diana's for decades.

RESERVATIONS
Not accepted

CREDIT CARDS
None

PRICES
À la Carte: £4.50–7

VAT/SERVICE
No service charged or expected

MISCELLANEOUS
Unlicensed, BYOB, no corkage

Farmer Brown
4 New Row, WC2

Farmer Brown is a sandwich bar by day and a pasta bar by night. The interiors of both locations are festooned with hanging sausages, fancy breads, dried herbs, ceiling fans, copper pots, old photos, and, at the New Row shop, a stunning collection of old-time radios. The sandwiches are huge, filled with layers of meat, cheese, lettuce, sliced tomatoes, and sprinkled with mustard sprouts. They are known for their salt beef (corned beef). According to the manager in one location, two American men come in every day for a salt beef sandwich for lunch, and one of them takes an extra home with him at night. If you are looking for breakfast between 7:30–11:30 A.M., try one of theirs. They are set apart from the mundane by their quality ingredients, including the same maize-fed eggs the Queen uses, homemade sausage, and the best bacon on the market.

In the evening, sandwiches give way to pastas at the Bedford Street location only. Eighteen varieties from plain spaghetti bolognese to fettucine with smoked salmon feed the starving. The rest of the menu tempts with salads, *ciabatta* or garlic bread, carrot cake, and a *tiramisu* made by the boss's sister that is worth saving room for, especially if you have never tasted this heady blend of espresso, lady fingers, and mascarpone cheese.

TELEPHONE
071-240-0230

TUBE
Leicester Square

OPEN
Mon–Sat, winter
Daily, summer

CLOSED
Sun (winter), Christmas

HOURS
Continuous service
Mon–Sat 8:30 A.M.–5 P.M.
(winter), 9 A.M.–6 P.M
(summer)

RESERVATIONS
Not accepted

CREDIT CARDS
None

PRICES
À la Carte: £1.50–6

VAT/SERVICE
No service charged or expected

MISCELLANEOUS
This location not open for pasta

Farmer Brown

32 Bedford Street, WC2

See Farmer Brown, previous page, for description. All other information is the same.

TELEPHONE: 071-836-7486
TUBE: Leicester Square
OPEN: Daily
CLOSED: Christmas
HOURS: Continuous service, 7:30 A.M.–midnight
PRICES: À la Carte: £3–9
MISCELLANEOUS: Pasta is served Mon–Fri from 5:30 P.M.; on Sunday, pasta is served all day long.

Fatboy's Diner

21–22 Maiden Lane, WC2

TELEPHONE
071-240-1902
TUBE
Charing Cross
OPEN
Daily
CLOSED
Christmas
HOURS
Continuous service
Mon, Tues 11 A.M.–11 P.M.,
Wed–Sat 11 A.M.–midnight,
Sun 11 A.M.–10:30 P.M.
RESERVATIONS
Not accepted
CREDIT CARDS
None
PRICES
À la Carte: £5–8
VAT/SERVICE
Service discretionary

Tourists, trendies, and teenagers love Fatboy's Diner, a real American imported diner with lots of chrome, stools at the counter with fry cooks behind, loud American music, and waitresses wearing bobby sox. Order the hot-breath hot dog topped with chili, swiss cheese, and raw onion; the ABC burger covered with avocado, bacon, and cheese; a thick malt; a banana shake or a slab of cherry pie, all served on paper plates with the Fatboy logo. Breakfast is served all day and brunch on weekends. Fatboy's memorabilia are for sale, and in the summer, picnic tables are set out on a raised platform covered in astroturf. No, it isn't the stuff gastronomic thrills are made of, but for a cheap bite that will take you back . . . *way* back, it is fun.

India Club

143 The Strand, WC2

TELEPHONE
071-836-0650
TUBE
Aldwych
OPEN
Daily for lunch and dinner
CLOSED
Holidays
HOURS
Lunch: noon–2:30 P.M.
Dinner: 6–9:30 P.M.

If you like unadorned Indian food, this is the Cheap Eats address to remember when you are low on cash. Even though it is on the Strand, it is easy to walk right past it without a second look because India Club is hidden up a flight of dark stairs. The clean but spartan canteen's interior has not changed ever, probably because there is nothing to it. The largely northern Indian food is not only cheap, but authentic, and the high number of loyal Indian patrons who eat here daily attests to this. For the price of a pre-fab burger, large fries, and a shake, you can have chicken tandoori, rice, mango chutney, and Indian tea. A vegetarian meal is equally reasonable, with vegetable or egg curry, *dal* (lentils), and *chile bhajias* (fritters) all costing less than £3 per dish. The eccentric service from long-suffering, white-coated waiters is efficient and courteous.

RESERVATIONS
Not accepted
CREDIT CARDS
None
PRICES
À la Carte: £3.50–9
VAT/SERVICE
Service discretionary
MISCELLANEOUS
Not licensed, BYOB, no corkage

Joe Allen
13 Exeter Street (*very* difficult to find; look for a brass plaque by the door), WC2

Joe Allen is a fashionable restaurant in a dark alley near Covent Garden. Accessible only to the determined (look for the brass plaque by the door), the popular spot is a faithful copy of branches in New York and Paris: brick walls, red-and-white-checked tablecloths, photos of film stars, blackboard menus, and stuck-up waiters serving good American food. The upscale see-and-be-seen crowd comes in after the theater to order bowls of chili con carne, plates of barbecue ribs with blackeyed peas, wonderful main course salads, and slabs of chocolate caramel cake or pecan pie. Insiders order the hamburger with everything; this one is not on the menu, so you have to ask for it. Even though the late-night diners and noise levels often seem too chic and loud for their own good, this is still a great place to grab a late meal and people-watch to your heart's content.

TELEPHONE
071-836-0651
TUBE
Covent Garden
OPEN
Daily
CLOSED
2 days at Christmas
HOURS
Continuous service
Mon–Sat noon–1 A.M.,
Sun noon–midnight
RESERVATIONS
Essential at night and on Sun
CREDIT CARDS
None
PRICES
À la Carte: £8–18
VAT/SERVICE
Service discretionary

The London School of Economics
Houghton Street between Aldwych and Kings Way (west end of Fleet Street), WC2

The London School of Economics (LSE) operates four cafeterias and two pubs, all open to the public. Its location near Fleet Street, Covent Garden, and Trafalgar Square makes it a good food stop if you are short on cash. The atmosphere feels like a self-service line in a Greyhound bus depot cafeteria, despite the fascinating mix of students from around the globe and a stray pin-stripe or two escaping from Fleet

TELEPHONE
071-405-7686
TUBE
Aldwych
OPEN
Something is open daily, except on holidays
CLOSED
Holidays

HOURS
Brunch Bowl: 9 A.M.–7 P.M.
(winter), 9 A.M.–4:30 P.M.
(summer). Pizza Burger: noon–
5 P.M. (winter). Robinson
Room: noon–2 P.M. (winter).
Student Union Cafe: 10 A.M.–
3 P.M. (summer), 9:30 A.M.–
6:30 P.M. (winter). Three Tuns
Bar: noon–2:30 P.M., 5–7 P.M.
(summer), noon– 3 P.M., 5–11
P.M. (winter). Beavers Retreat
Bar: noon–2 P.M., 5–7 P.M.
(summer), noon–2:30 P.M.,
5–9 P.M. (winter)

RESERVATIONS
Not accepted

CREDIT CARDS
None

PRICES
À la Carte: £1.50–5

VAT/SERVICE
No service charged or expected

Street prices. The subsidized meals are so unbelievably low cost, even for canteen food, that serious Cheap Eaters must pay attention.

The biggest of the cafeterias is the Brunch Bowl on the fourth floor of the LSE Old Building. On the same floor is the Pizza-Burger serving, naturally, pizzas and burgers. Then there is the Robinson Room on the third floor, the Student Union Cafe, the Three Tuns Bar, and Beavers Retreat Bar. Even though not all are always open, at least one or two will be, except on holidays. Keeping track of the opening and closing times could become a full-time job as they seem to change with the same degree of swiftness as student grade point averages. If you are determined to eat at a specific location, be sure to call ahead to verify the hours and whether they will be open.

Man Poh
59 Charing Cross Road, WC2

The Chinese Cheap Eats are at Man Poh.

TELEPHONE
071-734-5951

TUBE
Leicester Square

OPEN
Daily

CLOSED
Christmas

HOURS
Continuous service
11:45 A.M.–12:45 A.M.

RESERVATIONS
Not necessary

CREDIT CARDS
None

PRICES
À la Carte: £3–12
Set Price: Lunch £4, dinner
£8–25

VAT/SERVICE
No service charged

MISCELLANEOUS
Takeaway

The time to visit this restaurant on the edge of Chinatown is at lunchtime when they offer a breathtakingly low-priced set menu with three courses for around £4. While you won't be dazzled with subtle sauces and delicate seasonings, you will have a filling meal with lots of change left over to spend on something else.

You are given three choices: won ton soup, spring rolls, and fried rice; hot & sour soup, prawn crackers, and chicken curried rice; or sweet corn soup, prawn crackers, and sweet and sour rice. If you do not want a full three-course meal, there are nineteen à la carte items ranging from £3–4 per dish, including rice. These are available at both lunch and dinner. In the evening, there are other set menus, but the cheap thrill is gone—it is available *only* until 5 P.M.

Mövenpick
Leicester Square, WC2

Mövenpick Restaurant Marché and Swiss Bistro celebrate all things rich, hearty, and wonderful. From breakfast to dinner, you will dine well and economically at either of these two restaurants in the Swiss Center just off Leicester Square. You name it and they undoubtedly serve it, either upstairs in the Bistro that features sandwiches, salads, light meals, and ice cream delights rightfully called "dreams of ice cream." Or, let yourself in for a real dining treat and go downstairs to the Restaurant Marché, where the food is temptingly displayed and prepared while you watch from various food stations set around the large room. There is just so much offered that you really have to be careful that your eyes are not ten times bigger than your stomach.

I recommend browsing before making your final selection. Walk around the room and check out the omelette and fresh pasta stations, watch the chefs grilling steaks, lamb chops, fish, and chicken and wonder at the salad counter with at least twenty-five different ingredients available to make up a monumental salad. There is also a wine and coffee bar, a bread kiosk, a stir fry table, an area devoted to special dishes of the day, and a large dessert display with all the tempting delights baked here daily. After you are served, take your food to one of the nicely set tables positioned around the room and in various nooks and crannies, all decorated to look like Swiss farmhouse chalets. After 6 P.M. you can make a reservation and feast in a special room devoted to serving Swiss fondues and, my favorite Swiss delicacy, *raclette.* As the sweet lady sitting at the table next to me said, "Mövenpick is new to London, and we all love to come here. The food is so fresh, the variety enormous, and the service so welcoming that I wish I could eat here every day." I felt the same way and I hope you will, too.

TELEPHONE
071-494-0498

TUBE
Leicester Square

OPEN
Daily

CLOSED
Christmas

HOURS
Swiss Bistro: continuous service 11 A.M.–midnight. Restaurant Marché: continuous service Mon–Sat 8 A.M.–midnight, Sun & holidays 9 A.M.–midnight

RESERVATIONS
Only for Swiss fondue and *raclette,* served after 6 P.M.

CREDIT CARDS
DC, MC, V

PRICES
À la Carte: Swiss Bistro £3.50–6, Restaurant Marché £6–10

VAT/SERVICE
Service included

MISCELLANEOUS
No-smoking area; Happy Hour at Wine Bar from 5–7 P.M. The Swiss Center also houses a Bally shoe store and several shops selling Swiss Army knives, watches, and foods.

North Sea Fish Restaurant
7–8 Leigh Street, WC1

TELEPHONE
071-387-5892
TUBE
Russell Square
OPEN
Mon–Sat for lunch and dinner
CLOSED
Sun, Mon bank holidays, Christmas
HOURS
Lunch: noon–2:30 P.M.
Dinner: 5:30 P.M–11:30 P.M.
RESERVATIONS
Advised
CREDIT CARDS
AE, MC, V
PRICES
À la Carte: £8–10
VAT/SERVICE
Service discretionary
MISCELLANEOUS
Takeaway

On one side of the North Sea Fish Restaurant is a fish and chips takeaway, on the other a neatly dressed dining room with pink velvet chairs and varnished wooden tables. The only thing on the menu is fresh fish: sixteen varieties deep fried in pure peanut oil, sautéed, or grilled and served with homemade tartar sauce, chips (french fries), or boiled potatoes. The catch comes in every morning from the Billingsgate fish market. It arrives around 5 A.M., and the North Sea fishmonger spends the next few hours cutting it into serving-sized fillets. Best sellers are the cod, haddock, plaice, and skate, a bony fish that is an acquired taste for some. The portions are giant, leaving barely enough room for a slice of the homemade trifle or pineapple fritter for dessert.

The Original Carvery at the Strand Palace Hotel
The Strand, WC2

See The Original Carvery Cumberland Hotel, page 44, for description. All other information is the same.

TELEPHONE: 071-836-8080

TUBE: Charing Cross, Covent Garden, or Embankment

OPEN: Daily

CLOSED: Never

HOURS: Lunch: 12:30 P.M.–2:00 P.M.; Dinner: 5:30 P.M.–10 P.M.

RESERVATIONS: Advised for Sunday lunch

Palms
39 King Street, WC2

TELEPHONE
071-240-2939
TUBE
Covent Garden
OPEN
Daily
CLOSED
Christmas

Palms was one of the first restaurants in Covent Garden to specialize in pasta. The service is efficient but rushed, especially when a crowd is at the door waiting for your seat. The Italian fuel food served in megaportions is still an exceptionally fine value. The menu lists fourteen varieties, including spaghetti topped with mixed seafood, prawns, squid, scallops, and clams; a penne primavera; and fettucine with mushrooms and ham in a creamy sauce. Also available is tomato tortellini, cannelloni filled with ricotta cheese and spinach, and lusty lasagna. Each giant main-course salad is served in a glass mixing bowl with enough ingredients for four people. The best is the Creola: raw spinach, avocado, mushrooms, tomato, and crispy bacon tossed in a warm sweet and sour dressing. The grilled breast of chicken is as tender as butter and so is the marinated, chargrilled lamb. Desserts will threaten all dieters' willpower, especially the gooey Death by Chocolate, aptly described as "a death-defying mountain of chocolate sponge cake with chocolate mousse and cream." Only the brave should tackle this one.

HOURS
Continuous service
noon–midnight
RESERVATIONS
Not necessary unless 8 or more
CREDIT CARDS
MC, V
PRICES
À la Carte: £7–12
VAT/SERVICE
12½% service charge added to bill

Plummers
33 King Street, WC2

Plummers is perfect for a romantic dinner or a long, leisurely lunch with someone you are just getting to know. It looks small from the street, but there are actually three spacious rooms in the restaurant, all nicely done in soft greens with pink tablecloths, white linen napkins, fresh flowers, candles at night, and a back room with green hanging plants and an open skylight. The well-priced menu alternates English and American favorites. Clam chowder is listed between apple and Stilton soup and smoked herring and red onion salad. The Louisiana chicken casserole, a favorite since the restaurant opened fifteen years ago, combines breast of chicken in white wine with peppers, onions, tomatoes, and herbs. Cajun meatloaf is topped with a snappy red pepper sauce and Frencatelli's Venison, created by Queen Victoria's chef, is a casserole of prime venison in a sauce made from port wine, red currants, cinnamon, and lemon. Steak and kidney pie, fresh fish, grilled meats, and three vegetarian dishes round out the interesting menu. The desserts are all made here and are marvelous . . . except for one, the Atholl Brose, a weird melange of oatmeal, honey, whisky, and cream. Try instead the legendary

TELEPHONE
071-240-2534
TUBE
Covent Garden or Leicester Square
OPEN
Mon–Fri lunch and dinner, Sat and Sun dinner only
CLOSED
Lunch Sat and Sun, holidays
HOURS
Lunch: Mon–Fri 12:30–2:30 P.M. Dinner: Mon–Sun 5:30–11:30 P.M.
RESERVATIONS
Essential after 8 P.M.
CREDIT CARDS
AE, DC, MC, V
PRICES
À la Carte: 1 course £8.50, 2 courses £12, 3 courses £15
VAT/SERVICE
12½% service charge added to bill
MISCELLANEOUS
For pretheater dining, you can come back after the theater for coffee and dessert. Just inform your waiter.

banana and toffee pie or the chocolate and Grand Marnier mousse. The short wine list offers a few California and French vintages if you want to upgrade the house variety.

Poons
41 King Street, WC2

See Poons Restaurants, page 63, for description. All other information is the same.

TELEPHONE: 071-240-1743
TUBE: Covent Garden
OPEN: Mon–Sat
CLOSED: Sun, Christmas
HOURS: Continuous service, noon–midnight
RESERVATIONS: Advised in the evening
CREDIT CARDS: AE, DC, MC, V
PRICES: À la Carte: £15–25
VAT/SERVICE: Service discretionary, £1 cover in the evening
MISCELLANEOUS: Will omit MSG on request

Poons
4 Leicester Square, WC2

See Poons Restaurants, page 63, for description. All other information is the same.

TELEPHONE: 071-437-1528
TUBE: Leicester Square
OPEN: Daily
CLOSED: Christmas
HOURS: Continuous service, noon–11:30 P.M.
RESERVATIONS: Advised
CREDIT CARDS: None
PRICES: À la Carte: £11–14
VAT/SERVICE: Service discretionary
MISCELLANEOUS: Takeaway; will omit MSG if requested

Poons
27 Lisle Street, WC2

See Poons Restaurants, page 63, for description. All other information is the same.

TELEPHONE: 071-437-4549

TUBE: Leicester Square
OPEN: Daily
CLOSED: Christmas
HOURS: Continuous service, noon–11:30 P.M.
RESERVATIONS: Advised during peak hours
CREDIT CARDS: None
PRICES: À la Carte: £8–12
VAT/SERVICE: Service discretionary
MISCELLANEOUS: Takeaway

Porters English Restaurant
17 Henrietta Street, WC2

Porters is an attractive restaurant decorated with Covent Garden memorabilia, where you can bring the whole family, especially if you are footing the bill. Always arrive hungry, forget your diet, and order one of their famous pot pies or other English standbys and you will not go away disappointed. There are no starters, which leaves more room for the main event when you can sample any of eight pies, ranging from classic steak and kidney to more off-beat ones such as lamb and apricot or chicken and asparagus. Toad-in-the-hole, sausage and mash, bubble and squeak, spotted dick—no, these are not names from nursery rhymes, but some of the typical English dishes worth trying at Porters. For the novice these translate as sausage baked in batter; sausage and mashed potatoes; fried mashed potatoes, cabbage, and onions; and sponge cake with raisins and warm custard sauce. The bar turns out some very exotic cocktails. You can also order fine ales, a low-alcohol lager, or, if you have no further plans for the rest of the day, choose their Knockout Punch to go with your meal.

TELEPHONE
071-836-6466
TUBE
Covent Garden
OPEN
Daily for lunch and dinner
CLOSED
Christmas, Easter
HOURS
Lunch: noon–3 P.M. daily
Dinner: Mon–Sat 5:30–11:30 P.M., Sun 5:30–10:30 P.M.
RESERVATIONS
Essential during peak hours
CREDIT CARDS
AE, MC, V
PRICES
À la Carte: £7.50–11
Set Price: £15, including service, any pie, vegetables or salad, any pudding, tea or coffee, and ½ bottle of house wine
VAT/SERVICE
Service discretionary, 10% added for 5 or more
MISCELLANEOUS
Minimum charge £6 per person. Management may impose a 2-hour limit at a table.

The Rock and Sole Plaice
47 Endell Street, WC2

Regulars come from the neighborhood and around the globe to sample Ismet Hassan's excellent fish and chips. The last time I was there I met people from northern Cyprus and New Jersey who would never consider a trip to London complete without a meal at The Rock and Sole Plaice. My mail also indicates that

TELEPHONE
071-836-3785
TUBE
Covent Garden
OPEN
Mon–Sat
CLOSED
Sun, holidays

HOURS
Continuous service
11:30 A.M.–11 P.M.

RESERVATIONS
Not accepted

CREDIT CARDS
None

PRICES
À la Carte: £5–7

VAT/SERVICE
Service discretionary

MISCELLANEOUS
Unlicensed, BYOB, no
corkage; takeaway

scores of *Cheap Eats in London* readers add to the faithful followers as well. There are other things on the menu: steak and kidney pie, hamburgers, sausages, and some unadventurous desserts. Ignore these and pay attention *only* to the halibut, cod, salmon, plaice, skate, or Dover sole—or any other daily fish that may be offered. Whether you enjoy eating your fish at one of the nine indoor tables next to the gleaming kitchen; sitting at a picnic table on the sidewalk; or taking your food with you, you can always be assured of fresh fish that is perfectly deep-fried and so good you, too, will be back many times.

Salsa!
96 Charing Cross Road, WC2

TELEPHONE
071-379-3277

TUBE
Tottenham Court Road or
Leicester Square

OPEN
Mon–Sat evenings only

CLOSED
Days, Sun, Christmas, holidays

HOURS
Mon–Wed 5:30 P.M.–
12:30 A.M., Thurs 5:30 P.M.–
1 A.M., Fri–Sat 5:30 P.M.–2 A.M.

RESERVATIONS
Mon–Fri only

CREDIT CARDS
AE, MC, V

PRICES
À la Carte: £5–10

VAT/SERVICE
Discretionary for 1-7 persons;
10%, 8 or more

Everything restauranteur Bob Payton seems to touch turns into instant gold. Witness the Chicago Rib Shack (page 152) and The Criterion (page 32). Now it's Salsa!, the hot ticket South American theme restaurant that draws the young, the bold, and the beautiful. These stylish patrons in tune with the surroundings sample hot and cold tapas, sip exotic cocktails, and dance to a live Brazilian band. The idea is, if it's rhythmic and hot let's dance, and believe me after a pitcher or two of margaritas or the house pisco sour, the place is alive and moving with sambas, bossa novas, lambadas, and merengues. For best effect, arrive with a group about 9 P.M., spend the evening munching on chips, dips, thin pizzas, crostinis, potato skins, barbecued riblets, spicy chicken wings, and tiny fajitas. Then dance till you drop.

Smollensky's Balloon
105 The Strand, WC2

See Smollensky's Balloon, page 51, for description. All other information is the same.

TELEPHONE: 071-497-2101

TUBE: Covent Garden

Wolfe's
30 Great Queen Street, WC2

See Wolfe's, page 141, for description.

TELEPHONE: 071-831-4442, 4422
TUBE: Covent Garden
OPEN: Mon–Sat
CLOSED: Sun, two days at Christmas
HOURS: Continuous service, 11:30 A.M.–midnight
RESERVATIONS: Not necessary
CREDIT CARDS: AE, DC, MC, V
PRICES: Same pricing as other location
MISCELLANEOUS: Happy hour from 3–7 P.M., all drinks 30% less

Young Cheng
22 Lisle Street, WC2

See Young Cheng, page 55, for description. All other information is the same.

TELEPHONE: 071-287-3045
TUBE: Leicester Square
OPEN: Daily
CLOSED: Christmas
HOURS: Continuous service, noon–midnight
RESERVATIONS: Not necessary
CREDIT CARDS: AE, DC, MC, V
PRICES: À la Carte: £6–10, Set Price: £10–20 per person
VAT/SERVICE: No service added to bill, discretionary

WINE BARS WC2

Cork & Bottle
44–46 Cranbourn Street, WC2

New Zealander Don Hewitson was one of the first to introduce Londoners to the wine bar. For twenty-plus years he has devoted tremendous energy to this establishment, which offers outstanding food and wines in pleasant surroundings.

Please do not let the location, between a greasy fish and chips dive and a sex shop, deter you. Once down the stairs and in the basement, with its walls covered with prints and posters of wine-growing areas, you will be rubbing elbows with an attractive crowd that continually mobs this oasis of style just off Leicester Square.

TELEPHONE
071-734-7807
TUBE
Leicester Square
OPEN
Daily
CLOSED
Christmas
HOURS
Continuous service
11 A.M.–3 P.M., hot food
3 P.M.–5:15 P.M., cold food
available Mon–Sat 5:15 P.M.–
midnight, Sun 5:30 P.M.–
midnight

RESERVATIONS
Accepted only before
12:45 P.M. for lunch and 6 P.M.
for dinner
CREDIT CARDS
AE, DC, MC, V
PRICES
À la Carte: £9–12
VAT/SERVICE
Service discretionary

The food is all good, especially the ham and cheese pie and any of the grilled fish or meats. Hot and cold daily specials and imaginative salads such as lamb with salsa verde or Don's spicy cheese and apple salad fill the lunch and dinner groupies, while the wines from all over the world keep the drinkers happy. On Saturday and Sunday, the faithful turn up for brunch, which offers bucks fizz, smoked salmon, scrambled eggs, green salad, and a selection of cheeses.

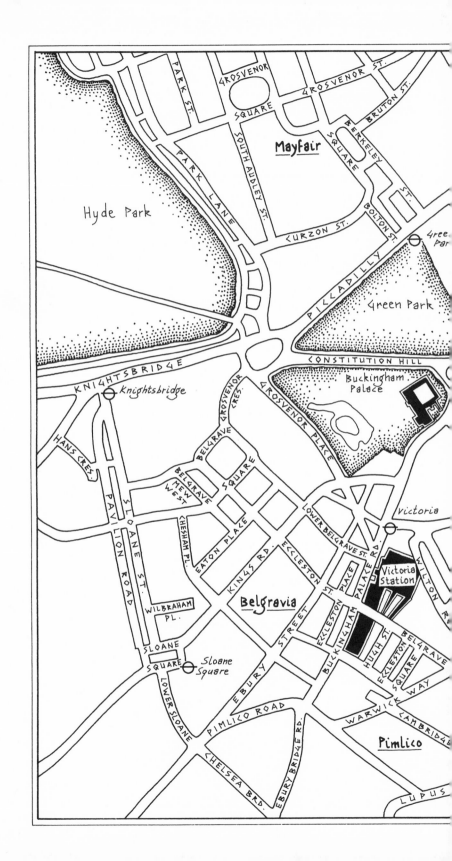

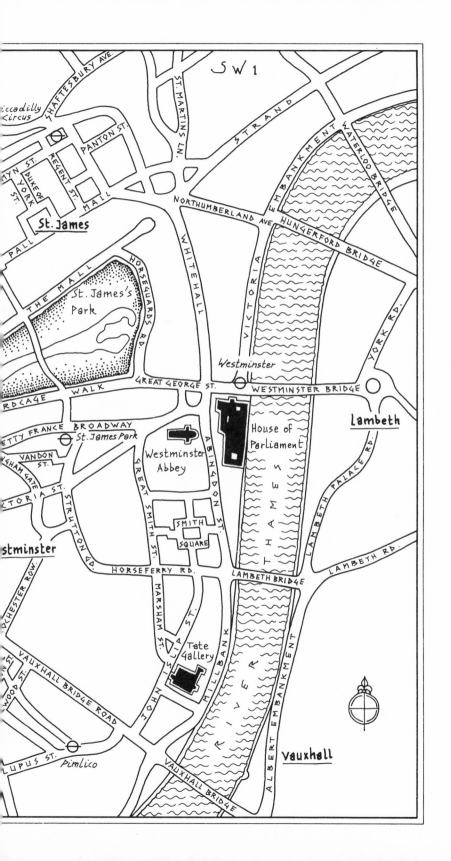

SW1 ✤ BELGRAVIA, THE MALL, PIMLICO, ST. JAMES'S, VICTORIA STATION, WESTMINSTER

The second Earl of Grosvenor owns two prime portions of London: Mayfair and Belgravia, both vying for most-expensive real estate status. Belgrave Square is now mainly embassies and at its center: ten acres of private gardens.

The Mall is the beautiful processional leading up to the gates of Buckingham Palace, where tourists gather faithfully each day hoping to catch sight of one of the royals, or at least just watching the Changing of the Guard.

Pimlico is far from Tourist Central, but it does have its admirers, especially those looking for a quiet area close to the River Thames and the Tate Gallery.

St. James's Square is the center of London's most gentlemanly district, and home to many wealthy residents. St. James's Park has all anyone could wish for with a royal park and pelicans descended from a pair given to Charles II.

In the Forecourt of Victoria Station is London's largest tourist information center. This area is not known for its sights, fine restaurants, or entertainment value. There are many good, inexpensive bed and breakfast hotels around Victoria Station, notably on Ebury Street (see *Cheap Sleeps in London*).

Westminster is home to the Houses of Parliament, Big Ben, and Westminster Abbey.

PUBS SW1

The Albert
52 Victoria Street, SW1

The Albert is a handsome pub positively bursting with atmosphere. Here you have it all: polished wood, original gas lamps, engraved glass windows that were removed and hidden during World War II, and a "division bell," which calls members of Parliament back to the House of Commons in time to vote. A set of old Victorian prints depicts the evils of drinking, and portraits of past prime ministers glare down at the diners in the restaurant. This is one of the few pubs where reservations are necessary if you hope to get a table during busy lunch hours. Eat downstairs and enjoy homecooked pub food while standing in very close proximity to your neighbor. If you are serious about your meal, reserve a table upstairs in the all-you-can-eat carvery. The lunch and dinner buffet simply groans with wonderful food: roast turkey, leg of pork, prime ribs, Scotch salmon, and vegetarian lasagna. All plates are garnished with vegetables or a fresh salad. Desserts are brought to your table on a three-tier trolley loaded with cakes, fresh fruits, and a tray of English cheese and crackers. Freshly brewed coffee completes the substantial repast. If you are in the area any Monday through Friday morning, stop in for one of their copious English breakfasts, served from 7:30–10:30 A.M.

TELEPHONE
071-222-5577

TUBE
St. James's Park

OPEN
Daily

CLOSED
Holidays

HOURS
Pub: Mon–Sat 11 A.M.–10:30 P.M.; Sun noon–3 P.M., 7–10:30 P.M.; food service, breakfast Mon–Fri 7:30–10:30 A.M.
Carvery: Daily continuous service noon–9:30 P.M.

RESERVATIONS
Not necessary

CREDIT CARDS
AE, DC, MC, V

PRICES
À la Carte: Pub £5–8, breakfast £5.95–7.95; carvery all you can eat lunch and dinner £16

VAT/SERVICE
No service charged or expected in pub, 10% service added to bill in carvery

The Antelope
22 Eaton Terrace, SW1

TELEPHONE
071-730-7781, 071-730-3169

TUBE
Sloane Square

OPEN
Daily

CLOSED
Holidays

HOURS
Mon–Sat 11 A.M.–11 P.M.,
Sun noon–3:30 P.M.,
7–10:30 P.M.
Lunch: Mon–Sat
noon–2:30 P.M.

RESERVATIONS
Not necessary

CREDIT CARDS
MC, V

PRICES
À la Carte: £6–8

VAT/SERVICE
No service charged or expected

The Antelope was built in 1780 for the workers who constructed Eaton Terrace. Later, it was used by the household staffs who worked in the neighborhood. You will notice that the pub has two front doors—one was for "upstairs" staff, the other for "downstairs." The popular British television series "Upstairs/Downstairs" was filmed around here and based on people living in the area.

A lunch visit to The Antelope will put you in close touch with those who reside in one of London's most exclusive neighborhoods, Belgravia. Despite the toney surroundings, the charming pub has a relaxed and welcoming feel to it. It is a good place to have a pint or two and wind down after a long day. It is also a comfortable spot to sip a glass of a little-known French, German, or Italian wine while eating a good pub meal. Try the steak and kidney pie, the roast beef, or a jacketed (baked) potato with a rich cheese filling. Desserts merit attention, especially chocolate trifle and rhubarb crumble. There are several rooms in the pub, but the back room with easy chairs and a roaring fire makes you want to settle in for the afternoon and forget all about seeing the next monument on your list.

Red Lion
2 Duke of York Street, SW1

TELEPHONE
071-930-2030

TUBE
Green Park

OPEN
Mon–Sat

CLOSED
Sun, holidays

HOURS
Continuous service
11 A.M.–11 P.M.

RESERVATIONS
Not accepted

CREDIT CARDS
AE

The tiny Red Lion pub just off Jermyn Street in the heart of Mayfair is a true jewel. It began as a gin palace. In the eighteen hundreds, William of Orange taxed beer, but not gin, making gin the "beer of that day." It has been said that this tax resulted in gin's killing more people at this time than all the wars William fought in Ireland. Today, much of the original pub remains intact. Look for the hand-etched, silver-leafed mirrors with each panel depicting a different English flower: the wrap-around mahogany bar which is a single piece of wood unjointed in the middle, and the gas rose ceiling lights. Outside by the entrance is a brass plaque with a polite notice:

"Customers wearing dirty work clothes will not be served." This is a dignified and quiet pub, serving a sophisticated crowd sandwiches every day, and on Fridays and Saturdays, fresh fish and chips and hot meat pies.

Star Tavern
6 Belgrave Mews West, SW1

It takes some searching to locate the Star Tavern because it is off the beaten track for most casual visitors. There is no actual pub sign, just a large star suspended from a metal bracket above the entrance. The pub is a friendly place that welcomes new faces alongside the old. The main ground-floor room is similar to a gentlemen's club. There are tables, chairs, a carpeted floor, globe lights, and revolving fans suspended from the ceiling. A real fire adds a welcoming touch on cool days. The cozy upstairs lounge has an open fireplace, a small bar in one corner, and large windows overlooking the cobbled mews below. The pub fare offers all the basics pub-goers know and love, from Monday to Friday for both lunch and dinner.

RESTAURANTS SW1

Arco Bars of Knightsbridge
46 Hans Crescent, SW1

Arco Bars of Knightsbridge is right across the street from Harrods. It reminds me of an American chain of coffee shops with its low prices, plasticized menus, and food that is several steps above fast food. There is zero in the ambiance department and no background music to soften the brightly lit room with seating in naugahyde-covered booths. Along one wall is a deli case with a string of sandwich chefs behind it. The food is predictable and quite good, especially if you order one of the breakfasts served from 7–11:30 A.M. Other reliable bets include pastas, daily specials, and sandwiches made to order. It is the type of place you can pop into anytime and get either a coffee and a piece of pie or a three-course meal with

PRICES
À la Carte: £3–6

VAT/SERVICE
No service charged or expected

TELEPHONE
071-235-3019

TUBE
Knightsbridge

OPEN
Daily

CLOSED
Christmas

HOURS
Mon–Sat 11 A.M.–11 P.M.,
Sun noon–3 P.M., 7–10:30 P.M.
Lunch: noon–3 P.M.
Dinner: 6:30–9 P.M.

RESERVATIONS
Not accepted

CREDIT CARDS
None

PRICES
À la Carte: £4 (lunch), £6–7
(dinner)

VAT/SERVICE
No service charged or expected

TELEPHONE
071-584-6454

TUBE
Knightsbridge

OPEN
Mon–Sat

CLOSED
Sun, holidays

HOURS
Continuous food service
Mon–Fri 7 A.M.–6 P.M., Sat
8 A.M.–6 P.M.
Breakfast: 7–11:30 A.M.

RESERVATIONS
Not accepted

CREDIT CARDS
None

PRICES
À la Carte: £2.50–7

VAT/SERVICE
Service discretionary

a glass of drinkable house wine. The best part is that you can be in and out for lunch or dinner in one hour and spend less than £10. In prime turf Knightsbridge, that is a Cheap Eat in London for sure.

Note: There is a smaller location in the Brompton Arcade.

The Footstool at St. John's Church
Smith Square, SW1

TELEPHONE
071-222-2779

TUBE
Westminster or St. James's

OPEN
Mon–Fri lunch; dinner on concert evenings

CLOSED
Evening and holidays when there are not concerts; Sat and Sun lunch and dinner when no concerts

HOURS
Lunch: 11:30 A.M.–2:45 P.M. (buffet), 12:15–2:15 P.M. (à la carte). Dinner: Mon–Fri concert evenings only 5:30 P.M.–after concert, Sat and Sun concert evenings only 6 P.M.–after concert

RESERVATIONS
Suggested for à la carte lunch

CREDIT CARDS
AE, MC, V

PRICES
À la Carte: Lunch £16–19; Buffet lunch or dinner £4–7

VAT/SERVICE
10% service charge for 6 or more, otherwise discretionary

St. John's Church on Smith Square is considered one of the masterpieces of English Baroque architecture. Since its completion in the early seventeen hundreds it has survived fires, lightning strikes, bomb attacks, and plans to tear it down. Now, thanks to the efforts of the Friends of St. John's, the church has been beautifully restored and is at the forefront of London's cultural and musical life. The church is the setting for the BBC's live Monday lunchtime concerts as well as a heavily subscribed evening series with guest artists.

The Footstool restaurant is in the crypt of the church. At lunch, two different pocketbooks are catered to. You have the choice of going through a self-service buffet line and selecting from hot and cold dishes, salads, baked potatoes with assorted fillings, and a range of inspiring desserts. Or you can sit at one of the formally set tables and order from the sophisticated, monthly changing menu. Diners are often entertained by a recital or a classical string quartet. In the evening when there is a concert, a lavish buffet is presented offering soups ladled out of hot cauldrons, tempting casseroles, roast meats, four or five salads, beautiful breads, cheeses, and desserts. You can eat as much or as little as you like and be charged accordingly. What better way to relax from the rigors of the day than to dine in one of the most beautiful churches in London, listening to the strains of Brahms or Beethoven, while sipping a glass of wine and enjoying a nice meal?

Gavvers
61–63 Lower Sloane Street, SW1

Anyone who has eaten at Gavvers agrees that it serves some of the best food they have ever had and offers absolute top value for their dining pound. Operated by the famed Roux Brothers, who are known for their outstanding culinary talents, Gavvers serves as a training ground for waiters, chefs, and other staff for their other restaurants, most notably La Gavroche, the first restaurant in Britain to receive three Michelin stars. The set two- and three-course lunches and dinners, which change daily, are bargains to behold, especially when you consider the high caliber of ingredients and preparation that go into each dish.

The small, two-room Gavvers is decorated in soft greens and natural woods. Plenty of space is left between the tables and banquettes. Fresh flowers, crisp linens, lovely table settings, nice paintings, and attentive service set the formal tone for the marvelous food to come. Just reading the menu is a gourmet pleasure. Depending on the season and your main course, you might begin with a salad of asparagus and marinated salmon or skewered mussels with vegetable noodles and saffron. Other choices might be the parcels of goat cheese with an endive salad or pea pancakes with broad beans and tomatoes. Sophisticated entrées include steamed sea bream with a brandade of vegetables, tournedos of halibut with grilled vegetables, a roast leg of rabbit wrapped in Parma ham with garlic sauce, or buttery potato chips with wood pigeon and foie gras. When it comes to desserts, do not even think of leaving without sampling something, even if you only have room to share one with your dining companion.

I am often asked where I like to eat in a particular city. Here is my answer for London. If I had only one meal to eat in London I would go to Gavvers, because everything I have eaten here has been well conceived and beautifully prepared. In fact, writing about it makes me wish I could go tonight. So that I won't be disappointed, I am going to reserve a table when I book my next flight to London.

TELEPHONE
071-730-5983, 071-823-4772

TUBE
Sloane Square

OPEN
Mon–Sat

CLOSED
Sat lunch, Sun, holidays

HOURS
Lunch: Mon–Fri
noon–2:30 P.M.
Dinner: Mon–Sat 7–11 P.M.

RESERVATIONS
Essential

CREDIT CARDS
DC, MC, V

PRICES
À la Carte: £23–27
Set Price: Lunch, 2 courses, £13.50; 3 courses, £16; dinner, 2 courses, £21; 3 courses, £27, includes ½ bottle of house wine

VAT/SERVICE
Service included with all set-price meals, otherwise discretionary

The Green Cafe
16 Eccleston Street, SW1

TELEPHONE
071-730-5304

TUBE
Victoria

OPEN
Mon–Fri

CLOSED
Sat, Sun, holidays

HOURS
Continuous service
6:30 A.M.–6:30 P.M.

RESERVATIONS
Not accepted

CREDIT CARDS
None

PRICES
À la Carte: £2.50–5

VAT/SERVICE
No service charged or expected

MISCELLANEOUS
Unlicensed

"Where do you eat lunch?" I asked the London cabbie who was transporting me back to my flat after a long working day. Believe it or not, he told me he has been going to the same place for almost forty years. You can bet that his recommendation was number one on my list the next day, and here it is—The Green Cafe, a family-run spot where people are not just customers, but treated as one of the family. The Fioris have been opening their door from Monday to Friday on this same site since 1955. Brothers Andrew and John run the upstairs operation and a father-in-law and his best friend hold the fort in the kitchen downstairs.

Only seven tables are set in a green room against a backdrop of beefy working-class regulars diving into Tums-inducing servings of a multitude of sandwiches, hot specials, and that holy grail of grease, the Full English Breakfast. You probably won't order the Spam fritter with chips and peas, or any soup other than the homemade minestrone because the rest are straight from Heinz, or the banana sandwich. Do consider their specialty, spaghetti bolognese, the braised lamb with vegetables, or any one of the *other* sandwiches made on their own bread. If you order with wild abandon, you will have a hard time spending more than £5.

Grumble's
35 Churton Street (off Belgrave Road), SW1

TELEPHONE
071-834-0149

TUBE
Pimlico

OPEN
Daily for lunch and dinner

CLOSED
Holidays

HOURS
Lunch: Mon–Sat noon–
2:30 P.M., Sun 1–3 P.M.
Dinner: Mon–Sat 6–
11:45 P.M., Sun 7–10:30 P.M.

Every table is usually filled at lunch and dinner by young, artistic types who appreciate Grumble's good food and wine served at non-inflationary prices.

The pine-paneled walls and closely packed bare wood tables and chairs create an informal look that is softened in the evening by fresh flowers and candles on each table, even those in the almost-airless basement. The noise level of music competing with conversation may be hard on some, but if you like Elton John, you probably won't mind.

The food leans toward French provincial, with the odd English dish and Sunday roast lunch thrown in for good measure. Starters range from snails in garlic butter to simple avocado and mozzarella salad sprinkled with fresh basil. Carnivores have loads of choices ranging from steak, chicken, lamb, or veal to roast duck. Vegetarians will have no worries with the spicy vegetable bake or Grumble's fish pie topped with mashed potatoes. Desserts are all made here and are loaded with guilty calories.

RESERVATIONS
Advised on weekends
CREDIT CARDS
AE, DC, MC, V
PRICES
À la Carte: £14
VAT/SERVICE
45p cover per person, 10% service charge added
MISCELLANEOUS
They are licensed but you can BYOB, £4 corkage.

La Campagnola
10 Lower Belgrave Street (far end of Ebury Street), SW1

Reliable restaurant tips often come from owners of family-run bed and breakfast hotels. These are people who have lived in the neighborhood and are always on the lookout for good value meals, not only for their guests, but themselves. Two of the best B & Bs on Ebury Street are the Cartreff House and the James across the street. (See *Cheap Sleeps in London.*) Both are well-run by Sharon and Derek James, who told me about La Campagnola, their favorite neighborhood restaurant, where they go most often to eat, and where they send their guests.

La Campagnola is a homey place with wooden tables, straw place mats, and pink paper napkins. By 9 P.M., neighborhood regulars fill every table, talking, laughing, and waving greetings. When ordering, they start with the chunky minestrone soup or a small version of one of the pastas, maybe *spaghetti alla carbonara* or *linguine al pesto*. Next, they might choose the veal stuffed with cheese and ham, covered in a mushroom cream sauce. This is no weight watcher special, but it is so decadently rich you will never forget it. Equally good is the breast of chicken stuffed with butter and garlic or the scampi cooked with mushrooms, tomatoes, herbs, and brandy. A light ending will be fresh figs in cream or the *zabaglione al marsala*.

TELEPHONE
071-730-2057
TUBE
Victoria
OPEN
Mon–Sat
CLOSED
Sun, holidays
HOURS
Lunch: noon–3 P.M.
Dinner: 6–11 P.M.
RESERVATIONS
Advised
CREDIT CARDS
AE, DC, MC, V
PRICES
À la Carte: £13–19
VAT/SERVICE
£1 cover, 10% service charge added to bill

La Fontana
101 Pimlico Road, SW1

TELEPHONE
071-730-6630/3187
TUBE
Sloane Square
OPEN
Daily
CLOSED
Holidays
HOURS
Lunch: noon–2:30 P.M.
Dinner: 7–11:30 P.M.
RESERVATIONS
Recommended
CREDIT CARDS
AE, DC, MC, V
PRICES
À la Carte: £20–26
VAT/SERVICE
£1.75 cover, service
discretionary

La Fontana has everything a good neighborhood restaurant should: a high standard of cooking, an on-the-job owner overseeing every detail, service by Italian waiters that is old world and polite in every way, and a dedicated clientele.

If you yearn for old-fashioned northern Italian food fixed without shortcuts, you have found your place. All dishes are prepared to order and can be tailored to each diner's taste. If you like truffles and are here between October and December, you owe it to yourself to indulge in this notable specialty of La Fontana. During this time, there is a separate menu featuring truffles in all guises, from risotto, gnocci, and ravioli starters to main courses of wild game, jugged wild duck, and veal sweetbreads. Any time you are here, the menu is varied and appealing. Sardine eaters won't soon forget the fresh sardine filets lightly sauteed in olive oil, sprinkled with garlic and parsley. Other noteworthy beginnings include the avocado filled with melted cheeses (gorgonzola, Parmesan, ricotta, bel paese, and mozzarella) and baked in the oven, or the homemade veal and chicken liver pâté flavored with port. Fish, free-range chicken, veal, and tender calf's liver make up the bulk of the main courses. Vegetables are extra, and I recommend the assorted seasonal vegetables or the salad of mixed, cooked vegetables lightly tossed in an oil and lemon dressing. After this avalanche of food, dessert may seem impossible, but the extraordinary zabaglione prepared tableside is the stuff dreams are made of . . . in other words, do not miss it.

Mario & Toni
76 Wilton Road, SW1

TELEPHONE
071-834-9224
TUBE
Victoria
OPEN
Daily
CLOSED
Sat & Sun lunch, Christmas
HOURS
Lunch: Mon–Fri noon–3 P.M.
Dinner: daily 5:30-11:15 P.M.

Mario & Toni's is consistently busy with just enough atmosphere and plenty of affordable Italian dishes to make it a recommended stop near Victoria Station. Comfortable pink paper-covered tables are set in two light blue rooms filled with framed art posters and hanging plants. Italian opera plays in the background adding the right touch to the mood of the place. The steady menu sticks to tried and true versions of minestrone, pasta basics, fish, shellfish, beef, and veal. While not worth a taxi ride across London, it is a local gathering spot you should try for lunch or dinner if you are nearby.

RESERVATIONS
Not necessary

CREDIT CARDS
AE, DC, MC, V

PRICES
À la Carte: £12–18

VAT/SERVICE
70p cover per person, 12% service added to bill

Mekong
46 Churton Street (off Belgrave Road), SW1

The cooking of Vietnam is a delicate blend of Thai, Cantonese, and Indonesian dishes highlighted by fascinating spice blends. The result is food that is light and subtly flavored. Mekong is a family-owned restaurant that draws a clientele eager to savor the fine Vietnamese food that is considered by many to be tops in London. Snacks and lunches are served upstairs in a whitewashed brick room. The aromas from the tiny kitchen below float upward, bringing people downstairs to the gaily decorated basement dining rooms. Fishnets, straw hats, streams of red-wrapped firecrackers, and pretty fans hang from the walls and ceiling. On warm nights you will wish you had your own fan, because as the crowd increases, the room gets hot and stuffy. No one seems to mind; they are too busy concentrating on the food to notice.

The menu, with over seventy choices, makes for good reading if you are familiar with the intricacies of this cuisine. Otherwise, rely on the waiter to help you to build a meal to suit the special tastes of your party or order one of the set menus. My favorite is the Saigon Feast, because it includes a sampling of eight dishes, including superb spring rolls, aromatic crispy duck, king prawns in garlic, and sizzling lamb pieces cooked with ginger and green onions.

TELEPHONE
071-834-6896, 071-630-9568

TUBE
Pimlico

OPEN
Daily for lunch and dinner

CLOSED
Holidays

HOURS
Lunch: noon–2:30 P.M.
Dinner: 6–11:30 P.M.

RESERVATIONS
Advised for dinner

CREDIT CARDS
MC, V

PRICES
À la Carte: £12–15
Set Price: £12–16

VAT/SERVICE
10% service charge added

MISCELLANEOUS
Takeaway

Olivo
21 Eccleston Street, SW1

Olivo is a *nuovo* Italian restaurant that has been a success since the day it opened, thanks to its delicious food. For the effort and ingredients put into every dish, it is an excellent value and you have to take your hat off to the imagination and ambition of the chef

TELEPHONE
071-730-2505

TUBE
Victoria

OPEN
Mon–Fri for lunch & dinner,
Sat dinner

CLOSED
Sat lunch, Sun, holidays

HOURS
Lunch: noon–2:30 P.M.
Dinner: 7–11 P.M.

RESERVATIONS
Essential for lunch and dinner

CREDIT CARDS
AE, MC, V

PRICES
À la Carte: £15–20
Set Price: Lunch only, 2
courses, £14; 3 courses, £16

VAT/SERVICE
£1 cover per person, service
discretionary

on most of his dishes. The strikingly simple interior has its walls painted in bright royal blue and sand with a marigold-stenciled border strip dividing the middle. Heavy cutlery and a small vase of fresh flowers sit atop paper-covered tables.

Lunch caters to office workers, offering only a set menu geared to faster and better meals for those with time limits. The pace is more leisurely at night when only an à la carte menu is available. As the evening wears on, a crescendo builds and by 10 P.M., every table is taken and the restaurant is in full form. Service by sweet Italian waitresses can be sluggish during this time.

The food has a Sardinian influence, making it appealing to those who like zing in their flavorings. Pasta portions are flexible; you can either order them as entrées or dine daintily on them as starters. One of the best is the *pizzocheri,* fresh wholemeal pasta with cabbage, leeks, and fontina cheese. You can skip this course altogether and have a substantial main course, perhaps roast quail with zucchini, pan-fried skate with balsamic vinegar, or venison with red wine and garlic. Desserts are not the chef's forte, but to finish in style, Italian style that is, order the *aranci sanguigni al prosecco* (blood oranges with *prosecco* wine) or *taleggio,* soft Italian cheese.

Peter's Restaurant
59 Pimlico Road, SW1

TELEPHONE
071-730-5991

TUBE
Sloane Square

OPEN
Mon–Sat breakfast, lunch,
dinner; Sun breakfast and
lunch

CLOSED
Sun dinner, holidays

HOURS
Continuous service
Mon–Sat 7 A.M.–10 P.M.,
Sun 7 A.M.–noon

RESERVATIONS
Not accepted

"Hey lady, anyone eating at Peter's should go into training, 'cause this ain't no sissy food!" barked the tattooed cabbie sharing my breakfast table the first time I ate here. He must have seen the look on my face as the waitress brought his breakfast platter overflowing with sausage, bacon, beans, fried eggs, fried bread, grilled tomatoes, and mushrooms all washed down with several cups of strong coffee. Peter's has been feeding London cabbies for thirty-three years, and has become almost hallowed ground for the many regulars who eat here. Salt, sugar, and calories definitely don't count at this typical blue-collar cafe where the artery-clogging grub is served in mountainous quantities. You can order less than the burly regulars do, but beware: this is not the home of tea and toast or nouvelle *anything*. If you miss the breakfast grease-out, there is always lunch or dinner, when you can roll up your sleeves and dig into one of the daily Italian specials or one of their popular chicken dishes that come with potatoes and three vegetables. No one stands on ceremony. Orders are placed at the counter, and as they are ready, the waitress shouts over everyone, "Who gets the fried liver and spaghetti?" Leave your mother-in-law home for this one, but if you are hungry, with no cholesterol or waistline worries, but a few in the cash department, Peter's is an experience you should not miss.

CREDIT CARDS
None

PRICES
À la Carte: £3.50–6

VAT/SERVICE
Service charge included

MISCELLANEOUS
Unlicensed, BYOB, no corkage

Stockpot—West End
40 Panton Street, SW1

See Stockpot Restaurants, page 52, for description.

TELEPHONE: 071-839-5142
TUBE: Piccadilly Circus
OPEN: Daily
CLOSED: Christmas
HOURS: Continuous service, Mon–Sat 8 A.M.–11:30 P.M., Sun noon–10 P.M.
RESERVATIONS: Not accepted
CREDIT CARDS: None
PRICES: À la Carte: £6–7, minimum charge £2.20 during peak hours
VAT/SERVICE: Service discretionary

Vandon House Hotel Restaurant
1 Vandon Street (off Buckingham Gate), SW1

The Vandon House Hotel Restaurant is as prim and proper as a British nanny. If you want glitter, glamor, and beautiful people, turn the page. If you like plain English cooking, simply served in a setting reminiscent of a retirement community, read on. The restaurant is open weekdays for morning coffee and lunch. The overwhelming number of older customers underscores the restaurant's appeal to a crowd that remembers what good value was and appreciates it

TELEPHONE
071-799-6780

TUBE
St. James's Park

OPEN
Mon–Fri for morning coffee and lunch

CLOSED
Dinner, Sat, Sun, holidays

HOURS
Morning coffee: 10 A.M.–noon
Lunch: noon–2 P.M.

when they find it today. When I was last there, I met four ladies—two sisters, a cousin, and a sister-in-law—who have been meeting here monthly for lunch for four years. They all come from outside of London, some traveling two to three hours by bus each way. When I asked why they *always* meet here for their lunch, the spry eighty year old said, "Because the food is just like home, we can afford it, and we feel so comfortable here."

There are daily specials. Certain customers would not think of missing the Monday pork chop with applesauce, the Tuesday roast lamb, or the roast chicken on Wednesday. On Thursday you will find roast beef and Yorkshire pudding and cod with duchesse potatoes on Friday. In addition, they offer meat pies, a Texas burger with onions, The All Day Breakfast, baked potatoes with fillings, and a salad bar. Hot treacle sponge with custard sauce, apple pie, spotted dick, and a variety of ice cream desserts round out the good line up of sturdy offerings.

Note: For details on the Vandon Hotel, see *Cheap Sleeps in London.*

Welcome
24 Broadway, SW1

Trying to find a decent place for lunch near Westminster Abbey that is not full of tourists eating poor-quality, overpriced food takes some doing. The Welcome is a plain-Jane restaurant that opens early for cabbies on shift change and closes just before dark. While it cannot be recommended as a gourmet find, it can be mentioned as a clean, reliable address for a blue-plate special lunch, a quick sandwich, or a bowl of soup between sightseeing rounds. The mob scene at noon might put some off, but if you wait until later, most of the hot food will be picked over. Best time to go is for a late breakfast, a delicious mid-morning cappuccino, or an early lunch. You can also order box lunches to go, with whatever you want in them. This is a very handy and almost life-saving tip if you are planning an overnight train trip and do not want to subsist on tired sandwiches that were made and wrapped days ago in a British Rail kitchen.

Note: Management has plans to change the name (unknown at press time) sometime in 1994. All else will stay the same.

VAT/SERVICE
Service charge included

MISCELLANEOUS
No public bathrooms, use pub next door; takeaway; box lunches to go

The Well
2 Eccleston Place, SW1

The area around Victoria Train and Coach Stations is overflowing with fast food parlors and greasy spoons with fly-specked windows, menus in four languages, and sweaty chefs standing in the doorway. However, all hope is not lost if you know about The Well, run in association with St. Michael's Church. All profits from The Well are used for the work at St. Michael's, and the gratuities collected are donated to a special monthly cause.

The roomy, lime-green interior is usually filled with a mixture of tourists and pensioners who lunch. The range of the cafeteria-style food is impressive and the quality is head and shoulders above any of the nearby competition. They make their own breads and raisin-filled scones and roast their own coffee. Hearty meat and vegetarian dishes, wholesome soups, nice salads, an assortment of crêpes, sandwiches, and a display of glorious cakes sold by the slice or whole are available from 9:30 A.M.–5 P.M. every day but Sunday and holidays.

TELEPHONE
071-730-7303

TUBE
Victoria

OPEN
Mon–Sat

CLOSED
Sun, holidays

HOURS
Continuous service, 9:30 A.M.– 5 P.M. Lunch: 1:30 P.M.–3 P.M., tea, cakes, and sandwiches available at other times

RESERVATIONS
Not accepted

CREDIT CARDS
None

PRICES
À la Carte: £4–7

VAT/SERVICE
Service discretionary and benefits a monthly cause of St. Michael's Church

MISCELLANEOUS
Unlicensed, BYOB, no corkage

WINE BARS SW1

Chimes
26 Churton Street, SW1

Over the years, English food has had a bad rap, and no wonder. Just thinking about overdone meats swimming in gluey gravy, surrounded by mushy peas, soggy chips, and limp carrots is enough to make anyone move on to something—*anything*—more interesting. However, after one meal at Chimes, faith

TELEPHONE
071-821-7456

TUBE
Pimlico

OPEN
Daily

CLOSED
Christmas
HOURS
Lunch: noon–2:30 P.M.
Dinner: 6–10:15 P.M.
RESERVATIONS
Suggested, especially at night
CREDIT CARDS
AE, MC, V
PRICES
À la Carte: £12–15
VAT/SERVICE
Service discretionary for fewer
than 6; 10% for 6 or more

is rapidly restored and opinions are guaranteed to change. Every day it is filled to the brim with locals eager to dip into a nostalgic bite of their heritage and past. The long menu makes for some interesting reading. Cottage pie, toad-in-the-hole, bangers and mash, Cumberland sausage, and a wide variety of individual meat pies such as chicken with gooseberries and ginger, fidget (ham, potato, onion, and apple), and Gloucestershire (lamb with rosemary and apples). These, plus a host of monthly specialties based on Olde English recipes have made Chimes a smart destination for those looking for the real thing in English food. Chimes also stocks a variety of draught ciders from major independent producers and many fruit wines, including elderflower, apple, damson, and gooseberry. For dessert, the puddings are a must, especially the treacle or apple crisp, served warm in their own casseroles and topped with rich vanilla ice cream.

A nice thing to remember about Chimes is that you can come here anytime they are open either for a full meal or a glass or two of their unusual wines.

Ebury Wine Bar
139 Ebury Street, SW1

TELEPHONE
071-730-5447
TUBE
Victoria
OPEN
Daily
CLOSED
Two days at Christmas
HOURS
11 A.M.–11 P.M.
Food service: Lunch noon–
2:30 P.M., dinner 6–10:30 P.M.
RESERVATIONS
Suggested
CREDIT CARDS
AE, DC, MC, V

The Ebury Wine Bar has developed a well-deserved reputation as one of London's premier wine bars serving consistently good food and excellent wines. The narrow interior combines the look and feel of a Paris bistro, with metal-based tables, wooden chairs, and bare floors. The professional crowd is smartly sophisticated, and it should be, considering the neighborhood boasts some of the most expensive real estate in London. The menu changes daily, displaying international and British cooking. Intriguing appetizers might include Gado Gado salad, a chiffonade of spinach and white cabbage with bean sprouts, hard-boiled eggs and satay sauce, or duck liver parfait with toast. Their main course sausage special, Cumberland sausages with mashed potatoes, fried onions, and gravy, is always a pleaser. The Sunday set lunch consists of a choice of two courses and always features a roast and seasonal favorites. The service is efficient yet friendly, and knowledgeable staff will take the time to answer questions and offer suggestions on the wines.

PRICES
À la Carte: £16
Set Price: Sunday lunch, £12 for any two courses

VAT/SERVICE
12½% service charge added to bill

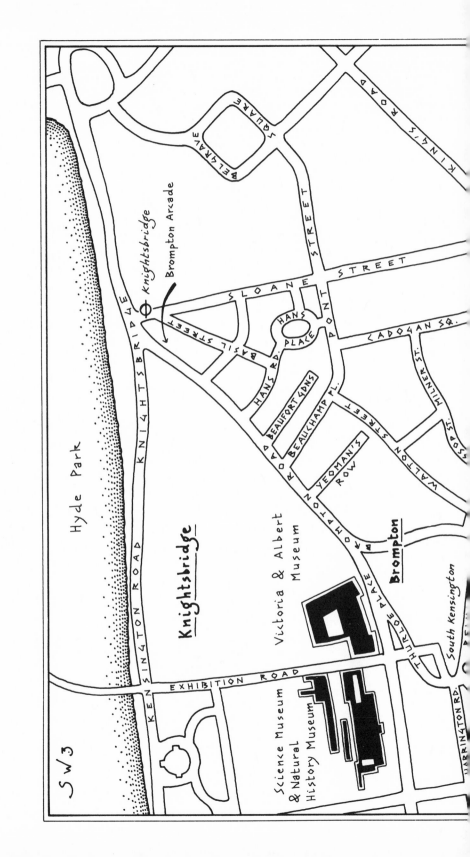

SW3 ✤ CHELSEA, KNIGHTSBRIDGE

Chelsea is where London preppies known as Sloane Rangers and Hooray Henrys live. Other famous residents have included Thomas More, Oscar Wilde, and Johnny Rotten and the Sex Pistols. The main thoroughfare is King's Road, a private road until the nineteenth century, extending from Sloane Square through Chelsea. Almost every designation along here requires a long walk or bus ride on #11 or #22. King's Road is best seen on a Saturday afternoon, when fashion victims make people-watching one of the best games in town.

Knightsbridge is the well-heeled shopper's paradise. Harrods, besieged by chauffeured limousines and taxis, is the centerpiece, beckoning Middle Eastern potentates and dowagers dragging poodles for a shopping spree. Smart boutiques line Sloane Street and trendy, *very* expensive shops make window shopping along Beauchamp Place something to behold.

PUBS SW3

Admiral Codrington
17 Mossop Street, SW3

Mention the Admiral Codrington pub to any Londoner and they will all agree—it's great! The Admiral Cod, as it is called, is one of the most popular and crowded pubs in Chelsea. The inside is very appealing, just what most people imagine a pub should be: wood paneling, old gas lamps, roaring fires in the winter, friendly barmen, and knots of regulars sitting around swapping lies and war stories. There is an outside patio along one side and a pretty, covered conservatory garden in back that is heated in winter. The pub is owned by Charrington Pubs and offers a fine selection of malt whiskeys in addition to its beer. The food is good and ranges from daily specials, soups, and sandwiches to grills, roasts for Sunday lunch, and homebaked pies for dessert. The prices are cheap enough and so is time. Expect *long* waits for your food order to arrive, which may be a tactic to encourage more spending at the bar.

TELEPHONE
071-581-0005

TUBE
South Kensington

OPEN
Daily

CLOSED
Sat, Sun dinner, holidays

HOURS
Mon–Sat 11 A.M.–11 P.M.; Sun noon–3 P.M., 7–10:30 P.M. Food service: Mon–Fri lunch noon–3 P.M., dinner 6–8 P.M.

RESERVATIONS
Not accepted

CREDIT CARDS
AE, MC, V

PRICES
À la Carte: £3.50–5.50

VAT/SERVICE
No service charged or expected

Bunch of Grapes
207 Brompton Road, SW3

What will the reluctant shoppers do while you are discovering the vast wonders of Harrods or scooping up bargains at the Reject China Shops on Beauchamp Place? They will go to the Bunch of Grapes pub on Brompton Road and happily spend the late morning or entire afternoon in this congenial spot. The pub is made up of a series of pleasant, paneled rooms with cut-glass mirrors and comfortable chairs. The meals

TELEPHONE
071-589-4944

TUBE
Knightsbridge

OPEN
Daily

CLOSED
Some holidays, call to check

HOURS
Mon–Sat 11 A.M.–11 P.M.;
Sun noon–2:45 P.M.,
7–8:30 P.M.
Food service: Mon–Sat
11:30 A.M.–8:30 P.M.,
Sun noon–2:45 P.M.

RESERVATIONS
Not accepted

CREDIT CARDS
AE, MC, V (food service only)

PRICES
À la Carte: £4.50–7

VAT/SERVICE
No service charged or expected

are all prepared here, using fresh ingredients—not frozen and microwaved as is the case in many pubs today. The pub is known for its ploughman's lunch (featuring Stilton, Brie, or cheddar cheese), meat pies, fish and chips, and daily roasts, all served non-stop from 11:30 A.M. until 8:30 P.M. When you return to meet your companion, you will probably hear "Back so soon?!?"

Please note: If some hot food runs out at noon you will be out of luck for that dish if you miss it. Knowing this, you are better off here for lunch, unless you don't mind a sandwich, cold meat plate, or salad for your dinner.

King's Head & Eight Bells
50 Cheyne Walk, SW3

TELEPHONE
071-352-1820

TUBE
Sloane Square

OPEN
Daily

CLOSED
Some holidays, call to check

HOURS
Winter: Mon–Fri noon–3 P.M.,
5:30–11:30 P.M.;
Sat noon–11 P.M.;
Sun noon–3 P.M., 7–10:30 P.M.
Summer: Mon–Sat noon–
11 P.M., Sun noon–3 P.M.

RESERVATIONS
Not accepted

CREDIT CARDS
AE, DC, MC, V

PRICES
À la Carte: £4–6.50

VAT/SERVICE
Service discretionary

The King's Head & Eight Bells is an historic Chelsea pub dating from the fifteenth century. Located on fashionable Cheyne Walk, it has always been a favorite haunt of the writers and artists who lived in the neighborhood. Famous occupants have included George Eliot at 4 Cheyne Walk and Swinburne at 16. Whistler painted his mother at No. 96, and J. M. W. Turner lived at 119. Mick Jagger and Keith Richards are more recent Cheyne Walk inhabitants. Now under new managers Rob and Sally Stacey, the pub kitchen offers homemade soups, chili, Guinness pie, and a Sunday roast lunch. Almost everything else is frozen, which doesn't make it bad, but when you can have something freshly made, why not? The comfortable pub is worth the hike from the Sloane Square tube stop. If you use a map and the Michelin Green Guide as you go along, you will find all sorts of interesting tidbits about this part of the city that will add to your visit to London.

RESTAURANTS SW3

Arco Bars of Knightsbridge
16 Brompton Arcade, SW3

See Arco Bars of Knightsbridge, page 113, for description. All other information is the same.

TELEPHONE: 071-583-3136
TUBE: Knightsbridge

Au Bon Accueil
19–21 Elystan Street, SW3

You will find Au Bon Accueil in a Chelsea neighborhood where nannies push prams and women wear pearls to the greengrocer. Just around the corner are several home-decorating studios displaying the latest word in fabrics and furniture for the well-dressed home. Only a block away is one of London's most talked-about restaurants, where prices for dinner equal most weekly budgets and reservations four or five weeks in advance are advised. That is why I was so happy to discover this reasonably priced French restaurant, which has been in the neighborhood for more than thirty years. The bright interior is unpretentious, yet comfortable, even though the pink-covered tables and chairs are closely placed. The blue-aproned waiters are professional and polite, but more important, the Gallic cooking is filling and tasty.

The unchanging menu displays a list of French favorites with a wide selection for each course. The robust *moules marinieres* (mussels in white wine) tops the list of appetizers. Other standbys are the escargots (snails) in garlic butter or the *oeufs en cocotte à la crème* (baked eggs in cream). The *croquettes de poisson* (fish cakes) were too rich and oily and the salade Niçoise was a bit heavy as a starter. The best entrées are the simple *poulet à l'estragon* (chicken in a tarragon cream sauce), a grilled fillet steak, or any of the fresh fish. Vegetables are extra and worth the additional investment. My favorite is the fennel *maison,* which is quickly deep-fried, giving new interest to

TELEPHONE
071-589-3718

TUBE
South Kensington

OPEN
Mon–Fri lunch and dinner; Sat dinner

CLOSED
Sat lunch, Sun, holidays

HOURS
Lunch: Mon–Fri 12:30–2:30 P.M.
Dinner: Mon–Sat 7–11:30 P.M.

RESERVATIONS
Advised on weekends

CREDIT CARDS
AE, DC, MC, V

PRICES
À la Carte: £18

VAT/SERVICE
£1 cover, service discretionary

this popular European vegetable. You can safely concentrate on the large-portioned appetizers and entrées here, because, with the exception of the house-made raspberry sorbet, the desserts are brought in and do not add much to the rest of the meal.

Beccofino
100 Draycott Avenue, SW3

TELEPHONE
071-584-3600, 071-581-3387
TUBE
South Kensington
OPEN
Mon–Sat for lunch and dinner
CLOSED
Sun, holidays
HOURS
Lunch: 12:30 P.M.–2:30 P.M.
Dinner: 7–11:30 P.M.
RESERVATIONS
Essential for dinner
CREDIT CARDS
MC, V
PRICES
À la Carte: £15
VAT/SERVICE
Service discretionary
MISCELLANEOUS
£9 minimum food charge

Warm sienna color tones, velvet banquettes, and soft background music create the mood of this outstanding Italian restaurant in Chelsea. Bouquets of flowers, tables set with heavy silver, and starched linens and superb service underscore the formal tone. It all sounds expensive, but the food and atmosphere add up to an unbeatable dining combination that guarantees many repeat visits. In fact, every time I am in London, I make a special point of reserving my first dinner here.

Trying to decide what to order is a problem, but a nice one. You could start with the tender arugula salad topped with thin slices of fresh Parmesan cheese or mushrooms and ripe tomatoes, lightly dressed in extra-virgin olive oil and balsamic vinegar. Or perhaps the garlicky grilled mushrooms or fat snails will appeal more. The homemade pastas and sauces are some of the best in London . . . period. And the risotto, bursting with seafood, garlic, and chili peppers in a light tomato sauce is, in a word, delicious. The veal picatta in lemon sauce, the grilled jumbo shrimp, and the roast chicken make good pasta alternatives, and so do any of the daily offerings. It is hard to save enough room for dessert, but the temptation is great when you see them displayed so seductively in the center of the room. The selections change daily, but the cloudlike custard is a must if it is there and so are the fat spring strawberries or sliced mangoes. Lingering over an espresso is the perfect ending to your excellent meal. When reserving, bear in mind that the best time to arrive is 8:30 or 9 P.M., otherwise, you could be dining alone.

Big Easy
332–334 King's Road, SW3

Arrive starved and be prepared to party the night away at the Big Easy on King's Road. Heel-kicking live music at night, a staff with youth on its side, and wild drinks with names like Beach Blanket Banana, Critical Condition, and Nitroglycerine keep the masses alive and pulsating. It all happens in a rough-hewn, big, barn-like building that serves a taste of almost-Cajun cooking. That's not all. The Big Easy is the home of ultimate Scotch prime steaks that range from 12 to 22 ounces *each* and come smothered with onions, pan-fried mushrooms, sweet peppers, and a Texas-size baked potato covered in sour cream or drenched in melted butter. Also touted are Monday night prime rib dinners, Gulf shrimp on Wednesday, Be Kind to Oysters on Thursday, hardshell Boston lobsters on Friday, and a country-style, hickory-smoked barbecue on Sunday. If you are an early bird and arrive between noon and 8 P.M., Monday through Friday, you can get soup or salad, a main course, and soft drinks for less than £6. If you are there from 5–7 P.M. Mon–Fri, you will get 25% off all menu items. With a sign saying "If you are in a hurry, we'll mail your lunch," you can guess speedy service is no virtue here.

TELEPHONE
071-352-4071

TUBE
Sloane Square, then bus #11, #19, or #22

OPEN
Daily

CLOSED
Christmas

HOURS
Continuous service
Sun–Thurs noon–midnight,
Fri–Sat noon–12:30 A.M.

RESERVATIONS
Not necessary

CREDIT CARDS
MC, V

PRICES
À la Carte: £8–12
Set Price: Early-bird special
Mon–Fri noon–8 P.M., £6;
Mon–Fri 5–7 P.M., 25% off all menu items

VAT/SERVICE
Service discretionary

Dan's Restaurant & Garden
119 Sydney Street, SW3

If I am in the mood for a lovely meal after browsing through the indoor antiques markets on King's Road, I walk down Sydney Street and just past the Chelsea Market go in the bright green door of Dan's. The airy interior is formally dressed in pink linens, nice crystal, and signature china. The select tables are in the back, where the ceiling can be rolled open on pretty days. The set menus offer three selections in each course of well-prepared, seasonally appropriate dishes. The à la carte menu is naturally more expensive, but the choices are larger. Starters might include a *feuilleté* of goat's cheese with salad, confit of duck with caramelized shallots, or a trio of smoked fish

TELEPHONE
071-352-2718

TUBE
Sloane Square, then bus #11 or #19

OPEN
Mon–Sat

CLOSED
Sat lunch, Sun, holidays

HOURS
Lunch: Mon–Fri 12:30–2 P.M.
Dinner: Mon–Sat 7:30–10:45 P.M.

RESERVATIONS
Suggested, especially in summer for garden area

CREDIT CARDS
AE, MC, V
PRICES
À la Carte: £20, 3 courses
Set Price: Lunch, 2 courses,
£8.50; 3 courses, £10.50;
dinner, 2 courses, £13.50;
3 courses, £16
VAT/SERVICE
Service discretionary

mousses. Main courses always include something for vegetarians. The roast pigeon with pigeon liver stuffing on toast was good, but a bit gamey. A better choice is the roast rack of lamb with rosemary, which is done to a pink-T. The lusty chocolate truffle cake with coffee bean sauce makes a dramatic sweet finale. The clientele is young, rich and Sloaney, and considers Dan's one of the best restaurants around. Even though the prices are on the high side, for a lunch or dinner with someone special, Dan's fills the bill.

Ed's Easy Diner
362 King's Road, SW3

See Ed's Easy Diner, page 35, for description. All other information is the same.

TELEPHONE: 071-352-1956
TUBE: Sloane Square, then #19 bus

The English Garden, The English House, and The Lindsay House

For a meal with someone special or simply to taste how fine British cooking really can be, reserve a table at one of these wonderful London restaurants. The English Garden and English House are converted Chelsea townhouses with food to match their stylish settings and clientele. The English Garden is patterned after a comfortable country home. Dining in the garden room, surrounded by floral murals, topiary trees, and masses of potted plants and flowers is a delightful experience. At the English House, the charm of dining in intimate rooms filled with chintz and lovely decorative furniture is pleasant, despite the close proximity of your dining neighbor. At the Lindsay House, you can enjoy a cocktail in the ground-floor dining room of this elegant seventeenth-century Soho house, then go up to the first-floor dining room for a quiet, romantic meal at a beautifully set table, surrounded by opulent fabric-covered walls, a huge marble fireplace, and gilt mirrors. The food in all three restaurants changes often and is always interesting and modern with perfect presentations of just-right portions. The à la carte meals can get mighty expensive, so ordering the set lunches (each location) and Sunday dinner (English House only) is a wise option. You could start with a smoked salmon mousse dressed with crab and dill or a galantine of duck with spiced vegetable preserve. The main course might be poached cod fillet with cheddar, celery, and horseradish crust; a pork roulade with two prune sauces; or a ragout of calf's liver and smoked bacon. The desserts are as inventive as the rest of the meal, especially the hot raspberry charlotte with vanilla custard or the steamed lemon sponge pudding with lemon curd sauce. A platter of petits fours and chocolates ends the meal. True, it will cost a bit more than most, but it is worth the extra for the memories that will linger long after you have left London.

The English Garden
10 Lincoln Street, SW3

See previous page for description.

TELEPHONE: 071-584-7272

TUBE: Sloane Square

OPEN: Daily

CLOSED: Christmas and some holidays (call to check)

HOURS: Lunch: Mon–Sat 12:30–2:30 P.M., Sun 12:30–2 P.M. Dinner: Mon–Sat 7:30–11:30 P.M., Sun 7–10:30 P.M.

RESERVATIONS: Necessary

CREDIT CARDS: AE, DC, MC, V

PRICES: À la Carte: 3 courses plus coffee, £32. Set Price: Lunch, 3 courses and coffee, £15.75

VAT/SERVICE: Service discretionary

MISCELLANEOUS: Two separate rooms for parties of 6–25 with £3 cover per person and menu to be arranged with management

The English House
3 Milner Street, SW3

See previous page for description.

TELEPHONE: 071-584-3002

TUBE: Knightsbridge

OPEN: Daily

CLOSED: Christmas and some holidays (call to check)

HOURS: Lunch: Mon–Sat 12:30–2:30 P.M., Sun 12:30–2 P.M. Dinner: Mon–Sat 7:30–11:30 P.M., Sun 7–10 P.M.

RESERVATIONS: Necessary

CREDIT CARDS: AE, DC, MC, V

PRICES: À la Carte: £32, 3 courses plus coffee. Set Price: Lunch Mon-Sat £15.75, Sun £19.75, includes 3 courses and coffee

VAT/SERVICE: Service discretionary

MISCELLANEOUS: On Sundays, *only* set menu available, private rooms for 6–12, £3 cover per person

The Lindsay House

See The Lindsay House (W1), page 38, for information.

La Bersagliera
372 King's Road, SW3

TELEPHONE
071-352-5993

TUBE
Sloane Square, then bus #11 or #19

OPEN
Mon–Sat for lunch and dinner

CLOSED
Sun, Christmas

HOURS
Lunch: 12:30–3 P.M.
Dinner: 7–11:45 P.M.

RESERVATIONS
Accepted only for 6 or more

CREDIT CARDS
None

PRICES
À la Carte: £11–14

VAT/SERVICE
Service charge included

Pasta partisans on modest budgets should not miss a visit to La Bersagliera. Stuck at the far end of King's Road from Sloane Square, it escapes most tourists, but not the neighborhood cognoscenti who have had it pegged for years. At midnight, every seat in the small room is filled with people eating, drinking, and having a good time. The closely placed marble-topped tables, along with the generally high noise level of the aggressive crowd standing in the aisles waiting for a table, make it uncomfortable for some. The service by mostly non-English-speaking Italian waiters is rough around the edges and at times unprofessional to the point of asking for the order the moment the menu is handed out, and presenting the bill *before* the meal has been served ... and both of these faux pas have happened to me twice! With these drawbacks, why do I continue to recommend it? Because the food, especially the homemade pasta, sauces, and breads, is just too good to ignore and the prices are definitely right for all Cheap Eaters.

Keeping in mind that the portions are *big,* start with *bresaola,* thinly sliced air-dried beef served with olive oil and lemon or the *insalata di mozzarella,* mozzarella cheese, tomato, and lettuce served with homemade pizza bread. This will leave plenty of room for one of the overflowing dishes of pasta and delicious sauces made in the tiny back kitchen by Lina Molino, the Italian mama who owns La Bersagliera. With the exception of the veal, the meat dishes do not quite live up to the standard set by the pasta. If you have dessert in mind, the crème caramel is the best.

Le Shop
329 King's Road, SW3

Crêpes and *galettes* are popular French snack foods that originated in Brittany. Le Shop was the first crêpe shop in London, and it is still one of the best because it only does one thing, and that is to make delicious crêpes. There are twenty-one *galettes*—crêpes made from buckwheat flour—on the menu. If you do not see one that appeals, you can build your own by mixing any of twenty-eight different fillings. Dessert crêpes made from white flour are listed in every combination imaginable or you can create your own from a long list of sweet fillings. Add a small salad, a glass of cider, and you will have a light and satisfying meal. Don't worry; these French pancakes are light as air and you will have room for at least two. The best place to enjoy your meal is at a table by the front window, where watching the fashion trendsetters preen and prance along this stretch of King's Road will probably be some of the most amusing people-watching you will do in London.

TELEPHONE
071-352-3891

TUBE
Sloane Square, then bus #11 or #19

OPEN
Daily

CLOSED
Christmas

HOURS
Continuous service noon–midnight

RESERVATIONS
For parties of 6 or more

CREDIT CARDS
MC, V

PRICES
À la Carte: £7–9

VAT/SERVICE
Service discretionary

MISCELLANEOUS
Minimum charge £2 per person, ½ portions available for children

Luba's Bistro
6 Yeoman's Row, SW3

Imagine the interior of a Russian *dacha* and you could be inside Luba's Bistro, a cozy, pine-walled restaurant in the heart of Knightsbridge. Long communal tables covered in red and white oilcloth are served by Russian waitresses wearing short black

TELEPHONE
071-589-2950

TUBE
Knightsbridge

OPEN
Mon–Sat for dinner only

skirts, frilly white embroidered blouses, and white stockings. They serve a mixture of hungry tourists and locals a wide sampling of Russian favorites such as borscht, blini, beef stroganoff, pork goulash, and *galubtzy*—stuffed cabbage served with sour cream.

A ten-percent discount is offered if you pay your bill *and leave* before 8 P.M. Of course, you can always go later, pay more, and not be hurried. The prices are very low for the area, but if you want an alcoholic beverage, you have to BYOB. Generally speaking, Luba's is more fun with several people.

My Old Dutch Pancake House
221 King's Road, SW3

See My Old Dutch Pancake House, page 83, for description. All other information is the same.

TELEPHONE: 071-376-5650

TUBE: Sloane Square (a long walk, but King's Road is great for shopping and browsing)

Nineteen
19 Mossop Street, SW3

The building has been a farmhouse, a chandlers, a greengrocer, and a workingman's cafe. In 1949, it became what it is today, the kind of homey bistro everyone wishes were in his or her neighborhood. The food is good, the prices reasonable, and the atmosphere welcoming both to lone diners or parties of eight. It is also a good place to see a cross-section of Chelsea dwellers, from pensioners out for their weekly lunch to the well-heeled professionals who live in the area's townhouses. The menu stays virtually the same, with a few specials added at lunch. This pleases the regulars, who always sit at the same tables and never consult the menu.

Begin with the onion soup with a cheesy top crust or the mushrooms sauteed with crispy bacon and garlic. The rack of lamb, steak, or veal escalope are winners in the main course section. Vegetarians have a wide choice, ranging from nut cutlets and gratinéed veggies to omelettes and pasta. Vegetables and potatoes are extra, but not by much. The best desserts?

Always the apple and blackberry crumble with cream, the chocolate layer cake, or an ice cream sundae.

Pasta Prego
1a Beauchamp Place, SW3

"What, another pasta place?" moaned my dining companion as we arrived at Pasta Prego, located on the Rodeo Drive of London, Beauchamp Place. At first, the restaurant seems plain, almost boring with its off-white interior dominated by banquette seating and a few green plants. Once your serving of their homemade pasta arrives, you quickly forget about the surroundings and concentrate on the food in front of you. You can play it safe and order spinach lasagna or fettucine primavera, but why not consider the linguine with tomato and garlic sauce loaded with clams, mussels, shrimp, and fresh squid, or the *crespoline alla fiorentina,* which is a ginger crêpe filled with whey cheese, spinach, and cream and baked in a cheese sauce. Salads can be ordered as side dishes or as whole meals; children eat for less and power desserts like the chef's Amaretto and banana pudding keep you off your diet for another day. In a posh area where even a beer can set you back £4, Pasta Prego is one to permanently place on everyone's Cheap Eats map of London.

TELEPHONE
071-225-1064

TUBE
Knightsbridge

OPEN
Daily

CLOSED
Christmas, New Year's Eve and New Year's Day

HOURS
Lunch: noon–3 P.M.
Dinner: 6–11 P.M.

RESERVATIONS
Advised

CREDIT CARDS
AE DC, MC, V

PRICES
À la Carte: £13–6

VAT/SERVICE
Service discretionary

San Frediano
62 Fulham Road, SW3

San Fred's, as insiders call it, is always jammed, always reliable, and always rewarding, thanks to the generous style and service that have characterized it for years. Long a favorite with South Kensington trendies, you can count on having well-prepared Italian staples of roasted peppers with olive oil and anchovies; avocado, tomato, and mozzarella salad; dried beef with fresh ricotta cheese; or *pasta e fagioli,* thick pasta and bean soup. Pastas come as appetizers or as main courses and include tagliolini in a smoked salmon and cream sauce, egg and spinach noodles with mushrooms and tomatoes, and cannelloni. Beef, veal, liver, and lamb keep carnivores happy and the

TELEPHONE
071-584-8375

TUBE
South Kensington

OPEN
Mon–Sat

CLOSED
Sun, holidays

HOURS
Lunch: 12:30–2:30 P.M.
Dinner: 7–11:30 P.M.

RESERVATIONS
Essential

CREDIT CARDS
AE, DC, MC, V

PRICES
À la Carte: £15–20

VAT/SERVICE
£1.50 cover per person, service discretionary

creamy *tiramisu* with fresh strawberries on the side keeps all sweet tooths satisfied.

Stockpot—King's Road
273 King's Road, SW3

See Stockpot Restaurants, page 52, for description.

TELEPHONE: 071-823-3175
TUBE: Sloane Square
OPEN: Daily
CLOSED: Christmas
HOURS: Continuous service, Mon–Sat 8 A.M.–11:45 P.M., Sun 1–11:30 P.M.
RESERVATIONS: Not accepted
CREDIT CARDS: None
PRICES: À la Carte: £6–7, £2 minimum charge for lunch and dinner
VAT/SERVICE: 10% service charge

Stockpot—Knightsbridge
6 Basil Street, SW3

See Stockpot Restaurants, page 52, for description.

TELEPHONE: 071-589-8627
TUBE: Knightsbridge
OPEN: Daily
CLOSED: Christmas
HOURS: Continuous service, Mon–Sat 8 A.M.–11 P.M. Sun noon–10:30 P.M.
RESERVATIONS: Not accepted
CREDIT CARDS: None
PRICES: À la Carte: £6–7, £2 minimum charge for lunch and dinner
VAT/SERVICE: 10% service charge

Upstairs Restaurant—Basil Street Hotel
8 Basil Street, SW3

TELEPHONE
071-581-3311
TUBE
Knightsbridge

The Upstairs Restaurant at the Basil Street Hotel inspires confidence in one's ability to dine well for less in these days of escalating food costs. Service is cafeteria style in a large room with pine tables and booths. You serve yourself from the line for the main course and drinks, and desserts are brought to your table. It is open for breakfast and lunch. At breakfast, you can get either the regular English breakfast with eggs, bacon, beans, tomato, and toast or just a coffee and Danish if you are taking a lighter approach. The best time to go is for lunch, when there is something for everyone from an all-you-can-eat cold buffet with over thirty meats and salads to the roast meat carvery with all the trimmings. In addition there are hot dishes of the day, vegetarian and fish offerings, and desserts. The most expensive item on the menu is the Lunch Special, which allows you to have a go at the buffet table and one hot dish for about £8.

OPEN
Mon–Sat for breakfast and lunch

CLOSED
Dinner, Sun, holidays

HOURS
Breakfast: 9–11 A.M
Lunch: noon–3 P.M.

RESERVATIONS
Not necessary

CREDIT CARDS
AE, DC, MC, V

PRICES
À la Carte: £2–8

VAT/SERVICE
Service discretionary

MISCELLANEOUS
No-smoking section

Wolfe's
24 Basil Street, SW3

Long recognized as the salvation of many a famished diner, Wolfe's is best enjoyed for what it is: a good place for a cooked-to-order hamburger, a large salad, or a guilt-inspiring dessert. If you wander too far from these, prices increase significantly. The big draw has always been Wolfeburgers, which are lifted out of the fast food lane by the quality of their beef and the charbroiling cooking process. All are accessorized with fresh vegetable purée and your choice of potato garnish—creamed, baked, fried, or croquettes. The chef recommends the hamburgers to be cooked "medium rare" and accepts no responsibility for the results if you order yours "well-done." For the under-12 set, Wolfe's has a children's menu with a small Wolfeburger or fried eggs with chips (french fries) and a salad. For everyone, there is a special dessert menu with a dozen or more ice cream creations, along with cakes, pies, tarts, and their unbelievably good specialty, a Waffle-Wolfe: two scoops of vanilla ice cream sandwiched between warm waffles and smothered in hot chocolate and whipped cream.

TELEPHONE
071-589-8444

TUBE
Knightsbridge

OPEN
Daily

CLOSED
Two days at Christmas

HOURS
Continuous service
11:30 A.M.–midnight

RESERVATIONS
Not necessary

CREDIT CARDS
AE, DC, MC, V

PRICES
À la Carte: £9–12

VAT/SERVICE
Service discretionary if bill under £40; if over, 12½%. Minimum charge £9, Sat £10 per person

TEAROOMS SW 3

Pâtisserie Valerie
215 Brompton Road, SW3

See Pâtisserie Valerie, page 56, for description.
TELEPHONE: 071-823-9971
TUBE: Knightsbridge
OPEN: Daily
CLOSED: Holidays
HOURS: Continuous food service, Mon–Fri
7:30 A.M.–7:30 P.M. Sat 7:30 A.M.–7 P.M. Sun
9 A.M.–7 P.M.
RESERVATIONS: Not necessary
CREDIT CARDS: AE, DC, MC, V only for orders of
£10 or more
PRICES: À la Carte: £2.50–3.50 for tea and pastry,
£5.50–8 for light meal with pastry and beverage
VAT/SERVICE: No service added to bill; 12½%
suggested
MISCELLANEOUS: Licensed for beer and wine

Richoux—Knightsbridge
86 Brompton Road, SW3

See Richoux, page 49, for description. All other
information is the same.
TELEPHONE: 071-584-8300
TUBE: Knightsbridge

Sonny's
39 Beauchamp Place, SW3

TELEPHONE
071-581-7012
TUBE
Knightsbridge
OPEN
Daily
CLOSED
Holidays
HOURS
Continuous service
Mon–Sat 9 A.M.–5:30 P.M., Sun
11 A.M.–5:30 P.M.
RESERVATIONS
Not accepted

It is true that good things come in small packages.
Sonny's is a tiny tearoom with an elegant address,
catering to an equally elegant clientele. When shopping at Harrods, Harvey Nicols, or along Beauchamp
Place, stop here for one of their famous sandwiches
served on wholemeal bread, a bagel or croissant,
creamy quiches, or teatime treats. The popular
chicken salad sandwich with chunks of roasted
chicken mixed with peppers, celery, and a tangy
cream dressing is served with a tomato and salad
garnish. Another delicious combination is the melted
Brie with cucumber and spring onions. All quiches

are baked with free-range eggs, Gruyère cheese, and fresh vegetables. Try the broccoli and ham or the spinach for wonderful renditions of old favorites. If it is before lunch, have one of their just-baked scones dripping with butter and jam or a slice of banana bread. I can enthusiastically recommend sinful desserts, especially the white chocolate cheesecake—a must for any card-carrying chocoholic. Another worthwhile splurge is the hot apple pie or crumble. Prices at Sonny's are below average for this expensive neighborhood, inspiring many repeat visits.

CREDIT CARDS
None

PRICES
À la Carte: £6–8, minimum charge £3.50

VAT/SERVICE
10% service added to bill

MISCELLANEOUS
Takeaway

WINE BARS SW3

Le Metro
28 Basil Street, SW3

Le Metro Wine Bar is around the corner from Harrods, a handy location if you, your shopping companion, or tag-along needs sustenance or a drop to drink while combing the shops in Knightsbridge. At Le Metro you can depend on good French food from *café* and croissants in the morning through to late suppers at night. In between they offer both light and substantial meals for lunch and dinner. Depending on the season, you may dine on sweet red pepper soup with green olive crostini, roasted red onion quiche with herbs and potatoes, pizza topped with chèvre, peppers, and zucchini, squid risotto with pinenuts and basil, or confit of duck with red wine. Every day there are at least two specials for both the starter and main course, as well as a tantalizing lineup of wonderful homemade desserts. Whenever I go, I always hope they have their banana bread with butterscotch or pear flan.

The wine list is as impressive as the menu. At any time there are at least ten bottles available by the glass, thanks to a Cruover machine, which works by drawing wine from the bottle and replacing it with inert gas to prevent oxidation. While here you can sample not only French and Californian wines, but those from Chile, New Zealand, and Australia.

TELEPHONE
071-589-6286

TUBE
Knightsbridge

OPEN
Mon–Sat

CLOSED
Sat evening, Sun, holidays

HOURS
Continuous service
Mon–Fri 7:30 A.M.–11 P.M.,
Sat 7:30 A.M.–7 P.M.

RESERVATIONS
Not necessary

CREDIT CARDS
AE, MC, V

PRICES
À la Carte: £4–10

VAT/SERVICE
Minimum charge £5 per person from noon–3 P.M., service discretionary

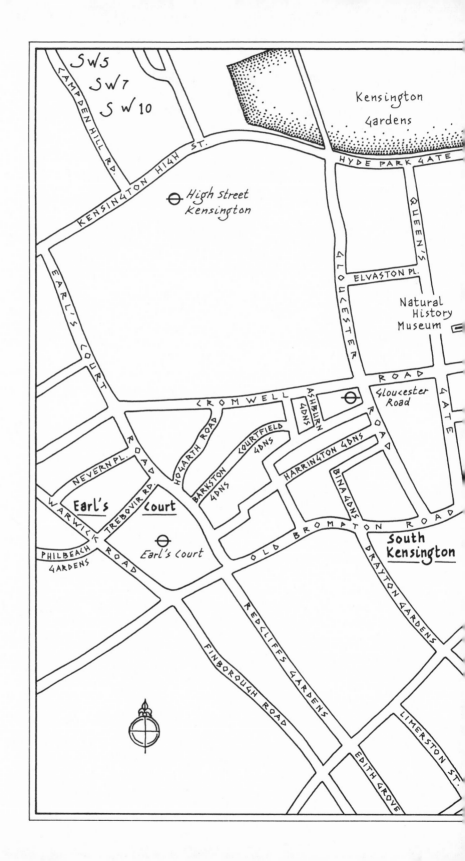

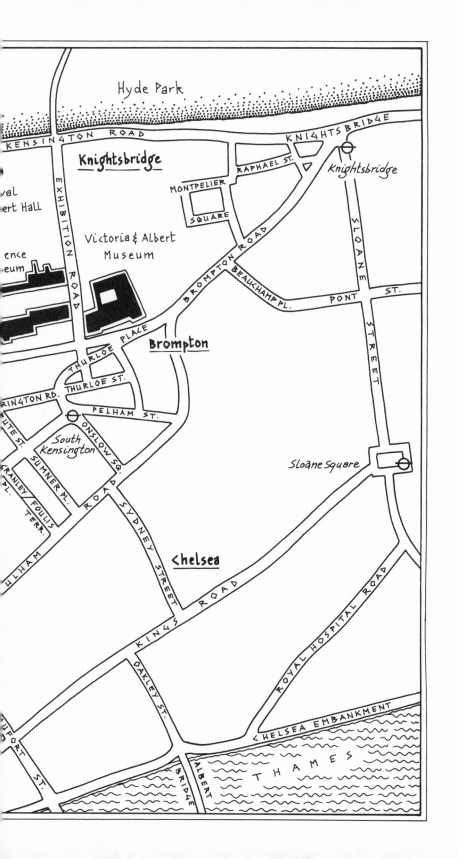

SW5 ✤ EARL'S COURT

Earl's Court is often called "kangaroo court" because it serves as the unofficial headquarters of England's Australian community. It is also a backpacker's heaven and hangout, thanks to the many low-priced (and low-quality in most cases) hotels and B & Bs. It is a dicey area at night, so watch out. There is a huge convention center and several exhibition halls here, but unless you are doing business there, this is not a top-choice area for most tourists . . . unless economy is your primary issue.

RESTAURANTS

RESTAURANTS SW5

Benjy's
157 Earl's Court Road, SW5

TELEPHONE
071-373-0245

TUBE
Earl's Court

OPEN
Daily

CLOSED
Holidays

HOURS
Continuous service
7 A.M.–9 P.M.

RESERVATIONS
Not accepted

CREDIT CARDS
None

PRICES
À la Carte: £2.50–6

VAT/SERVICE
Service discretionary

MISCELLANEOUS
Unlicensed

Benjy's claim to fame is breakfast, served day and night in a utilitarian coffee shop filled with a clientele of colorful poor and cash-strapped international Cheap Eaters. If you want to send your cholesterol level into overdrive and max out your fat gram allowance for the next two months, eat one of Benjy's breakfasts. More specifically, gorge on the Builder Breakfast. For about £3.50, you will be served a platter overflowing with bacon, two sausages, eggs, baked beans, toast, and all the coffee and tea you can consume. Lesser mortals can order smaller versions or à la carte. The menu also lists sandwiches, specials, and other dishes cooked according to the chicken-fried-steak school of culinary excellence. But remember, the *only* thing to consider here is breakfast. Two prominent signs say it all in terms of management attitude and service: "This is not the Ritz, so be prepared to share a table, you might make a friend," and "When there is a queue at the door, vacate your table promptly."

La Pappardella
253 Old Brompton Road, SW5

La Pappardella is one of London's best roll-up-your-sleeves Italian restaurants. By 9 P.M. a line waiting to get into this noisy trattoria is a common sight along Old Brompton Road. Once inside, seating is sardine style on red seats squeezed around little marble-topped tables. In the summer, the best tables are outside in the back garden where the tables have more space between them and the noise from the banter between the diners and the young waiters is less strident. Actually, this bright and colorful repartee only adds to the enjoyment of the inexpensive food that is good from first bite to last.

It is important to go easy with the appetizers and not be tempted to fill up before anything else arrives at the table. Begin with a light choice, say a *crostino saporito,* fried bread topped with mozzarella cheese and tomato sauce, or the grilled sardines with a splash of fresh lemon. All the familiar pastas are here, from *spaghetti al pesto* to lasagna, and all are made right here daily. One to remember is the *all'avocado,* a delicious combination of homemade thin green and yellow noodles covered in a decadently rich fresh avocado sauce. Pizza lovers are not ignored; they have more than eighteen choices, and carnivores over twenty preparations of veal, beef, and chicken. Portions are all oversized to begin with, but if you are feeling Herculean, larger helpings are always available. By the time you get to dessert, a scoop of ice cream or sorbet may be all you will be able to fit in. That is too bad, because the Pappardella Surprise, a mountain of whipped cream covered with fresh strawberries, almonds, macaroons, and liqueur is something else for sure.

Noorjahan
2a Bina Gardens, SW5

Where to go for some reliable Indian food? One choice is Noorjahan, a neighborhood favorite in an area that sports several restaurants featuring food from the subcontinent. Delicious tandoori chicken and

TELEPHONE
071-373-7777

TUBE
Earl's Court

OPEN
Daily for lunch and dinner

CLOSED
Holidays

HOURS
Lunch: noon–3 P.M.
Dinner: 6:30 P.M.–midnight

RESERVATIONS
Essential for dinner

CREDIT CARDS
AE, MC, V

PRICES
À la Carte: £9–17

VAT/SERVICE
Service discretionary

TELEPHONE
071-373-6522
TUBE
Gloucester Road or South
Kensington, both long walks
OPEN
Daily for lunch and dinner
CLOSED
3 days at Christmas, some
holidays
HOURS
Lunch: noon–2:45 P.M.
Dinner: 6–11:45 P.M.
RESERVATIONS
Suggested
CREDIT CARDS
AE, DC, MC, V
PRICES
À la Carte: £10–12
VAT/SERVICE
10% service added to bill;
£6.50 minimum
MISCELLANEOUS
Takeaway

lamb, plus a wide variety of curries headline the menu. If you are a beginner with Indian food, order the chicken *tikka masala,* one of the chef's specialties. Tandoori, or *tikka,* is a staple of northern Indian cooking. The meat, usually lamb or chicken, has been marinated in herbs and cooked in a *tandoor*—an Indian clay oven—which cooks the meat quickly, sealing in the juices and leaving the outside crisp. Noorjahan's version is cooked with ground almonds and cashews, fresh cream, yogurt, and mild spices. Add a vegetable, rice, and *nan*—the puffy, chewy Indian bread also cooked in the *tandoor*—and you will be all set. Old India hands will want to try one of the fourteen curries ranging from mild to explosive or one of the sweet and sour prawn dishes.

The service is always polite and helpful in explaining each dish, the food dependable time after time, and the mauve-colored dining room is simple, yet attractive, especially in the evening when the candles are lit. It all adds up to a nice dining combination if you like Indian food.

SW7 ✤ SOUTH KENSINGTON

South Kensington is a fashionable residential neighborhood with many nice hotels and restaurants. The Victoria and Albert Museum is one of the world's greatest museums of decorative art. Plan to spend some time here: the museum covers 100 acres. Also here is the Science Museum, Natural History Museum, and Royal Albert Hall.

PUBS SW7

King George IV
44 Montpelier Square, SW7

The King George IV is on one of London's prettiest squares in a neighborhood we all would live in if we could afford it. It is worth a visit if only to admire the surrounding townhouses, which look like cover subjects for *Architectural Digest*. It is only a few minutes by foot to Harrods and the bustle of Knightsbridge shopping, but this friendly Georgian pub seems miles away. You can sit outside or in, where there is a comfortable bar area with a roaring fire. A chalkboard menu lists all the usual sandwiches, hot dishes, salads, and daily specials one finds in most pubs. In addition, you can order seafood plates, nachos, or the Brompton Burger, a 6-oz. pure beef burger covered with cheese, bacon, mushrooms, onions, lettuce, and tomatoes and served with french

TELEPHONE
071-589-1016

TUBE
Knightsbridge

OPEN
Daily

CLOSED
Some holidays, call to check

HOURS
Mon–Sat 11 A.M.–3 P.M, 5–1 P.M.; Sun noon–3 P.M., 5–10:30 P.M. Food service: lunch noon–2:45 P.M., dinner 6–9 P.M., cold food & sandwiches No meals served Sat evening

RESERVATIONS
Not accepted

CREDIT CARDS
AE, DC, MC, V

fries. If you are in the mood for dessert, check the Blonde Bombshell, chocolate fudge cake with white chocolate frosting and white chocolate mousse inside. If that isn't enough, there is the Cheesequake, a chocolate brownie with cheesecake filling topped with another brownie and hot or cold toffee sauce. Weight Watchers didn't design these, but believe me, they are *good* even if they do send spasms of guilt through you.

Zetland Arms
2 Bute Street and Old Brompton Road, SW7

TELEPHONE
071-589-3813
TUBE
South Kensington
OPEN
Daily
CLOSED
Christmas and Easter
HOURS
Continuous food service
Mon–Sat 9 A.M.–10 P.M.,
Sun 10 A.M.–10:30 P.M.
RESERVATIONS
Not accepted
CREDIT CARDS
AE, DC, MC, V
PRICES
À la Carte: £5–7
VAT/SERVICE
Service discretionary

PRICES
À la Carte: £4–6
VAT/SERVICE
No service charged or expected

Offering breakfast, lunch, and dinner, the Zetland Arms is a good pub stop for a cheap, fast British snack or meal. Keep it in mind if you are en route to or from Christie's auction rooms on Old Brompton Road or visiting any of the museums in Kensington (the Victoria and Albert, Geological, Science, or Natural History). The menu contains the usual pub grub and while it is not the finest food you will eat in London, it is filling and very typical. The hot dishes and meat pies are homemade and the steaks cooked to order. If only one of you wants a beer and the other wants a banana split, both are possible. The crew is friendly and the pub is predictably busy most of the time, especially on warm days when all the outside wooden tables and benches are filled with young beer drinkers ogling the passersby.

RESTAURANTS SW7

Bistrot 190
190 Queensgate, SW7

TELEPHONE
071-581-5666
TUBE
Gloucester Road (taxi is better)
OPEN
Daily
CLOSED
Holidays

Bistrot 190 is full of pizzazz, partly because of the way it is put together. Bare floors dotted with tiny marble tables closely packed in a room bedecked with great prints and paintings, old mirrors, and garlands of flowers set the stage for this bustling spot. It is always filled to overflowing with a classy crowd that includes many London chefs in to sample owner Antony Worrall-Thompson's latest dishes. Bistrot

190 is the offspring of his more expensive Queensgate 190, which is in the basement of the Gore Hotel (see *Cheap Sleeps in London*). Worrall-Thompson describes his Bistrot menu as "Mediterranean. That means lots of grills and olive oil. It is sunny homecooking." The à la carte menu changes seasonally and displays a fondness for unusual combinations. To begin, order the basket of country breads with olives and tapenade. Then have a light appetizer such as chèvre on roasted celeriac or a chilled gazpacho, then settle into a dinner that may include a field mushroom risotto with wild garlic Parmesan. Other top picks could be chargrilled duck confit with braised endive, mash, and quince marmalade, or roast rabbit stuffed with spinach and served with lentils and mustard sauce. For dessert, the lemon tart is always on and is the top contender. You can't make reservations unless you are staying in the Gore Hotel, so arrive early or be prepared to wait up to one hour. Hope when you are seated that you can avoid the central tables on the main flight path of the wait staff, who despite their busy appearance, provide lackluster service once the rush is on.

HOURS
Lunch: Mon–Fri noon–3 P.M., 3–6 P.M.; Sat continuous service noon–12:30 A.M.; Sun noon–6 P.M. Dinner: Sun–Fri 6–11:30 P.M., Sat until 12:30 A.M.

RESERVATIONS
Not accepted

CREDIT CARDS
AE, DC, MC, V

PRICES
À la Carte: £15–20
Set Price: Afternoon 3–6 P.M., £8.50; Sun lunch, £15

VAT/SERVICE
Service discretionary

The Chanterelle
119 Old Brompton Road, SW7

The food, the setting, and the clientele are stylish at The Chanterelle, a smart restaurant on Old Brompton Road in fashionable Kensington. There is no à la carte, but the set menus change monthly for dinner and weekly for lunch. They offer interesting and imaginative meals along classic lines with at least five or six choices for each course. The service is friendly and attentive, without being overbearing. When ordering, stay with what has to be prepared to order, such as grilled fish, steak, or Toulouse sausages and pass on things that have contrived sauces or that can be made too far ahead and tend to dry out in a holding oven. The desserts are excellent, featuring cakes, mousses, ice cream, or sorbet. The wine list plays it safe with standard selections that are in keeping with the menu offerings. Because the price is so

TELEPHONE
071-373-5522

TUBE
Gloucester Road or South Kensington (a long walk; take a taxi)

OPEN
Daily for lunch and dinner

CLOSED
4 days at Christmas

HOURS
Lunch: noon–2:30 P.M.
Dinner: 7–11:30 P.M.

RESERVATIONS
Absolutely essential

CREDIT CARDS
AE, DC, MC, V

PRICES
Set price: Lunch, £12.50; Dinner, £21.50

VAT/SERVICE
Service discretionary

reasonable for this expensive area, every table is filled for both lunch and dinner, making booking at least one day ahead essential.

Chicago Rib Shack
1 Raphael Street, SW7

TELEPHONE
071-581-5595
TUBE
Knightsbridge
OPEN
Daily
CLOSED
Christmas
HOURS
Continuous service
Mon–Sat
11:45 A.M.–11:45 P.M.,
Sun noon–11 P.M.
RESERVATIONS
No reservations accepted on
Sat, otherwise accepted for
6 or more
CREDIT CARDS
AE, DC, MC, V
PRICES
À la Carte: £9–12
VAT/SERVICE
10% service added for 8 or
more, otherwise discretionary

American Bob Payton has made a fortune bringing American know-how and expertise to the restaurant business in London (see Salsa!, page 104, and The Criterion, page 32). Having met homesick Americans' and trendy Londoners' needs for deep-dish pizza and barbecued ribs and chicken, using only American recipes, and providing service by a preppie staff, his restaurants are hits even before they open. The Chicago Rib Shack in Knightsbridge near Harrods is no exception. Word has it that Princess Di has been in for a plate of Bob's tender baby back ribs. All the meats are smoked over apple wood in ovens especially imported to give the real taste of American barbecued meats. The rack of ribs is enough for a small family. Order the half-portion unless you are a fullback for the Chicago Bears. The combination platter with ribs, chicken, and barbecued beef is a good one to share along with an order of outstanding stuffed potato skins, overflowing with melted cheese and sour cream.

The desserts all sound and look great, but the chocolate cheesecake served with whipped cream and toasted almonds is the one to order, if you can get that far. The house wine is French or Californian, the beer American, and the cocktails something else.

Daquise
20 Thurloe Street, SW7

TELEPHONE
071-589-6117
TUBE
South Kensington
OPEN
Daily
CLOSED
Christmas

If you have been to Eastern Europe, you will recognize Daquise immediately for its front window crowded with green plants and the well-worn path down the center aisle of a room lined with booths and Formica-topped tables. During the morning and at teatime, this well-loved Polish gathering spot operates as a cafe where you will see a cross-section of families with small children, toothless pensioners, and dignified Polish émigrés sharing memories over glasses of steaming tea. If you arrive for lunch or dinner, chances are you will be seated downstairs, where the more appealing atmosphere resembles a Polish country cottage with bright table coverings and painted handicrafts scattered around the room. Order a shot or two of 100-proof vodka or a Polish beer while waiting for the robust specialties of beetroot soup, salted raw herring, boiled beef, *pierozoki* (pasta shells filled with seasoned ground meat), stuffed cabbage, and buttery homemade pastries.

Daquise is almost next door to the South Kensington tube station and handy to the museums in Kensington (Victoria and Albert, Natural History, Science, and Geological). The location, coupled with the incredibly low prices and sturdy food, makes this one restaurant no serious Cheap Eater in London can afford to miss.

HOURS
Upstairs: daily 10 A.M.–11:30 P.M., continuous service. Downstairs: Mon–Fri noon–3 P.M., 5:30–11:30 P.M. Sat and Sun noon–11:30 P.M.

RESERVATIONS
Not necessary

CREDIT CARDS
None

PRICES
À la Carte: £5–9
Set Price: Lunch £6.50, 2 courses with mashed potatoes, vegetable, and coffee or tea

VAT/SERVICE
Service discretionary

Gilbert's

2 Exhibition Road, SW7

Gilbert's is one of those wonderful hidden restaurants you always hope to find and seldom do. It is small, with only sixteen tables, around the corner from the South Kensington tube station. American co-owner Anne Wregg welcomes guests and her partner Julia Chalkey performs wonders in the kitchen, turning out confident adaptations of traditional French *bonne maman* food. A basket of homemade bread and a tub of sweet butter along with a bowl of assorted olives are brought to your table while you decide what to order. There are only two set menus, with choices that change every two weeks based on the freshest meat, fish, and produce of the season. Late winter starters might be a beet and orange soup or a broccoli salad with roasted peppers, capers, and olives. For a small supplement, the garlic soufflé is worth not only the little extra money, but the twenty minutes it takes to bake. To make sure no one leaves any room to spare, main courses are garnished with three fresh vegetables, potatoes, or a salad. The set menus do not include desserts, which are a tour de

TELEPHONE
071-589-8947

TUBE
South Kensington

OPEN
Mon–Fri lunch, Mon–Sat dinner

CLOSED
Sat lunch, Sun, holidays

HOURS
Lunch: Mon–Fri 12:30–2 P.M.
Dinner: Mon–Sat 7–10:15 P.M.

RESERVATIONS
Essential

CREDIT CARDS
AE, DC, MC, V

PRICES
Set Price: Lunch £13, 2 courses and coffee; dinner £15, 2 courses and coffee; Desserts £5 extra

VAT/SERVICE
12½% service charged for parties of 6 or more, otherwise discretionary

force, especially the chocolate tipsy cake, a creamy dark chocolate mousse floating on a bed of vanilla custard and garnished with fresh raspberries. A plate of rich, homemade fudge served with the after-dinner coffee will tempt you to buy a box to take with you. Because Gilbert's offers the qualities most people look for in a restaurant, it is always full, making reservations vital, as far in advance as possible.

Khobkhun
9a Gloucester Road, SW7

TELEPHONE
071-581-9514

TUBE
Gloucester Road

OPEN
Daily for lunch and dinner

CLOSED
Sun, holidays

HOURS
Lunch: noon–3 P.M.
Dinner: 6–11 P.M.

RESERVATIONS
Not necessary

CREDIT CARDS
MC, V

PRICES
À la Carte: £5–9
Set Price: £12.50–16.50, 3 courses, includes coffee or tea

VAT/SERVICE
10% service added to bill

MISCELLANEOUS
Takeaway

If you like different food and are not afraid to experiment, consider the exceptionally fine value offered at Khobkhun. I was first attracted to this narrow Thai restaurant because it looked so fresh and clean, with spring flowers in the window box outside and pretty blue and white dishes on linen-covered tablecloths inside. The best sign of all was the lunch crowd: all Thais. They obviously were on to something I needed to know more about. The Thais have a reputation for preparing hot and spicy food guaranteed to require potent antacid if caution and common sense are not exercised. The food here manages to capture the tastes, aromas, and delicacy of this cuisine without sacrificing Western digestion at the same time.

The menu, with over sixty selections, makes for tantalizing reading. Those with cast-iron stomachs can order the stir-fried squid with garlic and chilies or the fried pomfret (white fish) with a fiery sauce. The most popular dish, and certainly one of the best, is surprisingly mild and almost soothing. It is No. 72, fried noodles "Siam Style." It comes beautifully arranged on a tray with side dishes of prawns, eggs, bean sprouts, peanuts, and fried noodles. It is not only pleasing to look at, but delightful to eat. It addition to the à la carte choices, there are two set menus, but the best way to go here is to order individually according to your own taste.

Luigi Malone's
73 Old Brompton Road, SW7

Luigi Malone's is a great haunt for those seeking a vivacious and occasionally hectic atmosphere. Old gas lamps, ceiling fans, yellowed walls, wooden tables and chairs, and an assortment of semi-antique curiosities provide the decor for this American-style restaurant and bar. The far-reaching menu offers plenty to please everyone from vegetarians to Mexican foodies suffering the pangs of salsa withdrawal. Nachos, baby back ribs, chargrilled 8-oz. pure beef hamburgers with all the trimmings, stir fries, pizzas, pastas, sandwiches, steak and chicken fajitas, salads, and fattening desserts keep the diners definitely well fed. Monday through Friday from 11:30 A.M. to 3 P.M. there are daily lunch specials that include a third of a bottle of wine, the cocktail of your choice, or a beer. Happy hour between 3 and 6:30 P.M. overflows with thirty-something professionals in to lap up beer, wine, and crazy cocktails at reduced prices. Whenever you go, you are bound to have a good time and eat well in the bargain.

TELEPHONE
071-584-4323

TUBE
South Kensington

OPEN
Daily

CLOSED
Christmas

HOURS
Continuous service
11:30 A.M.–11:30 P.M.

RESERVATIONS
Not necessary

CREDIT CARDS
AE, MC, V

PRICES
À la Carte: £10–15

SET PRICES
Lunch £5–6, one course and wine, cocktail, or beer; dinner £7, one course

VAT/SERVICE
Discretionary until 6 P.M., then 12½% service added to bill

Texas Lone Star Saloon
154 Gloucester Road, SW7

See Texas Lone Star Saloon, page 63, for description.

TELEPHONE: 071-370-5625
TUBE: Gloucester Road
OPEN: Daily
CLOSED: Christmas
HOURS: Continuous service, Mon–Wed noon–11:30 P.M., Thurs–Sat noon–12:15 A.M., Sun and holidays noon–11:15 P.M.
RESERVATIONS: Essential after 7 P.M., but not accepted Fri or Sat night
CREDIT CARDS: None
PRICES: À la Carte: £4–11
VAT/SERVICE: 10% service charge
MISCELLANEOUS: Takeaway; minimum charge £4 after 7 P.M.; live music Mon–Sat nights; sweatshirts and T-shirts for sale

SW10 ✤ WEST BROMPTON

West Brompton is mainly a residential area.

RESTAURANTS

RESTAURANTS SW10

Chelsea Bun Diner
9a Limerston Street, SW10

TELEPHONE
071-352-3635

TUBE
Sloane Square (a very long walk; take bus #11, #19, or #31)

OPEN
Daily

CLOSED
Christmas

HOURS
Continuous service
7 A.M.–11:30 P.M.

RESERVATIONS
Not accepted

CREDIT CARDS
None

PRICES
À la Carte: £3–6

VAT/SERVICE
No service charged or expected

MISCELLANEOUS
Takeaway; unlicensed, BYOB, no corkage

Calling all Cheap Eaters in London to the Chelsea Bun Diner, which attracts hordes of bargain munchers from eighteen to eighty with its good-humored, casual ambiance, its low, low prices, and its wide-ranging menu. It has been on this site since the days of Jonathan Swift, who is reported to have bought a bun here for a penny. When you arrive, don't expect "decor" or gracious waiter service; do expect good food geared to big-league appetites, with portions that seem almost out of control. Consider the Chelsea Bun three-egg omelette, filled with ham, salami, cheese, tomato, mushrooms, two kinds of peppers, and onions, and served with chips (french fries) or a salad. It could feed three! The burgers range from regular to "all the way," with ham, egg, cheese, lettuce, and tomato sandwiched with a 100-percent beef patty. This comes with fries, a mixed salad, and relishes.

Breakfast served all day; potatoes stuffed, baked, fried, or mashed; tacos; pasta; meat pies; more than thirty sandwiches; and the famed Chelsea Buns (sticky cinnamon rolls packed with raisins and topped with cinnamon-sugar) keep the hard metal chairs filled from dawn until almost midnight. Don't have time to sit down and eat? Don't worry; they will prepare anything to go and even charge you less if you take it with you.

Ed's Easy Diner
335 Fulham Road, SW10

See Ed's Easy Diner, page 35, for description. All other information is the same.

TELEPHONE: 071-352-1952
TUBE: Sloane Square, then #19 bus

Parson's Restaurant
311 Fulham Road, SW10

Long a dining institution on Fulham Road, Parson's is a haven for families on budgets, young people on first dates, and tired tourists looking for easy food answers. The inside is bright and breezy, with lots of brass, glass, and wood and a staff sporting T-shirts and jeans. The formula-type food is instantly recognizable as the "chain-restaurant-in-the-mall" variety, with a children's menu, salads, sandwiches, and a host of daily specials, pastas, and hamburgers.

The two best deals to remember here are spaghetti and hamburgers. Often subtitled "The Old Spaghetti Factory," Parson's serves spaghetti with garlic bread and offers free second helpings, with your choice of three sauces: meat, tomato, or pesto, or a combination of all three. While the spaghetti is great if you want to go into carbohydrate overdrive, the half-pound all beef hamburgers with toppings of cheese, chili, barbecue sauce, guacamole, tomato, lettuce, and relish are other superman alternatives. The wine list is something you would expect to see in a far fancier spot. Prices for the wines from France, Australia, Chile, California, and Italy are reasonable and the nice thing is you can order just a glass of the really good stuff . . . not only of the plebeian house wine, as is usually the case.

TELEPHONE
071-352-0651

TUBE
South Kensington

OPEN
Daily

CLOSED
Christmas

HOURS
Continuous service
Mon–Sat noon–1 A.M., last order midnight
Sun 12:30 P.M.–1 A.M.

RESERVATIONS
Not necessary

CREDIT CARDS
AE, DC, MC, V

PRICES
À la Carte: £5–9

VAT/SERVICE
10% service charge for 6 or more, otherwise discretionary

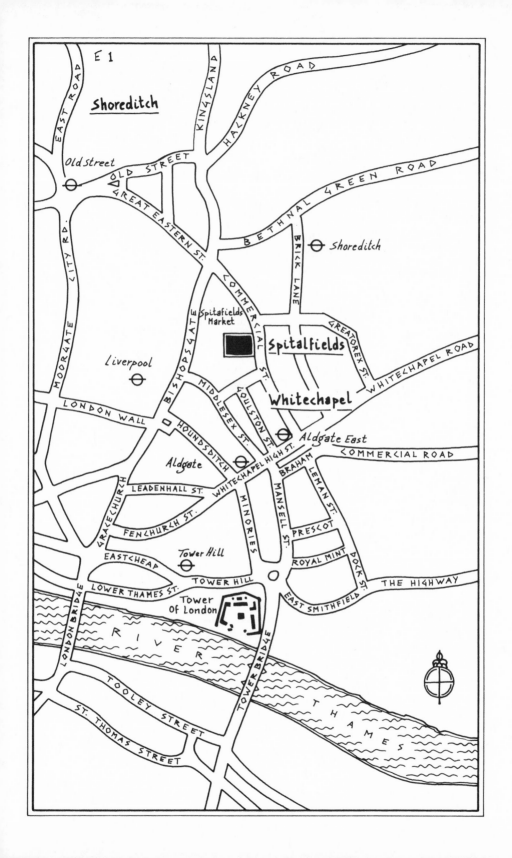

E1 ✤ SPITALFIELDS MARKET, WHITECHAPEL

Spitalfields refers both to the area and to the wholesale market that handles fruit, vegetables, and flowers. The market covers five acres to the east of Liverpool Street Station, on a site that was once a Roman burial ground. It opens weekdays around 5 A.M. and by 9:30 A.M. most of the selling is finished.

Whitechapel is a section of London's East End. On Whitechapel High Street, visit the Whitechapel Art Gallery, which has achieved fame for the excellence of its frequent exhibitions and contributions to the cultural life of the East End.

RESTAURANTS

RESTAURANTS E1

Bloom's
90 Whitechapel High Street, E1

You don't have to be Jewish to like Bloom's. Family owned, family run, and family loved, it is a well-known fixture in London's East End near Petticoat Lane Market. It is a legacy to the Jewish refugees who settled in the East End, and many regulars who remember those leaner days are still coming for the strictly kosher soul food served by polite oldtimers wearing white jackets and black trousers. For authenticity, start with calf's-foot jelly, chopped liver, or a cabbage borscht. There are many main courses, but the favorites are the hot salt beef (corned beef), homemade wurst and eggs, or the *gedempte,* meatballs that have been marinated, then braised. Whatever you do, order the potato *latkes* (potato pancakes) and the *tsimmis* (sweet carrot dumplings) to go with your meal. The warm *lockshen,* pudding made with clear thin noodles and golden raisins and dusted with sugar, is a dessert that delivers more than you imagine. Try it and you will see: it's great.

TELEPHONE
071-247-6001

TUBE
Aldgate East

OPEN
Sun–Fri

CLOSED
Sat and Jewish holidays

HOURS
Continuous service
Sun–Thurs noon–9:30 P. M.,
Fri noon–3 P.M.

RESERVATIONS
For Sun lunch

CREDIT CARDS
AE, MC, V

PRICES
À la Carte: £12–16

VAT/SERVICE
Service discretionary

MISCELLANEOUS
Rabbi and religious supervisor oversee kosher food preparation; takeaway

There is a convenient takeaway counter at the front entrance. Book ahead for Sunday lunch and recuperate from a morning battling the crowds at Petticoat Lane Market. This is the best time to enjoy the filling food and to drink kosher Israeli wines in an atmosphere that is as real as it is going to get.

Dino's Grill & Restaurant
76 Commercial Street, E1

TELEPHONE
071-247-6097
TUBE
Aldgate East or Liverpool
OPEN
Mon–Fri, Sun
CLOSED
Sat, Sun afternoon, holidays
HOURS
Continuous service
Grill: Mon–Fri 5 A.M.–5 P. M.,
Sun 7 A.M.–2 P.M. Restaurant:
Lunch only 11 A.M.–3:30 P.M.
RESERVATIONS
Not necessary
CREDIT CARDS
None
PRICES
À la Carte: Grill, £3.50–6;
restaurant, £10–11
VAT/SERVICE
Grill, no service charged or
expected; restaurant,
discretionary
MISCELLANEOUS
Takeaway

Dino Bragoli and his righthand gal Peggy have been running this down-home Cheap Eats outpost since the early sixties. It is a good, clean bet in an eyebrow-raising area around the Spitalfields wholesale fruit and vegetable market and Petticoat Lane. The emphasis is on back-to-basics food, the stuff we all loved before sundried tomatoes, chèvre cheese, and arugula became the buzzwords for cooks on their way up. Truckers and market workers arrive at the Grill around 5 A.M. for fry-ups of eggs, beans, bacon, sausage, chips (french fries), and slabs of fried bread. If you want something lighter, order one of their famous homemade Rock Cakes, which are similar to huge, buttery scones, studded with raisins. By 11:30 A.M., regulars stream in for steak and mushroom pie, overflowing plates of pasta and grilled meats, bangers and mash (sausage and mashed potatoes), and fried fish. The special of the house is pasta *al Dino,* spaghetti with a choice of sauces, topped with ham and/or a fried egg with a Parmesan cheese topping and run under the broiler. Let's just say it is different. Desserts? This is a meat and potatoes place, so desserts are not part of the main attraction.

In an effort to attract a wider clientele, the downstairs red brick basement has been turned into a separate restaurant with its own entrance. It has become a regular lunchtime haunt for local office workers who enjoy the low-key atmosphere and good Italian grub. The menu provides no surprises and no shocks either with its standard fare of pastas, chicken, and veal dishes and creamy, rich desserts.

Kosher Luncheon Club
Morris Kasler Hall, 13 Greatorex Street, E1

During the eighteenth century, Jewish refugees came to London in large numbers, gravitating to the East End. Eating houses were set up to feed them, many of whom arrived with only the clothes on their backs. The Kosher Luncheon Club is the last of these eating houses. The atmosphere in the large dining room looks like a movie set with colorful extras sitting at the white linen-covered tables, each with a number and a set of condiments in the center. You won't have to look far to see clusters of rabbis, old men with gray beards hanging to their chests, and pensioners who have eaten at the same table for years. The service is as down-to-earth as the food and its surroundings. If the waitress doesn't know you, after a few visits they make sure they do. In fact, if a regular does not come in for a day or two, someone from the restaurant goes to check up on them and takes meals to them if necessary. The emphasis is on fish and all the food is strictly kosher, with portions so big they can almost accommodate two. The pickled herring is delicious and so is the fried gefilte fish. The lemon sole is moist and flavorful and the *latkes*—potato pancakes—just like you wished your mother would still make. For dessert, the lockshen pudding or apple pie stand out from the bland custard or stewed prunes.

TELEPHONE
071-247-0039

TUBE
Aldgate East

OPEN
Sun–Fri

CLOSED
Sat, Jewish holidays, every evening

HOURS
Lunch: noon–3 P.M.
Dinner: closed

RESERVATIONS
Preferred, especially on Sunday

CREDIT CARDS
None

PRICES
A la carte: £7–10

VAT/SERVICE
50p "membership" charge per person; service discretionary

MISCELLANEOUS
Unlicensed

Tubby Isaac's
Goulston Street near Aldgate East tube station, E1

Almost since the turn of the century, the Isaac family has been selling jellied eels, rollmops (rolled-up pickled herring), mussels, oysters, fresh boiled crabs, prawns, cockles, and sea snails from a red and white cart near the Aldgate East tube station. Their fast food stand-up specialty is jellied eels, which is an acquired taste that takes a great deal of determination and practice. It is included here as a very British Cheap Eat appealing only to those eager to collect cuisine experiences. How do you eat a jellied eel,

TELEPHONE
None

TUBE
Aldgate East

OPEN
Daily

CLOSED
Main Jewish holidays, Christmas

HOURS
Continuous service
11 A.M.–11 P.M.

RESERVATIONS
Not accepted

CREDIT CARDS
None

PRICES
À la Carte: £1.50–4

VAT/SERVICE
No service charged or expected

MISCELLANEOUS
Not a restaurant—a pushcart;
takeaway and catering

which is boiled, then cut up and served in its own gelatinous consommé in a styrofoam cup? *Very* carefully. As anyone at Tubby Isaac's will tell you, the proper way to eat a jellied eel is to put a whole piece into your mouth, taking care to chew around the bone in the center. The lemon-colored jellied consommé in which the eels are served is helped by heavy doses of chili vinegar and chunks of bread from the bread bin.

Can't decide what to serve at your next party? Impress your friends with a spread from Tubby's— they cater!

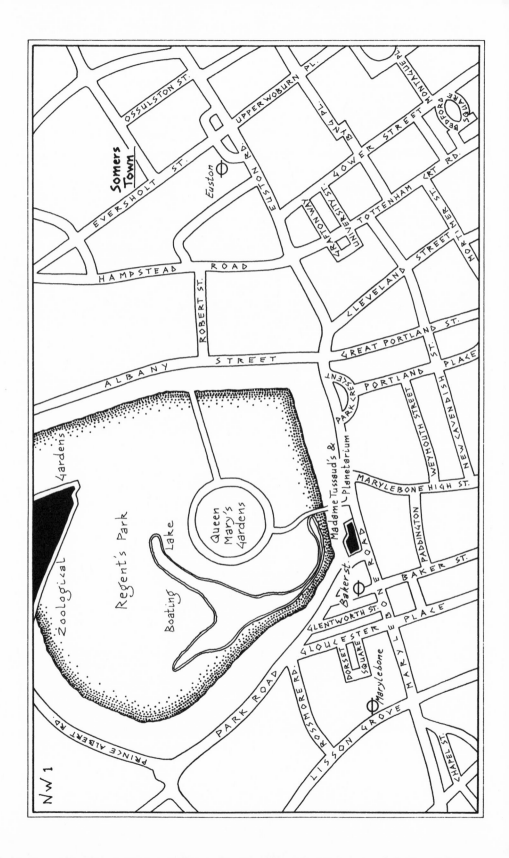

NW1 ✤ REGENT'S PARK, ST. MARYLEBONE CHURCH

Regent's Park was once Henry VIII's hunting forest and later provided London with hay and diary produce. Today, there is a boating lake, Queen Mary's Gardens, an open-air theater where Shakespeare is performed, and the London Planetarium. Also close by is Madame Tussaud's, overrated and packed, requiring lines lasting two to three hours during peak tourist season.

Since the fourteen hundreds, a church has stood on the site where the present St. Marylebone Church is now. This church was built in 1813 by Thomas Hardwick. It was there that Robert Browning married Elizabeth Barrett.

RESTAURANTS NW1

Great Nepalese
48 Eversholt Street, NW1

TELEPHONE
071-388-6737, 071-388-5935

TUBE
Euston

OPEN
Daily

CLOSED
Christmas

HOURS
Noon–2:45 P.M., 6–11:45 P.M.

RESERVATIONS
Preferred

CREDIT CARDS
AE, DC, MC, V

PRICES
À la Carte: £10–15
Set Price: Lunch £6.50,
£11.50; dinner £11.50; all
include 3 courses and beverage

VAT/SERVICE
10% service added to bill

The Great Nepalese gets my vote as one of the better Indian dining experiences in London. The outside is unremarkable. The inside, however, is pleasing with hand-carved wooden screens, a teak ceiling, and Nepalese masks and painted baskets on the walls.

A first visit usually means many returns to this friendly place, run by Gopal Manandbar and his two sons. Their service is professional, courteous, and helpful. They will suggest a menu for the uninitiated, selecting for taste, interest, and price. Basically, all the food is reasonable and the ingredients of high quality. There are many mild dishes and the kitchen will always adjust seasonings to suit a customer's taste. Specialties include tandoori dishes, curries made with duck, lamb, mutton, and pork. For dessert, try the homemade mango sherbert or the rice pudding. The best approach is to go with a group of four or more so you can sample a variety of dishes from the extensive menu.

St. Marylebone Cafe
17 Marylebone Road, St. Marylebone Church, NW1

Bill Sewell has a hit on his hands at The Place Below (see page 173). Recently, he opened this second church cafe venture, located across from Madame Tussaud's famous wax museum. This cafe is smaller and offers light breakfasts and canteen lunches to a growing audience eager to experience a variety of vegetarian dishes cooked with flair. Small and large salads showcase treats such as tabouli, carrot and orange, or broccoli and sweet corn. Handcrafted sandwiches filled with Stilton cheese and mango chutney or banana and peanut butter on wholemeal bread cost less than a burger at the corner fast food stop. Also available are soups, filled potatoes, several hot dishes plus the usual high-calorie, diet-defying desserts. The cafe is downstairs in the church in a white arched room that has changing art displays by local artists, and tables to share. It is a welcome oasis if you are anywhere nearby and are hungry when they are open.

TELEPHONE
071-935-6374

TUBE
Baker Street

OPEN
Mon–Fri

CLOSED
Evenings, Sat, Sun, holidays

HOURS
Continuous service
8:30 A.M.–3 P.M.

RESERVATIONS
Not accepted

CREDIT CARDS
None

PRICES
À la Carte: £4–6

VAT/SERVICE
No service charged or expected

MISCELLANEOUS
Takeaway; unlicensed, no BYOB

WINE BARS NW1

Cafe Suze
1 Glentworth Street, NW1

Cafe Suze is a pleasant wine bar and restaurant celebrating the food and drink of New Zealand. Instead of the traditional slice of limp quiche, boring salad, or lukewarm casserole, you can have anything from a platter of dips with fresh crudités and hot pita bread to a hearty beef stew, or their specialty, shelled green mussels in a creamy wine sauce, accompanied by an interesting vintage of red or white wine from New Zealand, France, Spain, or Alsace. It is a smart address to remember when you are in the mood for a quick meal or a snack on the run and want more than just a sandwich.

TELEPHONE
071-486-8216

TUBE
Marylebone

OPEN
Mon–Fri

CLOSED
Sat, Sun, holidays

HOURS
Continuous service
11 A.M.–11 P.M.

RESERVATIONS
Not necessary

CREDIT CARDS
AE, MC, V

PRICES
À la Carte: £5–10

VAT/SERVICE
Service discretionary

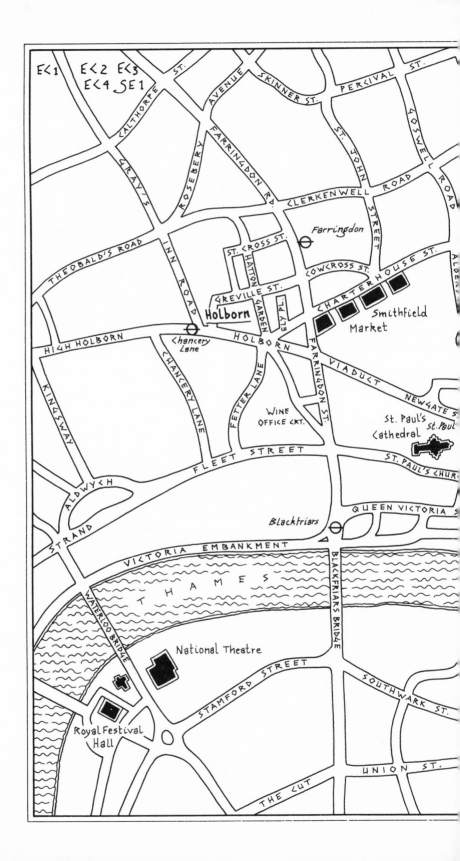

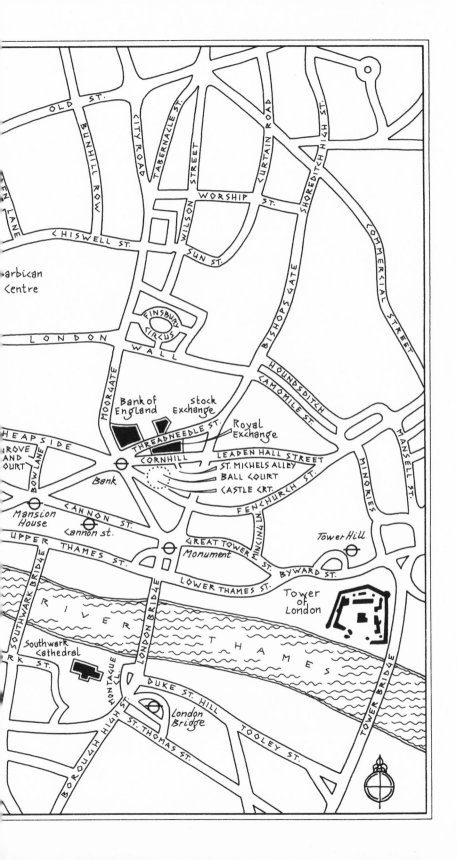

EC1 ✤ SMITHFIELD MARKET

Smithfield Market has been in operation since the twelfth century. It is London's main wholesale meat market and its annual turnover of 200,000 tons of goods makes it one of the largest meat and poultry markets in the world.

PUBS EC1

Fox & Anchor
115 Charterhouse Street, EC1

TELEPHONE
071-253-4838

TUBE
Farringdon

OPEN
Mon–Fri

CLOSED
Sat afternoon, Sun, holidays; the pub is open Mon–Fri from 6 A.M.–10 P.M., Sat 8 A.M.–1 P.M.

HOURS
Breakfast: Mon–Fri 7–10:30 A.M., Sat 8-10 A.M. Lunch: noon–2:30 P. M., Sat noon–1 P.M. Dinner: No food available after 2:30 P.M.

RESERVATIONS
Only if you want the mixed grill for breakfast, must call ahead to order

CREDIT CARDS
MC, V

The food served at the Fox & Anchor is a carnivore's dream and a cholesterol nightmare. The record for London's most gigantic breakfast stands unbroken at this pub, less than a block from the Smithfield Market (the world's largest wholesale meat market). As you can imagine, the market workers demand the best-quality meat and the Fox & Anchor serves it to them in abundance every weekday. The pub opens at 6 A.M. for workers to have an eye-opening pint or two before tucking into the morning repast, which is served from 7–10:30 A.M. Insiders generally ignore the menu and order the house favorite, which is not listed: the mixed grill. (If you want this, you must call ahead to order it.) Only hard-core meat lovers need apply for this gargantuan feast, which includes sausage, kidneys, steak, liver, black pudding, eggs, mushrooms, tomatoes, chips (french fries), and endless cups of potent coffee. If you feel you cannot do justice to the mixed grill, consider the lamb liver and kidneys or steak and eggs. If you can't bring yourself to down one of the heavy-hitting breakfasts, go for lunch and order their specialty, steak and kidney pie, a thick steak, or a large ham, cheese, tomato, or mushroom omelette. Don't pay attention to the salads, cold plates, or sandwiches—they don't measure up. This is a place where the protein-rich food is the *only* thing to order.

In 1992 the pub underwent a desperately needed renovation and is now restored to its original Victorian splendor. The chef still stands at the end of the bar in an open kitchen grilling the meats, which are served by smiling waitresses who know everyone. While the price tag for breakfast may seem high, you will actually save money because you won't need to eat for the rest of the day.

PRICES
À la Carte: £8–15

VAT/SERVICE
Service discretionary

Ye Old Mitre Tavern
1 Ely Place, EC1

Look for the old street lamp that marks the entrance to Ely Court, a narrow passageway linking Ely Place and Hatton Garden, a street lined with London's jewelry traders. In 1546, when the Bishops of Ely were lords over this part of London, the Mitre Tavern was built for their palace servants. Rebuilt in the late eighteenth century, its oak-paneled rooms are filled with original antiques and relics dating back to the origins of the pub. In the corner of the bar is the preserved trunk of a cherry tree that grew on the boundary between the Bishop of Ely's land and that leased to Sir Christopher Hatton, who was a great favorite of Queen Elizabeth I. In fact, she once danced the maypole around this tree. During the English Civil War, the tavern was used as a prison and a hospital, but judging from its size, it could only have held a handful of prisoners and patients. Today, the pub is popular with local office workers who treat it as their private club, and enjoy sitting and relaxing in a quiet atmosphere free from loud music or banging pinball machines. There is no hot food served, but it is a worthwhile stop for a freshly made sandwich and a pint of ale to savor one of London's most charming and authentic pubs.

TELEPHONE
071-405-4751

TUBE
Farringdon or Chancery Lane

OPEN
Mon–Fri

CLOSED
Sat, Sun, holidays

HOURS
Continuous service
11 A.M.–11 P.M.

RESERVATIONS
Not accepted

CREDIT CARDS
None

PRICES
À la Carte: £2

VAT/SERVICE
No service charged or expected

MISCELLANEOUS
Sandwiches only, no hot food

RESTAURANTS EC1

Cranks Smithfield
5 Cowcross Street, EC1

See Cranks Restaurants, page 31, for description. All other information is the same.

TELEPHONE: 071-480-4970
TUBE: Farringdon
OPEN: Mon–Fri
CLOSED: Sat, Sun, every evening, holidays
HOURS: Continuous service, Mon–Fri 7 A.M.–3 P.M.
RESERVATIONS: Not necessary

Diana's Dining Room
30 St. Cross Street, EC1

TELEPHONE
071-831-7261
TUBE
Farringdon
OPEN
Mon–Fri
CLOSED
Sat, Sun, holidays, 2 weeks at Christmas
HOURS
Continuous service Mon–Tues 8 A.M.–3:30 P. M., Wed–Fri 8 A.M.–8 P.M.
RESERVATIONS
Not accepted
CREDIT CARDS
None
PRICES
À la Carte: £4.50–8 for full meal
VAT/SERVICE
Service discretionary, minimum charge £3
MISCELLANEOUS
Takeaway

Diana's Dining Room is near the Leather Lane Market and the Hatton Garden jewelry merchants. Diana's sparkling clean spot, with thirty-six black bentwood chairs placed around marble-topped tables, is cozy and friendly. Along one wall is a collection of plates and on another a rotating show of daughter Janine's paintings. Diana does all the salads and sandwiches, her husband is in charge of the hot dishes and desserts, and Janine runs the restaurant and seats guests. Diana's salads are perfection. She offers at least ten a day, ranging from basic fresh fruit to the Middle Eastern favorite, taramosalata. The hot dish specialties include chicken and lamb shish kebabs, hot salt beef, and daily pastas. A blackboard menu lists each day's offerings and the rich desserts are all house made. If you want a lighter finish, order some of their delicious sugar- and fat-free flavored yogurt. From breakfast to teatime, everything is good, the portions are huge, and the prices are fair.

Nosherie Restaurant
12–13 Greville Street, EC1

TELEPHONE
071-242-1591
TUBE
Chancery Lane

The Nosherie Restaurant run by Esther Berner is like delis in New York used to be. For authentic Jewish food done the proper way with no shortcuts, motherly service, and budget-pleasing prices, The Nosherie is *the* place. This timeless breakfast and lunch cafe is located near the Hatton Garden jewelry merchants and has been feeding them and their families for thirty-five years. They specialize in salt beef (corned beef) and you can watch yours being sliced if you sit at the counter by the entrance. At the back are seats served by a staff of waitresses who grew up in the restaurant and have no plans to seek other work. Here a full menu is served with some regular and special items rarely seen. Just think about braised tongue with *latkes* (potato pancakes) or red cabbage, meat balls in tomato sauce with rice, boiled chicken, or wurst and eggs. To end your meal, select a piece of their famous Viennese apple strudel or cheesecake, which they make fresh each morning to keep up with the demand.

OPEN
Mon–Fri for breakfast and lunch

CLOSED
Dinner, Sat, Sun, holidays

HOURS
Continuous service
7:30 A.M.–3:30 P.M.

RESERVATIONS
Not accepted

CREDIT CARDS
None

PRICES
À la Carte: £6–11

VAT/SERVICE
Minimum charge £3.50 from noon–3 P.M.; service discretionary

The Pantry at St. Etheldreda's Church
14 Ely Place, EC1

If you find yourself shopping the stalls on Leather Lane or bargaining for diamonds in the jewelry shops along Hatton Garden, take a Cheap Eats lunch break in the oldest Catholic church in Great Britain. Built by the Bishops of Ely in 1290, it became one of London's greatest churches. It survived the great fire of 1666, but during the following century it deteriorated badly. In 1873, it was bought by the Fathers of Charity (Rosminians), making it the first medieval church in England to be restored to Roman Catholic hands. During World War II, the building was badly damaged, but through careful restoration, St. Etheldreda's is once again a busy pastoral church. One of London's oldest buildings, it is considered a fine example of Gothic architecture. Even if you don't lunch here, this is a lovely and interesting church to visit.

The Pantry, with its seven shared tables, is in the old cloisters. The nourishing boarding-school menu changes daily and is about as inexpensive as you will find in London. It would be absolutely impossible to spend more than £4 on a three-course lunch consisting of soup, roast lamb or chicken garnished with a choice of potatoes, and a vegetable or side salad, plus

TELEPHONE
071-405-1061

TUBE
Farringdon or Chancery Lane

OPEN
Mon–Fri for lunch only

CLOSED
Dinner, Sat, Sun, holidays

HOURS
11 A.M.–2 P.M.

RESERVATIONS
Not accepted

CREDIT CARDS
None

PRICES
À la Carte: £3–4

VAT/SERVICE
No service charged or expected

MISCELLANEOUS
Unlicensed. The church sponsors concerts once a month. Call for details.

a bowl of apple crumble with hot custard, and a cup of tea. Everything is made and served by sweet women, including one named Betty, who has been performing her labor of love for twenty-five years. All the diners know each other by name because most of them would never consider having their lunch any-place else. I shared my table with a man who worked nearby. He told me, "I eat here every day and if and when I retire, I shall still come here for my lunch. The food is good and it keeps me healthy." What more could anyone ask? All proceeds go to the church.

Note: Unfortunately, the church was damaged in the April 1993 bombing of the city of London. It is not known at press time when or if the Pantry will reopen, so before going please call.

Quality Chop House
94 Farringdon Road, EC1

TELEPHONE
071-837-5093
TUBE
Farringdon
OPEN
Daily
CLOSED
Sat lunch, holidays
HOURS
Lunch: Mon–Fri Noon–3 P.M.,
Sun brunch Noon–4 P.M.
Dinner: Mon–Sat
6:30 P.M.–midnight,
Sun 7–11:30 P.M.
RESERVATIONS
Essential
CREDIT CARDS
None
PRICES
A la carte: £18–22
VAT/SERVICE
Service discretionary

The Quality Chop House is a destination restaurant far afield from the basic tourist path. When you go, be sure to book a table and go by taxi. Otherwise you will find yourself on a long hike from the tube, through a part of London you won't like. The clock stopped ticking on the premises in 1869, when it first opened as a laborer's cafe. The interior is still the original, from the benches you will undoubtedly have to share, to the yellowing walls and black-and-white-tiled floor. In 1989, it was bought by Charles Fontaine, a former chef at La Caprice. Since then he has been highly praised for his fresh and simple preparations of old standards. It is important that you arrive starved and be prepared to indulge in a meat-lover's fantasy of grilled lamb chops, corned beef hash and eggs, Toulouse sausages with mash and onion gravy, or steak tartare. For daintier appetites, there is always an omelette or fresh fish. The line is long for the Sunday brunch, which features a jug of Buck's Fizzes or Bloody Marys, eggs benedict, or roast beef with all the fixings. Not planning ahead for dessert would be a serious mistake, since everything is made here from the ice cream and orange cheesecake to the comforting bread and butter pudding.

EC2 ✤ BARBICAN CENTER, THE CITY

The Barbican opened in 1984 and covers sixty acres. It is one of the most impressive and controversial buildings in London. It was built around the remaining portion of the old Roman wall as an ambitious scheme to promote The City as a residential area rather than only a place to come for work. It contains high-rise flats, shops, offices, pubs, the City of London School for Girls, the sixteenth-century church of St. Giles Cripplegate, The Museum of London, the London Symphony orchestra, and the Guildhall School of Music.

The City is an almost perfect square mile in the heart of London. During the week, The City teems with executives, office workers, and a constant rush of traffic. On the weekends and at night it becomes silent, populated by pigeons and the stray sightseer. It is the historic center of English law with Old Bailey here, and is recognized as the financial center of Europe with the Stock Exchange and the Bank of England dominating the area. It owes its lovely appearance to Sir Christopher Wren, who was the chief architect working after the Great Fire of 1666. He designed fifty-one churches to replace the eighty-nine that were destroyed.

RESTAURANTS

The Place Below   173

RESTAURANTS EC2

The Place Below at St. Mary-le-Bow
St. Mary-le-Bow Crypt, Cheapside, EC2

The Place Below is a brilliant example of how delicious vegetarian cooking really can be in the hands of a creative chef. Five years ago, Bill Sewell opened here and since opening day, has received awards and rave reviews for his meatless cuisine. The restaurant is located in the eleventh-century crypt of another of Sir Christopher Wren's masterpieces, St. Mary-le-Bow Church. Breakfast and lunch are self-service with the emphasis on quiches, soups, salads, and tempting desserts. Naturally, everything is prepared here. Special mention must go to the moist olive and garlic bread and old-fashioned lemonade. On Thursday and Friday nights, the lights are dimmed, candles lit, and charming waiters serve a set-price menu

TELEPHONE
071-329-0789

TUBE
St. Paul's

OPEN
Mon–Fri for lunch, Thur–Fri for dinner

CLOSED
Mon–Wed for dinner, Sat, Sun, holidays

HOURS
Lunch: Mon–Fri
7:30 A.M.–3 P.M.
Dinner: Thurs–Fri
6:30–9:30 P.M.

RESERVATIONS
Evenings only

CREDIT CARDS
None

PRICES
À la Carte: Lunch, £8–9,
minimum order £4
Set Price: Dinner, 3 courses
and service, £17.50; 2 courses
and service, £15.50

VAT/SERVICE
Service discretionary for lunch,
included for dinner

MISCELLANEOUS
Takeaway; unlicensed, BYOB,
no corkage

featuring a choice of two starters and two main courses with dessert extra. The changing dishes are exquisitely prepared and presented. When I was there, the offerings included butter bean, sage, and parsley soup or baby lettuce with asparagus and fresh Parmesan cheese, and for the entrée, three-mushroom tartlet (oyster, field, and shiitake) with cepe sauce, red cabbage, and celeriac and potato mash. The other choice was a red pesto pudding with a mixed-leaf and broccoli salad. The meal ended with either passion fruit ice cream, chocolate fudge cake, or rhubarb and strawberry purée.

EC3 ✤ TOWER OF LONDON

Perhaps the most famous castle in the world, the Tower of London was the largest fortress in medieval Europe and the palace and prison of English monarchs for five hundred years. It has also served as the nation's storehouse for weapons, public records, the Crown Jewels, and the Royal Menagerie.

RESTAURANTS

Poons	175
Simpson's of Cornhill	175

RESTAURANTS EC3

Poons
Minster Pavement, Minster Court, Mincing Lane, EC3

See Poons Restaurants, page 63, for description.
TELEPHONE: 071-626-0126
TUBE: Tower Hill/Monument
OPEN: Mon–Fri
CLOSED: Sat, Sun, holidays
HOURS: Continuous service 11:45 A.M.–10:30 P.M.
RESERVATIONS: Recommended
CREDIT CARDS: AE, MC, V
PRICES: À la Carte: £5–25; Set price: Lunch, £9
VAT/SERVICE: Service not included, discretionary
MISCELLANEOUS: Will omit MSG on request

Simpson's of Cornhill
38½ Castle Court at Ball Court, EC3

To find Simpson's of Cornhill (not to be confused with the touristy and overpriced Simpson's-in-the-Strand), walk along Cornhill, turn right on St. Michael's Alley, then right on Castle Court, walk until you come to Ball Court, and turn right again. To say it is a hidden find is the understatement of the year! The search is definitely worthwhile for this old-fashioned English food with old-fashioned prices to match. For my lunching pound, this is the best value in the part of London known as The City.

TELEPHONE
071-626-9985
TUBE
Bank
OPEN
Mon–Fri lunch only
CLOSED
Dinner, Sat, Sun, holidays
HOURS
Mon–Fri noon–3 P.M.
RESERVATIONS
Not accepted

CREDIT CARDS
AE, DC, MC, V

PRICES
À la Carte: £9–11

VAT/SERVICE
Service discretionary

The restaurant was founded in 1757, and for decades the traditions and customs of male-dominated London eating houses were strictly maintained. Not until 1916 were women admitted to this conservative male bastion. Today, women are welcomed in both the upstairs restaurant and in the downstairs grill room. The food is heavy and hearty, so skip the starters and concentrate on a main course of grilled meat or the daily hot joint (roast meat). You will have roast beef on Monday, ham on Tuesday, leg of lamb on Wednesday, and pork roast on Thursday. Friday it is lamb again. Liver and bacon, stewed rabbit, steak and kidney pie, and cold Scotch salmon are also on board and all equally recommended. For an after-meal savory, everyone orders the stewed cheese. This is a crock of melted Cheddar cheese mixed with Worchestershire sauce and seasonings to spread on toast. You *must* try one. It is the house specialty and the kitchen cannot turn them out fast enough.

Warning: You can't call for reservations because they don't take them. By 12:30 P.M. it is completely full, so for assured seating, plan to arrive at 12 sharp.

EC4 ✢ FLEET STREET, ROYAL COURTS OF JUSTICE, ST. PAUL'S CATHEDRAL

Nearly every national and provincial newspaper or periodical has had an office in or near Fleet Street. It is one of the most ancient streets in London and has had links with the printing trade since the fifteen hundreds. Now, most have their offices elsewhere.

St. Paul's Cathedral was created by Sir Christopher Wren after the Great Fire of 1666. Today, it retains its great dignity and grandeur even though it is overshadowed by huge tower blocks.

PUBS

RESTAURANTS

PUBS EC4

Black Friar
174 Queen Victoria Street, EC4

The main reason to visit the Black Friar pub is to see one of the richest and strangest pub interiors in London. This Art Nouveau fantasy, built in 1903 from designs by H. Fuller Clarke and sculptor Henry Poole, pays homage to the Dominicans or black friars who had a monastery on this site many years ago. The friars were known for being more interested in drinking than divinity and their devotion to the bottle sets the theme for this amazing building. Outside over the door stands a figure of a good-natured friar, hands folded across his impressive beer belly. Mosaics on either side show other friars eating, drinking, laughing, and having fun. The remarkable interior is replete with polished stone, colored marble columns, and bronze bas-reliefs. The room in back, known as the "Side Chapel," has a vaulted black, white, and gold ceiling and reflecting mirrors encircled by friezes of inebriated friars. They are accompanied by crouching demons, fairies, and carved alabaster animals. All

TELEPHONE
071-236-5650

TUBE
Blackfriars

OPEN
Mon–Fri

CLOSED
Sat, Sun, holidays

HOURS
11:30 A.M.–10 P.M.
Food service: Lunch
11:30 A.M.–2:30 P.M.

RESERVATIONS
Not accepted

CREDIT CARDS
None

PRICES
À la Carte: £3.50–5

VAT/SERVICE
No service charged or expected

around the room are mottoes of the friars: "Tell a gossip," "Finery is foolery," and "Haste is slow."

The main bar area has an enormous bronze canopied fireplace and a small horseshoe bar. The tiny wedge-shaped front part of the pub is where hot and cold lunches are served. The food is not as spectacular as the surroundings, but it is basic pub fare at reasonable prices.

Williamson's Tavern
1–3 Grovelands Court, Bow Lane, EC4

TELEPHONE
071-248-6280

TUBE
Mansion House

OPEN
Mon–Fri

CLOSED
Sat, Sun, holidays

HOURS
11:30 A.M.–8 P.M.
Food service: Lunch
11:30 A. M.–3 P.M.

RESERVATIONS
Not accepted

CREDIT CARDS
AE, DC, MC, V

PRICES
À la Carte: £4–6

VAT/SERVICE
No service charged or expected

Williamson's Tavern is appealing for its historic background, warm atmosphere, and better-than-usual food. Like many pubs in The City, it claims to be the oldest, a fact that is obviously determined in several creative ways. It does, however, mark the exact center of The City of London. Built after the Great Fire of 1666, it was a former Mansion House and the residence of London's Lord Mayors until 1753. The wrought-iron gates guarding the entrance leading down the leafy alley to the pub were presented by William III and Queen Mary to the Lord Mayor of London. Before its transition into a pub in the eighteenth century, it was Sir John Falstaff's home, and long before that the site of a Roman villa. The tiles used around the fireplace on the first floor were found ten feet below ground level during the most recent renovation one hundred years ago.

There are three parts to the pub: the Tavern Bar, a typical pub complete with loud music and pinball machines; the Library Bar, a quiet sanctuary on the ground level; and Martha's Bar downstairs, where a large variety of interesting wines are served. What to order to eat? The hands-down favorite is the house special: a 4-oz. sirloin steak sandwich, chargrilled and served with parsley or garlic butter, fried potatoes, and vegetable, all for less than £5.

RESTAURANTS EC4

Sweetings
39 Queen Victoria Street, EC4

If you like fresh fish superbly prepared, Sweetings is required eating.

"We don't take reservations, accept credit cards, or serve coffee—we *do* serve the best fish you will eat in London," states owner Graham Needham, who has been greeting his guests at this very popular fish restaurant for more than a quarter of a century. Generations of loyalists agree with Mr. Needham, and now fathers arrive with sons and grandsons on a regular basis. Sweetings has been on the same corner in London's financial district for over one hundred years. The only change seems to have been the prices. The yellowed walls, a front window loaded with tubs of wine, and customers milling around one of the long mahogany bars waiting for their favorite table served by their favorite waiter set the tone here day after day. The fish is fresh daily from the Billingsgate fish market and the oysters are supplied directly from West Mersea in Essex.

Every regular has his or her own favorite dish and would never consider experimenting with the Dover sole, salmon, smoked haddock, halibut, or crab salad unless it is their own special dish. Familiar desserts like bread and butter pudding, baked jam roll, and steamed syrup pudding, along with excellent wines sold by the glass or bottle, complement the meal.

TELEPHONE
071-248-3062

TUBE
Mansion House or Cannon Street

OPEN
Mon–Fri lunch only

CLOSED
Dinner, Sat, Sun, holidays

HOURS
Lunch 11:30 A.M.–3 P.M.

RESERVATIONS
Not accepted

CREDIT CARDS
None

PRICES
À la Carte: £21–25

VAT/SERVICE
Service discretionary

MISCELLANEOUS
Sandwich counter if you're in a hurry

Ye Olde Cheshire Cheese
145 Fleet Street (off Wine Office Court), EC4

Seventeenth-century chop houses were the forerunners of today's wine bars and this centuries-old bar and restaurant is one of the most famous. It is almost impossible to pick up a guide to London restaurants without reading something about Ye Olde Cheshire Cheese. Even though this notoriety brings flocks of international tourists to the door, the restaurant has managed to remain true to its beginnings. In the thirteenth century, the site formed part of a

TELEPHONE
071-353-6170

TUBE
Blackfriars

OPEN
Mon–Sat

CLOSED
Sun, holidays

HOURS
Mon–Sat noon–9 P.M.
Lunch: noon–2:30 P.M.
Dinner: 6–9 P.M.

RESERVATIONS
Suggested for dinner
CREDIT CARDS
AE, DC, MC, V
PRICES
À la Carte: £10–16
VAT/SERVICE
Service discretionary
MISCELLANEOUS
Can accommodate private
parties

Carmelite monastery. Rebuilt after the Great Fire of London of 1666, the pub preserves the atmosphere of intervening centuries through sixteen reigns of kings and queens. In the Chop Room, you can still see the long table where Dr. Samuel Johnson, Oliver Goldsmith, and Charles Dickens sat and dined. Pictures and artifacts throughout the multi-roomed pub portray the people, events, and times that have left their mark. Today, little has changed and you will still walk on the original wooden floors, sit on hard benches worn smooth, climb the rickety staircase leading to the upstairs rooms, and shuffle through sawdust tossed on the floor each day.

If "ye" appears before a menu item, that means it is English and a specialty of the house, as in Ye Famous Pie (steak and kidney) or Ye Olde Grylle. Prices lean on the high side for the predictable English fare, but for the historical value, it is definitely worth a visit, if you only step up to the bar and order a drink.

SE1 ✣ SOUTH BANK OF THE THAMES, SOUTHWARK

The South Bank Arts Center has been growing since 1951, when this Lambeth riverside site was chosen as a new hub for the arts in London. Included here is The Royal Festival Hall, The Queen Elizabeth Hall, Purcell Room, The National Theater Film Theater, The National Theater, and the Museum of the Moving Image.

Across the London Bridge from The City is Southwark, an area associated with entertainment from Elizabethan days. Shakespeare's plays were performed at the Rose Theater and his Globe Theater is nearby. Southwark Cathedral is a fine example of Gothic architecture.

PUBS SE1

The Anchor
34 Park Street, SE1

The Anchor is an eighteenth-century pub with a maze of rambling corridors joining low-ceilinged dark rooms with open fires and wooden benches. At the Anchor, you can wine and dine, or just eat. In all, there are five small bars, three restaurants, and an outdoor terrace with a spectacular view across the Thames to St. Paul's Cathedral. The upstairs formal restaurant serves large doses of English food at prices most Cheap Eaters will find over budget. That is not to say that enjoying a rack of lamb or a grilled fish while sitting at table number 6 or 7 with their inspiring views is an experience you should miss. The pub used to play host to William Shakespeare, whose Globe Theater is close by, and later on, Dr. Samuel Johnson had a special room where he wrote his famed dictionary. In the Clink Room, named after the notorious debtor's prison that stood around the corner on Clink Street, police sticks and billy clubs are on display.

TELEPHONE
071-407-1577/3003

TUBE
London Bridge

OPEN
Daily

CLOSED
Christmas

HOURS
Mon–Sat 11 A.M.–11 P.M.; Sun noon–3 P.M., 7–10:30 P.M. Food service: lunch, Pub noon–2:30 P.M., restaurant noon–3 P.M.; dinner, pub 6–10 P.M., restaurant 7–10 P.M.

RESERVATIONS
Suggested for the restaurant

CREDIT CARDS
AE, DC, MC, V

PRICES
À la Carte: Pub, £4–7; restaurant, £17–20

I think this is one of the more interesting pubs in London, so be sure and stop by, if just for a beer and a look around.

George Inn at Southwark
77 Borough High Street, SE1

The George Inn is a taste of London as it was fifty years after Columbus discovered America, when Henry VIII reigned and Sir Francis Drake was sailing around the world. The inn has stood on this spot since Elizabethan times and is the last galleried coaching inn from that period still standing in London. The current inn is only one quarter of its original size and dates from 1542. It was rebuilt in 1676, following the Great Fire of Southwark. Its purpose then was to provide food, drink, and lodging for travelers en route to Kent and the port of Dover. Inside the walled yard, tradesmen had offices, plays were performed, and musicians played, while lords and ladies relaxed in front of roaring fires after their strenuous journeys. Later on, Charles Dickens ate and drank here. But he only became a patron after he had become rich and famous. As a child, visiting his father in the Marshalsea prison just down the road, he would have been too poor to enter. In *Little Dorritt* he has Pip go into The George to write begging letters. Today, the inn is part of the National Trust for the Preservation of Historic Sites and still provides food and drink to its many customers every day.

The ground-floor bars are small, with bare wooden floors and benches. In the back bar is a parliamentary clock, from the time when Parliament imposed a tax on all timepieces. Some of the old coaching bedrooms with latticed windows overlooking the cobblestone courtyard are now part of the Coaching Rooms Restaurant. More bedrooms make up the George Room Restaurant. The Talbot Room above it is reported to be haunted. The large courtyard has picnic tables and benches and in summer is full of people eating and drinking. The menus in the various eating areas of the inn highlight all the English favorites: roast meats, grilled lamb chops, hot and cold pub food, meaty sandwiches, and fattening desserts.

RESTAURANTS SE1

The Chapter House
Southwark Cathedral, Montague Close, SE1

Looking for a reasonably priced lunch served in a historic setting? Consider dining in a church. Whenever you find yourself exploring Shakespeare's Globe Theater and lunchtime rolls around, head straight for Southwark Cathedral, across the Borough High Street from the London Bridge tube station. Built in the twelve hundreds, the church is the oldest-surviving Gothic church in London. Because of its location, the cathedral had close ties to Elizabethan actors and dramatists. A monument and stained glass window commemorate William Shakespeare, and his brother, Edward, is buried here.

The cathedral's Chapter House Restaurant was opened by Queen Elizabeth II in 1988. The menu devotes itself primarily to pizza, with a few pastas, sandwiches, soups, salads, and homemade desserts along for the ride. In an area not known for its fine dining choices, The Chapter House serves food that is not only reliably good, but charitable as well. Ten percent of the restaurant profits go to the church and if you order the Pizza Veneziana, 25p will be given to the Venice in Peril Fund. To date, more than £300,385 has been paid to the fund. No matter how you calculate it, that is a lot of pizza.

TELEPHONE
071-378-6446

TUBE
London Bridge

OPEN
Mon–Fri

CLOSED
Sat, Sun, evenings, holidays

HOURS
Continuous service
10 A.M.–4:30 P.M.

RESERVATIONS
Not accepted

CREDIT CARDS
AE, DC, MC, V

PRICES
À la Carte: £6–9

VAT/SERVICE
Service discretionary up to 7, then 12½% added to bill

PUBS

No greater institution has ever been developed to further human happiness than that of a good public house.
—Dr. Samuel Johnson

The word pub comes from public house, and in that phrase lies the essential character of this British institution. The British pub is a place licensed by the government where people can come together and freely talk. Every traveler going to London considers a visit to a pub to be as important as seeing the Changing of the Guard at Buckingham Palace and the Crown Jewels at the Tower of London. As a visitor you can rely on being made welcome and enjoying yourself in a pub. In some, the welcome after a few pints will be more enthusiastic, and in only a few will you be politely ignored.

Pubs date back to Roman times, when they began as taverns offering overnight accommodations and entertainment for travelers. In the thousand or so years since they were first introduced in Britain, people have talked about them, written about them, laughed and played in them, and relied on them for food, drink, and companionship. Pubs have been the haunt of highwaymen and smugglers, artists and writers, criminals and comics, and ordinary people. Nowhere else in England can you find such a diversity of pubs as in London. Around almost every corner will be the welcoming door of a pub, and they include many of the most ancient and historic buildings in the capital city. In fact, there are over five thousand in greater London, and more per square yard in The City than in any other part of England.

Until the early twentieth century, pubs set aside different sections for different groups of customers. The tradesmen drank in the public bar and were shielded from the gentry, who drank in the lounge behind etched-glass "snob screens." Until 1970, few pubs were open to women alone and those that were, were unsavory to say the least. Even today, pubs have a strong aura of masculinity, and a woman alone in a pub has yet to win social acceptance from everyone.

The Slug and Lettuce, Spotted Dog, Widow's Son, Dog & Duck, the Sugar Loaf, the Rose and Crown, the Three Stags—silly made-up names? No, names of pubs you can find in London today. It was the Roman invaders who first required innkeepers to display signs outside their premises to guide the illiterate masses. In 1393, Richard II introduced legislation that every inn should be clearly signed so travelers might swiftly find shelter from the robbers and murderers who stalked them. By pub signs you can identify loyalties and great events that date back to these early times. The Crown, for example, originated in the Middle Ages, when innkeepers felt it necessary to display their loyalty to the monarchy. The Rose and Crown commemorated the end of the conflict between the red rose of Lancaster and the white rose of York. The Stag was an early religious symbol, and the Sugar Loaf recalls the way sugar was sold many years ago.

English pubs are national institutions similar to cafés in Paris and coffeehouses in Vienna. For millions of Londoners, their local pub is a home-away-from-home, where they gather at the same time every day to meet their friends, catch up on local gossip, argue over politics, discuss the dreary weather, and cheer their favorite sports team.

A pub takes on the flavor of its neighborhood and location, and in many busy metropolitan pubs, the clientele changes almost hourly. Many regulars meet for lunch. Others get together in the afternoon for a game of darts. In the evening, they stop by on their way home after work for a relaxing pint or two, and after dinner they come back to watch a sporting event on the "telly." The clientele in a pub represents a cross-section of society, from the blue-collar workers in the rowdy East End to the aristocrats in Belgravia and Mayfair. In The City, expect to see lawyers in pinstriped suits discussing their cases. In Bloomsbury, known as literary London, you can mix with students and tweedy professors. The Hooray Henrys (British yuppies) crowd the Chelsea pubs, and farther west along the banks of the Thames, writers, actors, and artists fill their favorite pubs.

PUB ETIQUETTE AND SURVIVAL TECHNIQUES

1. You can offer to buy the barman a drink, but *never* tip him or anyone else working behind the bar.

2. In a pub, stick to beer, not wine or fancy mixed drinks.

3. Be prepared for no-nonsense service. You order your food from the food area and drinks from the bar. You pay for each separately at the time of service. In busy pubs you are often given a number when you place your food order, and when it is called, you return to the food service area to get your plate of food.

4. If the Englishman next to you offers to buy you a drink, it is okay to accept, but you should offer him the next round.

5. Conversation is part of the reason people go to pubs. Barside chats are quick and easy ways to meet people, but don't expect an invitation to that person's home. The easiest way to start a

conversation is to talk about the beer served in that particular pub. Then fall back on the weather and the latest sports scores before getting into heavier topics of the Crown and taxes.

6. The best pub food is usually in a pub that also has its own restaurant.

7. When pub food, or "pub grub," as it is called, is described in *Cheap Eats in London* as *good*, that means good by general pub standards. The quality of pub food, which is often frozen and microwaved to order, must never be compared to that of restaurants, because it is aimed at a clientele who want a quick, filling bite to go with their beer.

8. If you are ordering a hot dish, stick with the daily specials listed on the chalkboard. If you want a sandwich, ask for a "freshly cut" one, which means it will be made to order for you. A "ready made" one probably was made way ahead of time and its freshness might be questionable.

9. If you want to relax in a pub and be assured of getting a good place to sit, arrive after 2 P.M. or before 6 P.M. If you do this, be aware that you might not get a hot meal.

10. If you want to experience pub life at its fullest, go for lunch or around 5:30 in the evening when everyone stops by for a pint or two on the way home for the day. At lunch, don't expect always to get a place to sit. More often than not, an Englishman will stand with a pint in one hand and his plate of food in the other and somehow manage to finish both without spilling a drop.

11. You must be eighteen years old to drink in a pub. Children under fourteen are not allowed in pubs at all, but may go into a pub restaurant.

12. Pub hours are governed by Parliament. Pub hours were extended in 1988 to 11 A.M.–11 P.M., Monday through Saturday, and noon–3 P.M. and 7–10:30 P.M. on Sunday. Depending on the pub, its location, and type of trade, there are certain variations. You can be sure, however, that no drinks will be served before or after these opening and closing times.

13. Ten minutes before closing time you will hear the closing bell, which signals that you have ten more minutes to finish your drink before the pub closes and you are asked to leave.

PUB FOOD

For Cheap Eaters in London, pub food is a godsend because it is so filling, so cheap, and so British. If you want to eat in pleasant, but often very crowded surroundings, and without punishing your pocketbook, where do you go? To a pub, of course. But you must be forewarned. At lunch most pubs are wall-to-wall people, and getting a seat requires either arriving early, or a stroke of good luck. Also keep in mind that the food is filling and fattening; don't even *think* of counting calories or monitoring your fat or cholesterol intake on your pub outings.

Even though pub food all tends to look, smell, and taste the same after awhile, it is the soul and comfort food most Britishers grew up on. Several standbys you will find in most pubs are meat pies, the ploughman's lunch, and a roast joint served for Sunday lunch. The pies are usually steak and kidney or shepherd's—which is diced meat and vegetables covered with gravy, topped with mashed potatoes, and baked in a casserole. The ploughman's lunch is a good accompaniment to a pint of English bitter. It consists of a piece of crusty bread served with a large chunk of Cheddar or Stilton cheese with chutney and a pickle on the side. On Sunday, you can expect to have some sort of roast served with potatoes, vegetables, and all the appropriate trimmings. Beyond these staples, pub food varies from wrapped sandwiches of undetermined length of life to hot and cold buffet spreads, lasagna, salads, and in some instances desserts such as spotted dick or apple pie.

ENGLISH BEER

Visitors to England are often bewildered by the number of brews available in most pubs. In some, there are as many as two dozen ales alone. Every pub will always have at least one bitter, plus stout, lager, and a wide range of bottled beers. One of the major attractions of English beer is this wide variety. No two are alike, even if they have the same general name, such as bitter, stout, and so on. The taste of each depends on the techniques used by the brewery for that particular type of brew.

Asking for "a beer" will get you nowhere. You must specify not only the type and the brand, but the amount you want: a pint or half pint. For the novice, the best thing to do is to tell the barman the type of beer you like: light, dark, heavy, loaded with the flavor of hops, low alcohol, and so on, and let him suggest something. Part of the fun is experimenting and you may try three or four before you settle on a favorite.

While it is beyond the scope of *Cheap Eats in London* to present an in-depth discussion of English beer, the following should shed some beginning light on this confusing subject.

BITTER

If you want to drink what the locals do, order a pint of bitter, a clear yellowish beer with a strong hops taste. This traditional British beer is the most popular, but it is hard for many Americans to get used to because it is never chilled—that would ruin the taste. The best bitter is real ale. Because of the "real ale" movement of the past few years, most pubs now serve brews that are still fermenting when they are delivered. Real ale is alive and continues to mature in the cask and has to be pumped to the bar where it is served by the barkeep by a hand pump. The taste of real ale is best at 56°F. It comes in two grades: ordinary and best, or special, which is stronger.

ALE

Ale is weaker and a little sweeter than bitter. Light or pale ale is bottled and served at room temperature.

EXPORT ALE

Stronger than ale, it is also bottled.

LAGER

If you want to drink what most Americans call beer, ask for a cold lager and stress the world *cold*. This brew is served in bottles or on draught and there are over twenty-five varieties.

SHANDY

An equal mixture of bitter and lemonade or ginger beer. Definitely an acquired taste.

STOUT

Strong, dark, rich, creamy brew with the foam lasting from the first sip to the last. Guinness is the most popular.

U.S. brands are expensive. Remember "When in Rome . . ." and drink English beer while you are in London.

PUB CRAWLS

Guided pub walks, or pub crawls, meet in the early evening near tube stations, tour a neighborhood, and visit several typical pubs along the way. It is a good way to become better acquainted with London and to have a party while doing it. Check with your hotel or the London Tourist Authority for brochures on guided walking tours of London. There are several companies operating and they generally seem about the same. These outings last two or three hours and are worth the nominal fee. They go rain or shine, even if you are the only one going.

LISTING OF PUBS

Admiral Codrington	129
The Albert	111
The Anchor	181
The Antelope	112
Black Friar	177
The Britannia	66
Bunch of Grapes	129
The Chandos	89
Fox & Anchor	168
George Inn at Southwark	182
The Globe	90
King George IV	149
King's Head & Eight Bells	130
Lamb	78
Museum Tavern	79
Queen Charlotte's Restaurant & Pub	80
Red Lion	112
Shepherds Tavern	26
The Sherlock Holmes	90
Star Tavern	113
Williamson's Tavern	178
Ye Old Mitre Tavern	169
Zetland Arms	150

TEAROOMS

Everything stops for tea.
　　　—Popular English saying

Name one other drink which cools, which warms, which calms and which cheers all at once. There aren't many drinks like tea.
　　　—Anonymous

Whether served in plastic foam cups or in fine, translucent bone china, tea is serious business in England. More than 180 million cups are consumed *daily* in Britain, according to the British Tea Council.

For three-hundred years, tea has been part of every level of British society. In the seventeenth century, it was so expensive that tea caddies had locks on them. Now it is the cheapest drink after tap water.

English tea was served during the Regency days by the Duchess of Bedford to fill the gap between lunch and dinner. Victorian ladies drank tea in the drawing room while nannies passed the scones and tarts to the nursery set. A century ago, tearooms were about the only public place a lady could venture unchaperoned, yet maintain her good reputation. The first recorded English tearoom was a woman's idea. In 1864, the manager of a bread shop near the London Bridge started serving tea to her favorite customers and before long everyone wanted some. She then asked the bakery if she could sell pots of tea with scones. The result was a huge success. Tea shops became a part of the nation's heritage and part of every English person's childhood.

A proper English high tea in a lovely setting is a pleasant and filling alternative to a big lunch or dinner. It is also theater at its best, complete with pots, dishes, special silverware, trays, and hovering waiters in fancy dress. Many London tourists associate teatime with the elaborate offerings at Brown's Hotel, the Ritz, or Fortnum & Mason. Tea at the Ritz Hotel on Piccadilly is as famous as dinner at Maxim's in Paris, only slightly less expensive, and almost as difficult to get a table for. Few Londoners dress to kill and pay in excess of £20 to sip tea at a fancy address. Instead, they go to a neighborhood tearoom. These informal tea places usually do not have a set tea with scones, sandwiches, and fancy pastries, but they do offer good value and a nice atmosphere where you can have a cup of tea and a sinfully rich treat that will keep you going until dinner, or in many cases until the final curtain call at the theater.

If tragedy should happen, the ultimate cure is always a cup of tea. It doesn't matter if you get hit by a truck or lose all of your money, a cup of tea will make things right again. It is the English solution to all the world's ills.

LISTING OF TEAROOMS

Wine Bars

Wine, the plasma of life.
  —Mary Gregg Misch

Wine bars offer new dimensions to dining out in London. In order to survive the competition, the newer wine bars serve better food as well as a wider variety of wines. In many places you can have anything from a smoked salmon salad to a three-course meal at prices lower than you would pay for the equivalent in a nice restaurant.

For many, wine bars are attractive alternatives to pubs. Not only is the food better, there is usually a place to sit and the crowd is quieter and more upmarket. They are also less crowded and smoky and seldom have blasting jukeboxes or loud pinball machines drowning out conversation. They tend to be busy during the lunch hour and after work, but if you avoid those peak hours, you should find them relaxing settings where you can go and drink a variety of wines and sample a selection of foods especially chosen to go with the vintages being served. Most of the staff in wine bars are well-versed on their bar's particular wines and are willing to spend time helping you decide what to try.

LISTING OF WINE BARS

QUICK REFERENCE LISTS

ALPHABETICAL LIST OF RESTAURANTS, PUBS, WINE BARS, AND TEAROOMS

W

Y

Z

BIG SPLURGES

These restaurants are suggested for those with more flexible budgets or anyone looking for special occasion dining.

CHEAP EATS IN LONDON BY TYPES OF FOOD

Daquise	152
Dell'Ugo	34
Ebury Wine Bar	124
Gavvers	115
Gilbert's	153
Grumble's	116
Le Metro	143
Le Shop	137
Luba's Bistro	137
Mövenpick	99
My Old Dutch Pancake House	83, 138
Nineteen	138
October Gallery Cafe	85
O'Keefe's	43
Parson's Restaurant	157
Salsa!	104
Wolfe's	104, 141

FISH/FISH & CHIPS

Costas Grill	69
Geales Fish Restaurant	69
The Fryer's Delight	81
North Sea Fish Restaurant	100
The Rock and Sole Plaice	103
Sweetings	179
Tubby Isaac's	161

GREEK/MIDDLE EASTERN

Costas Grill	69
Halepi	60
Konaki	82
Mayfair Greek Tavern	40
Phoenicia	70

INDIAN

Great Nepalese	164
India Club	96
Indian YMCA Cafeteria	38
Khan's	61
Noorjahan	147

ITALIAN

Amalfi Ristorante	26

George Inn at Southwark 182
The Globe 90
King George IV 149
King's Head & Eight Bells 130
Lamb 78
Museum Tavern 79
Queen Charlotte's Restaurant & Pub 80
Red Lion 112
Shepherds Tavern 26
The Sherlock Holmes 90
Star Tavern 113
Williamson's Tavern 178
Ye Old Mitre Tavern 169
Zetland Arms 150

SANDWICHES

Arco Bars of Knightsbridge 113, 131
Farmer Brown (lunch) 95
The Green Cafe 116
Hungry's 37
Mr. Christian's 74
Paul Rothe & Son 46
Rabin's Nosh Bar 48
Woolley Brothers Food Hall 86

SOUTHEAST ASIAN

Bahn Thai (Thai) 27
Khobkhun (Thai) 154
Malaysian Dining Hall (Malaysian) 39
Mekong (Vietnamese) 119
Melati (Indonesian & Malaysian) 41
Nahar Cafeteria—Mara House (Indonesian &
  Malaysian) 61

TEAROOMS

The Fountain Restaurant at Fortnum & Mason 36
Maison Sagne 55
The Muffin Man 71
Pâtisserie Cappuccetto 56
Pâtisserie Française 64
Pâtisserie Valerie 56, 142
Richoux 49, 142
Sonny's 142

VEGETARIAN

WINE BARS

CHEAP EATS IN LONDON MAPS

GLOSSARY OF ENGLISH FOOD TERMS

> The English have really everything in common with the
> Americans, except of course language.
> —Oscar Wilde

The English speak English, we speak American. It doesn't matter
that we share the same language, London is still a foreign capital and
you are a foreigner in it. True, you won't have the serious communica-
tion problems you would have in Moscow or Tokyo, but you will have
to deal with some different meanings and terms. *To queue* is to line up
(and you will find yourself doing this too often). A *subway* is an
underground walkway, but the actual underground transportation system is referred to as *the underground* or *the tube*. If you are going to see
a stage play, you are going to *the theatre* and for a film, you head for the
cinema. The following list of food terms and related words should help
you sort out any dining dilemmas.

B

banger	sausage
bangers and mash	sausages and mashed potatoes
bank holiday	legal holiday, many restaurants and pubs closed
bap	soft bun like a hamburger bun
bill	check (restaurant)
biscuit	cookie or cracker
black or white?	black or milk/cream in your coffee?
broad bean	lima bean
bubble and squeak	mashed potatoes mixed with cabbage and fried (sometimes leftover meat is added)

C

caff	inexpensive cafe; pronounced "caff," to rhyme with half
chicory	endive
chips	french fried potatoes
cooker	stove
Cornish pasties	meat, onion, and veggies wrapped in pastry
cottage pie	similiar to shepherd's pie, but meat is ground
courgettes	zucchini
crisps	potato chips

crumpet	like an English muffin, but with bigger holes and more of them
cuppa	cup of tea or coffee (slang)

F

fish and chips	cod, plaice, or skate dipped in batter and deep fried, served with chips (french fries), vinegar, and salt
French beans	green beans
fry-up	fried breakfast of eggs, sausage and/or bacon, and fried bread, with additions of mushrooms and tomatoes depending on the poshness of where you are eating

G

grease-out	see *fry-up*

J

jacketed potato	baked potato
jam	jelly
jelly	Jell-O
joint (meat)	roasted meat (leg of lamb would be a joint of lamb)

L

Lancashire hot pot	mutton and vegetables in a rich sauce, cooked in a pastry crust

M

mange tout	snow peas
marrow	squash
martini	straight vermouth (to get a real martini, ask for a double gin with ice)
mince	hamburger meat

O

off-license	retail liquor store
other half	either another half pint of beer or your spouse, depending on your location

P

peckish	a little bit hungry
pickled wally	pickled dill cucumber
ploughman's lunch	pub lunch consisting of cheese or pâté with bread, pickle, and sometimes chutney or an onion

pub grub	pub food
publican	manager of a pub
pudding	dessert
puds	desserts

R

rasher (bacon)	slice
ring	to call on the telephone as in "to ring for a booking" (to call for a reservation)

S

salt beef	corned beef
sausage and mash	sausage and mashed potatoes
Scotch egg	hard-cooked egg encased in ground sausage and bread crumbs and fried
shepherd's pie	diced meat and vegetables covered with gravy, topped with mashed potatoes, and baked in casserole
spirits (drink)	liquor
spotted dick	steamed sponge cake with diced fruit and raisins, served warm with soft custard sauce
steak and kidney pie	mixture of steak, kidneys, and mushrooms in gravy baked in crust or topped with one
strawberry fool	fresh whipped cream mixed with strawberries
sultana	raisin
sweet	dessert
sweets	candy
Swiss roll	jelly roll

T

tatties	potatoes
toad-in-the-hole	sausage baked in batter, served plain or with ale gravy
top-up	refill
treacle	molasses
treacle pudding or sponge	delicate sponge cake steamed in its own brown sugar sauce; best served warm with custard sauce
trifle or tipsy cake	sherry-soaked sponge cake, layered with raspberry preserves, and topped with cold custard sauce and whipped cream

W

Welsh rarebit	melted Cheddar cheese and mustard served on toast
whitebait	tiny whole fish, deep-fried

READERS' COMMENTS

Please take a few minutes to send your comments, tips, new finds, or suggestions. There are some places I have no doubt missed and maybe you know something new and good that has popped up since this was written. Be sure to include the name and address of the restaurant, as well as the date you were there, and any other information you think is important. Send it to Sandra A. Gustafson, *Cheap Eats in London,* c/o Chronicle Books, 275 Fifth Street, San Francisco, California 94103.